AF540389

REGIONAL DEVELOPMENT AND LEVELS OF LIVING IN INDIA

Contents

Foreword

I am pleased to write a foreword of the book entitled "Regional Development and Levels of Living in India", jointly edited by Anil K. Thakur and Dalip Kumar. The authors have analytically examined the issues related to the subject matter. No doubt, this subject is exposed to limitations of field data. But the authors have done good job even with such limitations. The book examines the aspects of regional disparities and the widening variations in the levels of living even after 60 years of India's independence. India has witnessed a rapid economic growth in recent years and crossed the 30 years image of 'Hindu' rate of growth. It has emerged as a vibrant nation—to realize the status of a global economic power in the 21st century. Yet, the nation holds the picture of high incidence of poverty, illiteracy, poor infrastructure development, and poor health record—all of which are essential for better levels of living. In the land of diversities, economic growth becomes meaningful only if it caters to the dire needs of teeming millions, so that the vast masses can strive to live a better life and with dignity.

The variation in the levels of living is the direct consequence of deficiencies in India's planning process and implementation mechanism. The present state of affairs is far behind the constitutionally defined goal of a welfare state as well as the ambitious vision of achieving the status of an economic super power. It is high time to inject major refinements in the concept as well as process of planned development, viz. market economy. India needs to bring new thinking for accelerated economic growth. The levels of living should be judged by levels of disposable as real income per person. Real income means income in terms of purchasing power. Level of living depends on personal income and consumption expenditure of a household. The level of income or expenditure higher than this means better conditions of living. The proportion of personal consumption expenditure is distributed among the various items of consumption.

The book consisting of 21 chapters provides good insights into the issues relating to widening regional disparity and distorted picture on levels of living. Future researchers in this area would receive good impetus from this book for improving the methods of data collection and the desired analytical tools. This would also help towards improved planning process and plan implementations procedures. The authors have done a lot of groundwork to make the book worth reading and useful as reference material on these issues.

The contributions to this volume raise many of the fundamental issues pertaining to regional development and levels of living. I wish and hope that the book will receive wider circulation amongst planners, academicians, and interested economic researchers. The two editors are complimented for doing an excellent work.

DR. SATISH C. JHA
Member, Economic Advisory
Council to the Prime Minister

Preface

This book 'Regional Development and Levels of Living' is an outcome of the 10th Annual Conference of Economic Association of Bihar, which was organised by the Department of Economics, C.M. Arts College, Dharbhanga, Bihar during March 29-31, 2007. We are thankful to Professor T.S.P. Singh, the Conference President of the Economic Association of Bihar for his valuable guidance and immense cooperation.

The success of the conference was reflected in the lively debate among all the paper writers and discussants. The session attracted more than 20 papers, including the concern of economists for a sensitive topic, which is likely to have a major impact on the state as well as Indian economy. We are also grateful to all the paper writers for incorporating the desired comments and revising their papers.

We extend our heartfelt thanks to Prof. Chandrika Prasad, Principal, C.M. Arts College, Darbhanga and his colleagues, and all the teaching and administrative staff of the College for their active support in organising and making this conference a success. Thanks are also due to the General Secretary, Economic Association of Bihar who spent enormous time and energy for organising the conference and facilitating the publication of this book.

Our special appreciation is due to Dr. Anjani Kumar Jha, the Chairman, Development of Indian Society and Culture (DISC), Dr. Rajesh Jaiswal, Associate Fellow, National Council of Applied Economic Research, New Delhi for a helping hand in bringing out this publication. We are indebted to many friends, colleagues, and teachers for their careful guidance and constant support.

We would like to acknowledge Mr. G.S. Bhatia and his staff of M/s Deep and Deep Publications Pvt. Ltd., New Delhi deserve thanks for all the designing, typesetting and printing work to bring out this volume. We would like to confess that despite the best possible efforts against all odds, the quality and outlook of the book may not be upto the desired level. Utmost care has been taken to minimize the errors.

ANIL KUMAR THAKUR
DALIP KUMAR

List of Contributers

Abhishek Kumar Pandey, Research Scholar, Department of Economics, University of Allahabad, UP.

Anand Kishore, Lecturer in Economics, S.L.K. College, Sitamarhi, Bihar.

Arun Kumar Thakur, Head, P.G. Department of Economics, R.D.S. College , Muzaffarpur, BRA Bihar Univerity, Muzaffarpur, Bihar.

Binay Kumar Singh, Department of Economics, Y.N. College, Dighawara, Saran.

Binodanand Bharti, T.G.T., Kendriya Vidyalaya, Muzaffarpur, Bihar.

D.B. Goswami, P.K. Roy Memorial College, Dhanbad, Jharkhand.

D.M. Diwakar, Professor of Economics, Giri Institute of Development Study, Lucknow.

Dalip Kumar, National Council of Applied Economic Research, New Delhi.

G.C. Tripathi, Professor, Department of Economics, University of Allahabad, UP.

Gagan Kumar, Lecturer in Economics, S.L.K. College, Sitamarhi, Bihar.

H.C.L. Das, PG Department of Economics, M.S. College, Motihari, Bihar.

Kumar Ratnesh, Sr. Lecturer, Department of PG Studies and Research in Economics, Pt. J.N. PG College, Banda, UP.

Kunal Vikram, P.K. Roy Memorial College, Dhanbad, Jharkhand.

M. Narasimhlu, Former Professor and Head, Department of Economics, Osmania University, Hyderabad.

M.S. Gupta, Department of Commerce, R.K.D. College, Patna, Bihar.

Manindra Kumar Singh, Department of Economics, M.A.M. College, Naughachia, Bhagalpur.

Md. Tarique, Department of Economics, BRA Bihar University, Muzaffarpur, Bihar.

Mirtunjay Kumar, Department of Economics, B.N.M. Vanijya Mahavidyalaya, Madhepura, Bihar.

N.C. Jha, Reader and Head, Department of Economics, Madhupur College, Madhupur, Dumka, Jharkhand.

N.K. Thakur, Marketing Manager, GNFC Limited, Lucknow, UP.

Niraj Kumar, Lecturer in Economics, HNK Inter-College, Ara, Bihar.

Parmanand Singh, Reader in Department of Economics, BNM College, Barhiya, Bhagalpur University.

Poonam Jaiswal, Research Scholar, Department of Economics, University of Allahabad.

R.V. Dadibhavi, Professor, Department of Economics, Karnataka University, Dharwad, Karnataka.

Rabindra Nath Ojha, Lecturer, Department of Economics, R.D.S. College, Muzaffarpur, BRA Bihar Univerity, Muzaffarpur, Bihar.

Ramesh Kumar Singh, Department of Economics, G.N.M. College, Parsathuan, Rohtash, Bihar.

Ravi Ranjan, Lecturer in Department of LSW, AI Collage, Bihar Shariff, Nalanda.

S.K.L. Das, Head, Department of Economics, P.K. Roy Memorial College, Dhanbad, Jharkhand.

S.T. Bagalkoti, Reader in Economics, Karnataka University, Dharwad, Karnataka.

Sandhya L.S. Singh, Post-Doctoral Fellow, M.U., Bodh Gaya.

Satendra Prajapati, Department of Commerce, Gaya College, Gaya.

Shashi Bhushan Singh, Reader in Department of Economics, C.M. Arts College, Dharbhanga, LNM University, Dhabanga

Surendra Kumar, Department of Economics, S.S. College Jahanabad, Magadh University, Bodh Gaya, Bihar.

T.N. Singh, Research Scholar, Department of Commerce and Management, LNMU, Dharbhanga, Bihar.

Ugra Mohan Jha, Former President, Economic Association of Bihar, Former Director, Agro Research Centre, Bhagalpur University, Bhagalpur, Bihar.

Abbreviations

APCE	Average per capita Consumption Expenditure
BCI	Business Confidence Index
BLI	Basic Literacy Index
BUMARU	Bihar, Madhya Pradesh, Rajasthan, Orissa and Uttar Pradesh
CBR	Crude Birth Rates
CDR	Crude Death Rates
CIS	Competitiveness of Indian States
CSO	Central Statistical Organisation
DRDA	District Rural Development Agency
DWCRA	Development of Women and Children in Rural Areas
EPI	Expanded Programme on Immunization
EPW	Economic and Political Weekly
FAI	Fertilizer Association of India
FAO	Food and Agricultural Organization of the United Nations
FDI	Final Index of Development
FDI	Foreign Direct Investment
FPS	Fair Price Shop
GCI	Growth Competitiveness Index
GCR	Growth Competitiveness Rates
GDP	Gross Domestic Product
GDS	Gross Domestic Saving
GKY	Ganga Kalyan Yojana
GSDP	Gross State Domestic Products
HDI	Human Development Index
HHs	Households
ICMR	Indian Council of Medical Research
IDI	Infrastructure Development Index

ILO	International Labour Organization
IMD	Institute of Management Development
IMI	Infant Mortality Index
IMR	Infant Mortality Rates
IRDA	Integrated Rural Development Programme
LEI	Life Expectancy Index
MCH	Mother and Child Health
MDGs	Millennium Developments Goals
MMR	Maternal Mortality Rate
MPCE	Monthly Per Capita Expenditure
MT	Matric Tonnes
MWS	Minimum Well Scheme
NFHS	National Family Health Survey
NGO	Non-Governmental Organization
NHDP	National Human Development Report
NHFDC	National Housing Finance Development Corporation
NHP	National Health Policy
NIEPA	National Institute of Educational Planning and Administration
NIN	National Institute of Nutrition
NPC	National Productivity Council
NREGS	National Rural Employment Guarantee Scheme
NRHM	National Rural Health Mission
NSDP	Net State Domestic Product
NSSO	National Sample Organisation
OBCs	Other than Backwards
OECD	Organisation for Economic Cooperation and Development
ORT	Oral Dehydration Therapy
PCI	Per Capita Income
PCNSDP	Per Capita Net State Domestic Product
PDS	Public Distribution System
PHC	Primary Health Centres
PQLI	Physical Quality of Life Index
QLI	Quality Life Index
QLQI	Quality of Life and Work Index
SDM	Standard Deviation Method
SEZ	Special Economic Zone
SGRY	Sampurna Grameen Rozgar Yojana

SGSY	Swarnajayanti Gram Swarozgar Yojana
SITRA	Supply of Improved Toolkits for Rural Artisans
SPCL	Statistics of Price and Cost of Living
STD	Standard Deviation
TAC	Technical Advisory Committee
TRYSEM	Training of Rural Youth for Self-Employment
UHDR	United Nations Human Development Report
UN	United Nations
UNDP	United Nations Development Programme
UNO	United Nations Organisation
UNESCO	United Nations Educational, Scientific and Cultural Organisation
UPA	United Progressive Alliance
USA	United States of America
USAID	United States Agency for International Development
WEF	World Economic Forum
WHO	World Health Organisation

Introduction

Imbalances in regional infrastructural availability have been a major reason behind lopsided development in India. Continuous study of economic trends and rates of growth in different areas and of the programmes bearing on the less developed regions is useful in formulating programmes for more balanced regional development. Once a minimum in terms of national income and growth in different sectors is reached, without affecting the progress of the economy as a whole, it becomes possible to provide many directions for a larger scale of development in the less developed regions. Underdeveloped areas which need special attention have to be more closely identified, their resources surveyed and the factors influencing their development.

The idea of regional development originated with Stalin who wanted to develop each region in the former Soviet Russia in such a way that in the event of an invasion, the occupation of any region by the capitalist powers might not cripple the economic power of the country. Regional development began to receive attention in the Western countries in the 1930, on welfare considerations. Specially, the need was to relieve from (i) mass unemployment and distress in the depressed regions, such as the northern and western industrial regions of the UK, which had suffered severely during the depression, and (ii) poverty and backwardness in regions such as Appalachia in the US and Italian South, which had been by-passed in the course of the economic development of these countries (Nath, 1970). The pressure for development of backward regions is stronger and the most persistent among regional development pressures and, it can be harnessed in support of the political objective of creation of separate States. (Nath, 1971)

The concept of regional development in India originated during the Second Five Year Plan. A region means a state within the Union of India like Bihar, UP or any other States. But for the purpose of planning, a region may be an area within a state, as example, North Bihar, South Bihar, East UP and West UP, etc. It is an economic entity within a state. The concept of a 'region' also needs to be defined more clearly. There are regions within States as well as those which extend beyond them and, depending upon the purpose in view, different concepts may be employed. Within every State, there are areas, which are more under-developed than others. As explained earlier, problems of regional development also arise in a variety of other contexts, as for instance, in areas around major projects, areas where new resources are being developed, and around metropolitan regions.

In areas, which are less developed, and lag in education are among the greatest handicaps in achieving rapid economic progress. Expansion of the general educational-base through the programmes of free and compulsory primary education and facilities for technical training is likely to make a steadily increasing contribution to the development of the less developed regions. Financial provisions for these programmes have been made in the States plan, but it is necessary to ensure that the resources earmarked for the development of primary education in the less developed areas and for the education of girls are effectively utilised. Facilities for the training of engineers, doctors, agricultural specialists, craftsmen and others are already being distributed throughout the country. The requirements of the population of relatively less developed areas in which new industrial projects may be located should be particularly borne in mind when programmes for technical, vocational and secondary education are implemented.

Development potentials of different regions need to be studied in relation to the possibilities, which arise from, advances in science and technology. For example, the handicaps of certain regions such as Assam, Gujarat and Rajasthan arising from lack of deposits of coal may be materially reduced as hydel power, oil and atomic energy become available. From a long-term point of view, this factor is of great importance in regional development. Similarly, improvements in transport and communications are already bringing distant regions nearer, as for instance in the case of Assam, Jammu and Kashmir and parts of Orissa, Madhya Pradesh and Rajasthan, and making it possible for them to share. more fully in the general economic advancement. Increase in the supply of electric power and the extension of rural electrification important factors in opening up of new possibilities of regional development. (Planning Commission, 1961)

The level of living can be usefully defined as real income per person after investment. By real income is meant income in terms of purchasing power. Level of living depends on personal income and consumption expenditure of a household. A level of income or expenditure higher than this means better conditions of living. The proportion of personal consumption expenditure is distributed among the various items of consumption. While comparing the levels of living of the people in terms of the level of expenditure as a whole and on individual items of expenditure, we are beset with the problem of price. We can also overlook the problem of prices, as also the problems connected with the supply of goods and services by the state, which is known to have an impact on the level of living. One important aspect of the indicator of the levels of living is their utility from the point of view of measurement of the degree of inequality in the levels of living at the state level.

The measurement of levels of living depends on so many indicators like health, food consumption and nutrition, level of education, level of employment and condition of work, housing status, social security, quality of clothing, types of recreation and entertainment, communication, quality of transportation, levels of aged population and its economic freedom, etc. We have also discussed health related indicators like CBR, CDR, IMR, life expectancy, housing status, drinking water and toilet facility, levels of aged population, etc. The especially in terms of health indicators. The levels of living can be usefully defined as real income per person after investment. By real income is meant income in terms of purchasing power. Level of living depends on personal income and consumption expenditure of a household. A level of income or expenditure higher than this means better conditions of living. The proportion of personal consumption expenditure is distributed among the various items of consumption. In this paper authors are going to discuss only health-related indicators like CBR, CDR, IMR, Life Expectancy, Housing status, Drinking Water and Toilet facility, Levels of aged population, etc. For the first, differences in the life expectancy between the richest and poorest countries is over 40 years, says the World Health Organisation's World Health Reports, 2008. Japan has the longest life expectancy at 81 years 6 months, while Zambia is the shortest at 32 years 8 months whereas world's average life expectancy is 67 years. Authors-duo make several recommendations which include increase in public expenditure in health sector, poverty-reduction, availability of safe drinking water and improved sanitation, health education, health insurance schemes for BPL people, encouragement to traditional low cost Indian system of medicine and popularization of Yoga.

"Growth Competitiveness Index and Regional Inequality" is written by Md. Tarique. Author's attempt is to find out the existing regional disparity among states and that is obvious from the standard values of overall competitiveness index of different states. Although Bihar is at the lowest level in terms of several parameters but there seems to be a silver lining in terms of broad parameters like economic strength, business efficiency, governance quality, human resource and infrastructure. The need of the hour is to reap the benefits of the approaching opportunities by utilising the strength.

The chapter on "Regional Development and Disparity: In Levels of Living in India" is contributed by H.C.L. Das. Levels of living depend on the size of national income as well as manners of distribution of the national income. This makes difference between developed and developing nations. The author concludes that there is earnest need to coordinate the dispersal process and development of agriculture through a scheme of agro-based industries.

The Chapter on "Levels of Living of Industrial Workers in India: A Study of their Family Budget Survey and Consumer Price Index Numbers" is jointly written by Mirtunjay Kumar, Ratnesh Kumar and Bijay Kumar Singh. The authors refer to various surveys on poverty conducted since 19th century. The Labour Bureau adopted the widely accepted concept of the levels of living, while conducting the survey during 1958-59. Family budget surveys of industrial workers in India Provide material for study into the living conditions and behaviors patterns of working class people. In less developed countries, family living surveys are the most direct ways of knowing the essential informations about the population for future planning. Presently Cost of Living Index, Retail Price Index and Consumer Price Index are generally used in appropriate circumstances in different countries with practically no difference in their connotations.

The chapter on "Level of Living of Child Labour—A Case Study" is the contribution of M.S. Gupta. By survey, the author finds that the working conditions of the child labour are far from satisfactory, as their employers do not adhere to laws made for the prohibition and regulations of child labours. Workers are not given weekly holidays, wages are dismally low and the overall findings of the study go against the sprit of Supreme Court decisions in M.C. Mehta *v/s* State of Tamil Nadu case. The author makes several recommendations to check this social evil. For this there is need of strong will power, dedicated welfare activities, change in societal attitude and of course the constructive role of mass media.

"Infrastructure and Inter-Regional Disparities in India" is written by G.C. Tripathi, Poonam Jaiswal and Abhishek Kumar Pandey. All through the planning process, more stress was given on balanced regional development to realise the objective of growth with social justice. Despite that severe regional disparities exist as poverty is concentrated in few states. The authors suggest for multi-pronged strategy to reduce regional disparities. It needs modified development strategy with major thrust on education, health and nutrition to accelerate the human capital formation. Region-specific and product-specific policies are required to achieve growth with human face.

The chapter on "Glaring Regional Disparities in Economic Development in India" is authored by Niraj Kumar. The ultimate goal of development is the improvement in the quality of life which depends not only on material prosperity but also on social and welfare services, satisfaction, self-reliance, self-esteem and economic freedom. The author concludes by emphasising the importance of balanced regional development in a federal structure even in the phase of liberalisation and globalisation. Hence, there is need to re-examine the pattern of development, greater coordination between center and states, improvement in human resources, and expansion of service sector in backward regions to promote small scale and agro-based industries.

"The Regional Disparities in Economic Devlopment : Comparative Analysis" is presented by S.K.L. Das and Manindera Kumar Singh. The convergence theorem of Barrow postulated that in the wake of accelerated economic growth, initially some regions with affluence resources grow faster than others. But gradually due to the law of diminishing marginal return, the growth rates converge resulting into the bridging of gaps in the levels of income of different regions. But it did not happen so. Despite poverty reduction, some states have very high poverty ratios. There is simmering unrest in several less developed regions. Without major initiatives at the national level, it may further accentuate the crisis and threaten the crisis and threaten social harmony, national integration and sustainable development.

The chapter on "Health Situation in India: Regional and Gender Disparities: An overview" is written jointly by Arun Kumar Thakur and Rabindra Nath Ojha. India is still far behind its objecting of ensuring good health to its citizens due to poverty, illiteracy, malnourishment and lack of modern health facilities. The National Rural Health Mission is an effective step in the direction of integrated, comprehensive and effective primary health care. For the success of health programmes, there is need to ensure full community participation and target. Each and every district/blocks, by deferring the priorities by states.

The chapter on "Regional Disparities in Levels of Agricultural Development: A Comparative Study of North-East Region" is authored jointly by N.K. Thakur and Shandhya L.S. Singh. Agriculture sector and rural economy are the dynamic path of development of rural areas. Without it there can be no sustainable development. Authors make a few recommendations like stimulation of agricultural growth, diversification of agriculture, Agricultural research and extension, flood control and credit facilities, etc.

The chapter on "Regional Development and Level of Living" been written by Ravi Ranjan and Satendra Prajapati peeps through regional imbalances in pre-reform and post-reform periods. The states with larger population like Bihar, UP and MP have been acting as a drag on the growth process of Indian economy. Some States have picked up while some forward states witness decelerating trends in the growth rates in recent years. Under liberalisation and globalisation, private sector has opted to play pivotal role. The growth of forward states and regions are ensured at the cost of other backward regions. This is the natural characteristic of private economic system.

The chapter on "Levels of Living of Agricultural Labour in Bihar during 1985-2001: An Analysis" is presented by Ramesh Kumar Singh. The author tries to throw light on indicators like size of holdings in Bihar, level of wages of agricultural worker, per household assets and loans on wage earner households in Bihar and minimum per capita consumption expenditure for rural consumer, etc. There has been some improvement in the wages and consumption but rising indebtedness and lack of employment opportunities are the causes of concern. Hence there is need of creation of employment opportunities, land reforms and pro-active role of village panchayats.

"Regional Development and Level of Living on the Edge of SGSY in Jharkhand" authored by D.B. Goswami and Kunal Vikram is based on a case study conducted in the Chas Block in Bokaro District. It is an attempt to examine the various aspects of Swarnajayanti Gram Swarozgar Yojana

(SGSY). There have been significant increase in G.N.P. and per capita income but the gap between rich and poor, between educated and illiterate has been on increase. The authors understand that SGSY is a comprehensive scheme of self-employment for rural poor.

The chapter on "Regional Development and Levels of Living in India" is written jointly by Gajan Kumar and Anand Kishore. In terms of extent of poverty, food security, inflationary trend of essential commodities, availability of safe drinking water, human development and access to education, the chapter finds wide disparities among states. In the post-liberalisation era, those states which benefited more have better infrastructures and other resources. The authors conclude that backward states like Bihar, UP, Rajasthan and Orissa are lagging behind in terms of selected human development indicators like life expectancy, infant mortality rate, birth rates, death rates as well as the national average in terms of access to education.

The chapter on "Regional Development and Levels of Living in India—A Case of North-East Region" is contributed by N.C. Jha. Regional disparities are not only in India but also global problem. Regional development is not only a political flavour but also an economic necessity for the backward states as it contains the power to breakthrough the circle of poverty. The author finds some improvement in the level of living in North-eastern states but the outcome of liberalisation and economic reforms are centered to certain pockets. It will have some adverse impacts on the future Indian economy. He concludes with the suggestion that there is need for formulation of appropriate programmes to address the educational and economic backwardness of backward states and to enhance the much expected levels of living.

The chapter on "Regional Disparities and Human Development" is a case study conducted by T.N. Singh and Binodanand Bharti. The authors find that Bihar is India's least developed state. Its plight has further worsened due to its bifurcation in 2001. They suggest that transformation of Bihar's economy is very essential to increase productivity in agriculture sector and output in an agrarian society. There is need to pull out the people from agriculture and deploy them in industry. Hence the fate of Bihar lies in the fact that agriculture is enabled to provide push towards industrialisation.

The last paper on "Bihar Road to Economic Development" authored by Ugra Mohan Jha has made attempt to find the road and various stumbling blocks to development. Main challenge to Bihar's economy is agriculture, which had nose-dived to 2.7 per cent while manufacturing, and service sectors have registered the growth rates of 11.3 per cent and 11.2 per cent respectively. The state is more dependants on Central allocation to finance public investment and development programs but unfortunately Bihar shows the lowest utilisation rate for Central funds. The author gives a few pragmatic policy prescriptions and recommendations for economic development of Bihar, which should not be seen in an isolated and insulated term.

For assessing levels of development in different regions, indicators of development based on agricultural production, industrial production, investment, unemployment, electricity consumption, irrigated area, value of output by commodity producing sectors, level of consumption expenditure, road mileage, primary and secondary education and occupational distribution of population, are useful, but they must be compiled on the basis of accurate statistical data and should be strictly comparable for different States or regions.

References

Hagen, E.E. (1959), Population and Economic Growth, *American Economic Review*, 49:310-327 (June).

Ganguli, B.N. and D.B. Gupta (1976), *Levels of Living in India : An Inter-State Profile*, S. Chand & Company Ltd, New Delhi.

Nath, V. (1970), Regional Development in Indian Planning, *Economic and Political Weekly*, Volume V, Issue 3-5, Special Article, p. 247.

Nath, V. (1971), Regional Development Policies, *Economic and Political Weekly*, Volume VI, Issue 30-32, pp. 1601-03.

Philip E. Enterline, and William H. Stewart (1962), Health Program Requirements to Offset Effects on Levels of Living, *American Journal of Public Health*, Vol. 52, No. 3, pp. 401-09.

Planning Commission (1961), Third Five Year Plan, Planning Commission, Government of India, August 3, 1961.

Sharma, Sanchita (2008), Rich Live Longer, Poor Die Younger, *The Hindustan Times*, 15 October, 2008, Quated from World Health Report (WHR), 2008.

United Nation (1953), Determinants and Consequences of Population Trends, *Population Studies*, No. 17, New York.

A Note on Inter-Regional Disparities in Irrigation Development in India

M. Narasimhulu

INTRODUCTION

One of the important problems faced by India today is inter-state and inter-regional disparities. This is particularly evident after introduction of economic reforms. For the last two decades, the world is moving towards new economic order due to failure of Marxian and Keynesian systems. More than fifty developing countries including India has undertaken introduction of economic reforms. No doubt the policies of Jawaharlal Nehru and Indira Gandhi laid foundations of economic development and social justice but could not answer to the challenges faced by India by 1990. By this time, we have faced the situation of a stagnant and sick India with poverty, unemployment, inflation, black money, mounting burden of external and internal debt, fiscal imbalances, balance of payments, disequilibrium and wage goods scarcity, smuggling, inefficient cultivation and the problem of regional imbalances. The Central Government was forced to create more and more separate States. Still the demand for creation of separate States is continuing. By 1991 June, Indian Economy was on the verge of collapse. Foreign exchange balance was just sufficient to pay import bill for a week or so and not been able to meet foreign debt payments commitment. Foreign lenders and NRIs lost their confidence in our country. Capital was flying out of our country. We were about to default our foreign loans. There was despair and gloom all around.

(a) Before industrial revolution in the World manufacture output India's share was 17.6 per cent. UK's share was 9.3 per cent, USA's share was 2.3 per cent. But by 1900 India's share declined to 1.7 per cent, UK's share increased to 18.5 per cent and USA's share increased to 23.6 per cent.

(b) During the period 1871-1947 the rate of growth of India was 1.5 per cent per annum whereas, UK and USA exceeded India's annual growth rate, rate of saving in India in 1947 was 5 per cent.

We had prominent place among the world countries in 1950s. India's industrial sector was bigger than Taiwan, South Korea. Share of our exports was higher than that of China, South Korea, Singapore, Indonesia and Malaysia. The level of poverty was more in the above countries than India but by now all these countries have surpassed us. Today these countries export more than what we do. Their industry is more competitive than ours. They have higher level of foreign exchange reserves than us. All these countries have eradicated poverty (except China). Their per capita income is 3 to 4 times more than ours. Their people are more literate than us. They have more health care facilities and enjoy higher quality of life than an average Indian.

Due to several reasons India lagged behind these countries. One of the important problem that is faced by India is multi-linguist system, difference in natural endowment. Some areas are highly advanced. Some are very poor. According to Prof. C.H. Hanumantha Rao, after the implementation of Green Revolution, inter-personal, inter-regional and inter-state disparities have increased in India.

Today, we are facing problem of regional disparities in the production of energy availability of irrigation, transport facility, IT, health, education, etc. Therefore, it is necessary to have balanced regional development in all sectors in all regions to control separatist tendencies. It is difficult to discuss all types of disparities in an article like this. Therefore, in this paper, we have made an attempt to find out the inter-state and inter-source irrigation disparities in the country. This is based on secondary data for the year 2002-03 as the published data is available upto this year only. We have calculated inter-source disparities for each state by giving ranks to each indicator and finally we applied total rank score method to explain the regional disparities in irrigation development in India and measures taken to solve this problem which will lead to balanced regional development.

STATEMENT OF THE PROBLEM

There exists nexus between irrigation development and economic development via agriculture development. In developing countries agriculture technology is an important aspect to determine the development. However, there exists international, inter-state and intra-state disparities in various aspects of development including irrigation development. Those countries, states and regions which are endowed with huge potential of irrigation facilities have achieved higher rate of growth of the economy including human development. The areas which lagged in irrigation facilities remained backward, poverty ridden and not in a position to meet the basic needs of day-to-day life. In short, irrigation development plays an important role in determining the destiny of the people.

In this article an attempt is made to discuss the disparities in irrigation development in India.

INTERNATIONAL DISPARITIES IN IRRIGATION DEVELOPMENT

We would like to discuss the percentage of irrigated area to total cropped area in some of the countries along with their annual growth rate of agriculture sector.

It is evident from the data given in Table 1, that the countries which have the highest percentage of irrigated area to total cropped area have exhibited highest rate of growth of agriculture sector. For example, among the eight countries for which data is given in Table 1, Pakistan having highest irrigated area as percentage to total cropped area (81.1%) also has highest rate of growth of agriculture sector (3.7%). Canada is having 1.7 per cent of the cropped area as irrigated area and the rate of growth of agriculture sector is also low. Therefore, we feel that irrigation development is a crucial aspect in agriculture development which in its turn leads to higher growth rate of economy.

Though percentage of irrigated area is crucial for economic development but irrigation development (percentage of area irrigated to total cropped area) is not uniform among all nations of the world. Therefore, some of the countries are developed, some are developing, some more are backward or remained underdeveloped countries. This aspect is considered in the Table 1.

The data given in Table 2 shows some countries which have highest percentage of irrigated area to the total cropped area. Among the countries considered in Table 2, Egypt is in the first place with 100 percentage of irrigated area, Pakistan, Bangladesh and China are better than India. So far as the availability of irrigated land is concerned. Therefore, there is a need to increase irrigated area as a percentage to total cropped area in India to achieve full employment, equitable distribution of wealth and income as well as to remove poverty. The studies on poverty have become next only to disparities in the contemporary economic literature.

So far we have considered a broad sketch of disparities among countries as to the percentage of irrigated area in the total cropped area. Therefore, we would like to discuss the inter-state intra-state and intra-source disparities in the irrigation sector in India.

TABLE 1

Statement Showing the Percentage of Irrigated Area to Total Cropped Area in Some of the Countries vis-à-vis Rate of Growth of Agricultural Sector

Sl. No.	*Name of the Country*	*Percentage of Area Irrigated to Total Cropped Area 2000-02*	*Annual Rate of Growth of Agriculture Sector 1990-2003*
1.	India	33.7	2.7
2.	Pakistan	81.1	3.7
3.	Bangladesh	52	3.1
4.	Iran	45.1	3.3
5.	Canada	1.7	0.5
6.	Germany	4	1.5
7.	France	13.3	1.3
8.	Mexico	23.1	1.9

Source: Statistical Outline of India, 2005-06, pp. 260, 266, published by Tata Services Ltd., Department of Economics and Statistics, Bombay House, Mumbai.

TABLE 2

Statement Showing the Percentage of Irrigated Area to Total Cropped Area in Some of the Countries for the Year 2000-02

Sl. No.	*Name of the Country*	*Percentage of Area Irrigated to Total Cropped Area, 2000-02*	*Rank*
1.	Egypt	100.0	1
2.	Pakistan	81.1	2
3.	Korea Republic	60.4	3
4.	Japan	54.7	4
5.	Bangladesh	52.0	5
6.	Israel	45.8	6
7.	Iran	45.1	7
8.	China	35.9	8
9.	India	33.7	9

Source: op. cit., pp. 266.

INTER-STATE DISPARITIES IN IRRIGATION IN INDIA

The net area irrigated as a percentage to total cropped area is varying among the Indian states both in percentage as well as in absolute terms. For example, the State of Delhi stands in the first place though it is a small State more urbanised is having 24,000 hectares of cultivated land all of which is irrigated (i.e., 100%). Punjab is in the second place with 43,72,000 hectares which represent 95.6 per cent irrigated area to total cropped area. Himachal Pradesh is in the 3rd place with 1,02,000 hectares of irrigated area representing 85.8 per cent. Thus, the inter-state disparities are taking place in the Indian states which is harmful to the country. Generally the developed states try to exploit the backward states. Therefore, the backward regions in the state fight for separation of State. Thus after independence, number of states have been created in India such as Arunachal Pradesh, Chhattisgarh, Haryana, Gujarat, Jharkhand, Manipur, Meghalaya, Mizoram, Nagaland, Tripura and Uttaranchal, etc. But its not stopped here. The backward regions which form part of the State are demanding for the creation of the separate States. Telangana region in Andhra Pradesh, Vidarbha region and Konkan region in Maharashtra, Boda region in Assam, Gurkaland in West Bengal are demanding the governments for the creation of separate state. Therefore, there is a need to develop infrastructure of both types of economic and social and particularly irrigation uniformly in all parts of the country. With this in view the government of Andhra Pradesh has launched the programme of Jalayagnam in the state by present ruling Congress party. The data pertaining to the above discussion is given in the following Table 3.

On the basis of the data given in Table 3, it is evident that the percentage of irrigated area to total cropped area is 40 per cent in India. All those states which have less than 40 per cent of irrigated area are considered as backward and above 40 per cent of irrigated area are considered as advanced. Accordingly, Andhra Pradesh, Arunachal Pradesh, Assam, Chhattisgarh, Goa, Gujarat, Himachal Pradesh, Jharkhand, Karnataka, Kerala, Madhya Pradesh, Maharashtra,

Manipur, Meghalaya, Mizoram, Nagaland, Orissa, Sikkim, Tripura are the backward states in irrigation. The only few states which are advanced in irrigation development are Delhi, Haryana, Jammu and Kashmir, Punjab, Rajasthan, Bihar, Tamil Nadu, Uttar Pradesh, Uttaranchal and West Bengal. Thus inter-state disparities are prevailing in so far as irrigation development is concerned. However, this will give only a rough idea about inter-state disparities in irrigation among the Indian states. For example, Delhi is having only 29,000 hectares of cultivated area which is a meager area but all of it is irrigated. Therefore, it is getting 1st rank, whereas Assam is having more irrigated area that is 174 thousand hectares which is getting 29th rank (last rank) with only 6.23 per cent of irrigated area which is higher than Delhi. Therefore, what is required is to find out the share of each state's percentage of irrigated in India in the total cropped area in India as a whole which is attempted here below:

Percentage Share of Irrigated Area in the Total Cropped Area in the Indian States during the Period 2002-03

The data pertaining to the above is given in the following Table 3.

On the basis of the data given in Table 4, it is clear that, inter-state disparities in the irrigation development prevailing. This we have worked out on the basis of the data given in statistical abstract of India for the year 2002-03 in thousand hectares. In percentages as well as in ranks, U.P. stands as the first state among the 29 states (for which data is published) with 12,232 thousand hectares of irrigated land. The share of irrigated area in the country's irrigated area works out to 23.02 percentage getting the first rank. Second place goes to Madhya Pradesh with 4494 thousands hectares of irrigated land with 8.46 per cent of country's irrigated land. Rajasthan, Punjab, Andhra Pradesh are in the position of 3rd, 4th and 5th ranks respectively. Sikkim is in the last rank. BIMARO states are not that poor in irrigated area though they are known as backward states. Nagaland, Meghalaya, Tripura, Manipur are relatively poor in the irrigation development due to natural situation. Bihar though known as backward state in economic development, its

TABLE 3

Statement Showing the Percentage of Irrigated Area to Total Cropped Area (net) during the Year 2000-03

Sl. No.	*Name of the State*	*Irrigated Area in 1000 hectares*	*Irrigated Area as Percentage to Total cropped Area*	*Rank*
1.	Andhra Pradesh	3614	37.14	11
2.	Arunachal Pradesh	42	25.61	16
3.	Assam	174	6.23	29
4.	Bihar	3462	60.47	5
5.	Chhattisgarh	1068	22.47	19
6.	Delhi	29	100.00	1
7.	Goa	24	17.02	24
8.	Gujarat	2994	31.12	12
9.	Haryana	2967	85.80	3
10.	Himachal Pradesh	102	18.72	21
11.	Jammu and Kashmir	300	40.93	9
12.	Jharkhand	164	9.27	27
13.	Karnataka	2515	25.57	17
14.	Kerala	379	17.19	23
15.	Madhya Pradesh	4494	30.95	13
16.	Maharashtra	2971	16.90	25
17.	Manipur	40	25.81	14
18.	Meghalaya	59	25.65	15
19.	Mizoram	16	17.78	22
20.	Nagaland	65	20.06	20
21.	Orissa	1300	22.89	18
22.	Punjab	4038	95.60	2
23.	Rajasthan	4372	40.46	10
24.	Sikkim	9	7.76	28
25.	Tamil Nadu	2310	50.32	7
26.	Tripura	40	14.29	26
27.	Uttar Pradesh	12232	73.70	4
28.	Uttaranchal	347	43.76	8
29.	West Bengal	2980	55.66	6
30.	India	53131	40.01	—

Source: CMIE, March 2006, Agriculture, pp. 26-27, Mumbai.

TABLE 4

Statement Showing the Percentage of Irrigated Area in Each State in the Total Irrigated Area of the Country 2002-03

Sl. No.	Name of the State	Irrigated Area in 1000 hectares	Irrigated Area as Percentage to Total cropped Area in the Country	Rank
1.	Andhra Pradesh	3614	6.80	5
2.	Arunachal Pradesh	42	0.08	23
3.	Assam	174	0.33	18
4.	Bihar	3462	6.52	6
5.	Chhattisgarh	1068	2.01	14
6.	Delhi	29	0.06	26
7.	Goa	24	0.05	27
8.	Gujarat	2994	5.64	7
9.	Haryana	2967	5.58	10
10.	Himachal Pradesh	102	0.19	20
11.	Jammu and Kashmir	300	0.56	17
12.	Jharkhand	164	0.31	19
13.	Karnataka	2515	4.73	11
14.	Kerala	379	0.71	15
15.	Madhya Pradesh	4494	8.46	2
16.	Maharashtra	2971	5.59	9
17.	Manipur	40	0.08	25
18.	Meghalaya	59	0.11	22
19.	Mizoram	16	0.03	28
20.	Nagaland	65	0.12	21
21.	Orissa	1300	2.45	13
22.	Punjab	4038	7.60	4
23.	Rajasthan	4372	8.23	3
24.	Sikkim	9	0.02	29
25.	Tamil Nadu	2310	4.35	12
26.	Tripura	40	0.08	24
27.	Uttar Pradesh	12232	23.02	1
28.	Uttaranchal	347	0.65	16
29.	West Bengal	2980	5.61	8
30.	India	53131	100	—

Source: Compiled from Table 3.

position is not bad (with 6th rank) next only to Andhra Pradesh. The position of Bihar in irrigated area is better than developed states like Gujarat (7th rank), West Bengal (8th rank), Maharashtra (9th rank). It is surprising to note that the developed states like Tamil Nadu (12th rank), Karnataka (11th rank) are worse than Bihar. Thus inter-state disparities are prevailing in the Indian states in irrigation development. These disparities have to be removed by taking special measures so that there will be peace in the country otherwise demand for creation of separate states will increase.

However, the above analysis gives a broader view of inter-state disparities in irrigation development in the country. The above type of analysis generally followed by the scholars in the traditional way. As Keynes said classical economics is not only misleading but also disastrous (J.M. Keynes : General Theory of Employment, Interest and Money by Dudly Dillord), same way the above analysis also not scientific. Therefore, we would like to follow the total rank score method to scientifically analyse the inter-state disparities in irrigation development in India in the following pages.

SCIENTIFIC APPROACH TO ANALYSE THE INTER-STATE DISPARITIES IN INDIA IN IRRIGATION DEVELOPMENT

We feel it necessary that instead of taking total irrigated area, it is proper to take source-wise irrigated area in the country so that we will be in a better position to explain the inter-state disparities in irrigation development. For example among the Indian States one state is predominant in canal irrigation, another state is predominant in tanks, well and other sources respectively. By giving ranks to each source to all the states and finally by adding ranks of each state for all sources, we will calculate the total rank score and find out the inter-state disparities in irrigation development. The details pertaining to the above discussion is given in the Table 5.

Canal Irrigation in Indian States

According to the data compiled and presented in Table 5, it is clear that, if we take inter-state source-wise

TABLE 5

Statement Showing the Source-wise State-wise Irrigated Area in India during the Year 2002-03 in '000 Hectares

Sl.. No.	Name of the State	Canal Irri-gation	Tank Irri-gation	Well Irri-gation	Irri-gation by other sources	Total Rank Score	Status of source
1	2	3	4	5	6	7	8
1.	Andhra Pradesh	1209 8.1 (3)	426 22.1 (1)	1842 5.5 (8)	137 5.3 (6)	18	VI
2.	Arunachal Pradesh	— — ()	— — ()	— — ()	42 1.6 (13)	13	III
3.	Assam	152 1.0 (16)	— — ()	2 0.0 ()	20 0.8 (18)	34	XIV
4.	Bihar	966 6.5 (5)	111 5.8 (5)	2251 (6.7) (6)	134 5.2 (7)	23	X
5.	Chhattisgarh	734 4.9 (11)	52 2.7 (9)	197 0.6 (14)	85 3.3 (9)	43	XVIII
6.	Delhi	2 0.0 ()	— — ()	24 0.1 (18)	2 0.1 (21)	42	XVII
7.	Goa	4 0.0 ()	— — ()	20 0.1 (19)	— — ()	19	VII
8.	Gujarat	382 2.6 (14)	13 0.7 (12)	2590 7.7 (5)	9 0.4 (22)	53	XXII
9.	Haryana	1433 9.6 (2)	— — ()	1522 4.5 (10)	11 0.4 (20)	32	XIII
10.	Himachal Pradesh	4 0.0 ()	— — ()	13 (0.0) ()	85 3.3 (10)	10	I
11.	Jammu and Kashmir	275 1.8 (15)	3 0.2 (14)	2 0.0 ()	20 0.8 (19)	48	XXI

(Contd.)

1	*2*	*3*	*4*	*5*	*6*	*7*	*8*
12.	Jharkhand	17	27	75	45	60	XXV
		0.1	1.4	0.2	1.7		
		(20)	(11)	(17)	(12)		
13.	Karnataka	886	239	1033	357	26	XI
		5.9	12.4	3.1	13.8		
		(8)	(4)	(12)	(2)		
14.	Kerala	100	49	116	115	52	XXII
		0.7	2.5	0.4	4.5		
		(18)	(10)	(16)	(8)		
15.	Madhya Pradesh	748	94	2988	665	22	IX
		5.0	4.9	8.9	25.7		
		(10)	(7)	(4)	(1)		
16.	Maharashtra	1040	—	1931	—	11	II
		6.9	—	5.7	—		
		(4)	()	(7)	()		
17.	Manipur	—	—	—	40	15	V
		—	—	—	1.5		
		()	()	()	(15)		
18.	Meghalaya	59	—	—	—	19	VII
		0.4	—	—	—		
		(19)	()	()	()		
19.	Mizoram	15	—	—	—	21	VIII
		0.1	—	—	—		
		(21)	()	()	()		
20.	Nagaland	—	—	—	65	11	II
		—	—	—	2.5		
		()	()	()	(11)		
21.	Orissa	882	100	134	184	35	XV
		5.9	5.2	0.4	7.1		
		(9)	(6)	(15)	(5)		
22.	Punjab	962	—	3074	2	34	XIV
		6.4	—	9.1	0.1		
		(7)	()	(3)	(25)		
23.	Rajasthan	960	8	3377	27	38	XVI
		6.4	0.4	10.0	1.0		
		(7)	(13)	(2)	(16)		
24.	Sikkim	—	—	—	9	23	X
		—	—	—	—		
		()	()	()	()		
25.	Tamil Nadu	614	422	1263	11	47	XX
		4.1	21.9	3.8	0.4		
		(13)	(2)	(11)	(21)		
26.	Tripura	13	2	2	24	54	XXIV
		0.1	0.1	0.0	0.9		
		(22)	(15)	()	(17)		

(Contd.)

1	2	3	4	5	6	7	8
27.	Uttar Pradesh	2711	66	9251	203	14	IV
		18.1	3.4	27.5	7.9		
		(1)	(8)	(1)	(4)		
28.	Uttaranchal	103	—	202	42	44	XIX
		0.7	—	0.6	1.6		
		(17)	()	(13)	(14)		
29.	West Bengal	701	313	1716	250	27	XII
		4.7	16.3	5.1	9.7		
		(12)	(3)	(9)	(3)		
30.	India	14972	1925	33625	2584	—	
		100	100	100	100	—	

Notes: 1. The figures in the 1st line (horizontal) indicate 1000s of hectares.
2. The second line figures (horizontal) which are indicate percentage of each source in the country's total for each State.
3. The figures in the parantheses indicate rank of each source for each State in the Country.

Source: Table 3.

information for canal irrigation, Uttar Pradesh is in the first place. Haryana is in the second place and Andhra Pradesh is in the 3rd place in the country. In canal irrigation the position of Tripura (22nd rank), Mizoram (21st rank), Jharkhand (20th rank), Meghalaya (19th rank) are very backward. The States such as Assam (16th rank), Chhattisgarh (11th rank), Gujarat (14th rank), Jammu and Kashmir (15th rank) are medium developed. This shows these states are not highly developed as U.P., Haryana and Andhra Pradesh but better than North-Eastern States. So if we take only one source that is canal irrigation we get this type of result. But this canal irrigation will not give proper idea of irrigation development in a State.

Tank Irrigation in Indian States

If we consider the tank irrigation, Andhra Pradesh is in the first place, second place goes to Tamil Nadu and 3rd place goes to West Bengal. In tank irrigation Tripura (15th rank), Rajasthan (13th rank), Jammu and Kashmir (14th rank), Gujarat (12th rank), Jharkhand (11th rank). These States are backward in tank irrigation. It is surprising to note that in States like Arunachal Pradesh, Assam, Delhi, Goa, Haryana, Himachal Pradesh, Maharashtra and North-Eastern States.

There is no tank irrigation at all. So the inter-state variation the tank irrigation in Indian states is prevailing.

Well Irrigation in Indian States

In well irrigation, Uttar Pradesh is in the first place. Rajasthan is in the 2nd place, Punjab is in the 3rd place, Madhya Pradesh is in the 4th place, Gujarat is in the 5th place, Bihar is in the 6th place, Maharashtra and Andhra Pradesh are in the 7th and 8th places in well irrigation. The states like Goa, Chhattisgarh, Jharkand and Kerala, Orissa are in the backward position in well irrigation. It is surprising to note that, Bihar is a unique state which has 5th rank in canal and tank irrigation respectively 6th and 7th rank in well irrigation and other sources. We see that the position of the state of Bihar is good so far as irrigated area is concerned, though Bihar is treated as a backward State in economic development.

Irrigation under Other Sources in Indian States

So far as irrigation under other sources in Indian States is concerned Madhya Pradesh is in the 1st place. Karnataka is in the 2nd place, West Bengal is in the 3rd place, Uttar Pradesh, Orissa, Andhra Pradesh, Bihar are in the 4th, 5th, 6th and 7th places respectively Punjab, Sikkim, Tamil Nadu, Gujarat and Haryana are in the backward position in this aspect.

In short when we consider inter-state and inter-source irrigation development, we have got the above result but if we go by intra-source the result is different. Therefore what is needed is to give the ranks to each state for each source and add up rank of each state to get the proper idea of inter-state and inter-source disparities in irrigation development among the Indian states, which is generally referred to as total rank score method.

Total Rank Score of Various Sources of Irrigation in Indian States

Under this method Himachal Pradesh is in the 1st place, Maharashtra in the 2nd place, Arunachal Pradesh in the 3rd place, Uttar Pradesh is in the 4th place, Manipur is in the 5th place and Andhra Pradesh is in the 6th place. These States can be considered as developed States from the point of view of irrigation (Please see Table 5).

The States such as Jharkhand (25th rank), Tripura (24th rank), Gujarat (23rd rank), Kerala (22nd rank) are backward in irrigation development but developed in other sectors. Other States are in the middle level of development in irrigation.

CONCLUSION

Every effort is to be made by Planning Commission for the removal of inter-state, inter-sectoral inequalities in the country which will pave the way for peace and cultured civilized society otherwise, problem of law and order, backwardness, unemployment, strikes and lockouts will continuously take place in the country.

What is needed is to give priority to development of irrigation particularly in those areas where the States are backward as well as whose percentage of irrigated area, in the total cropped area is less than all India level. The problem is solvable by allocating more and more funds to irrigation development both plan grants, non-plan grants.

In this connection, mention may be made the case of Andhra Pradesh. Here inter-source as well as inter-regional disparities are prevailing. So far as canal irrigation is concerned Guntur district is in the first place, for tank irrigation Vizianagaram district is in the first place, for well irrigation it is Warangal district which is in the first place and for other sources of irrigation Visakhapatnam district is in the first place.

When we take regional analysis Andhra Pradesh State is divided into three broad regions or six zones. These are:

1. Coastal Andhra
2. Rayalaseema
3. Telangana

So far as net irrigated area is concerned, Coastal Andhra is in the first place, Telangana is in the second place and Rayalaseema is in the third place. Thus there prevails inter-regional and inter-source disparities in irrigation development in Andhra Pradesh. Therefore, the people of backward irrigation development that is Telangana and Rayalaseema are struggling for the creation of separate State would for them. Keeping this in the mind at present State Government lead by Congress Party is giving highest priority in its budgetary allocation in each year to irrigation development since it came to power in the name of Jalayagnam. For this purpose not only State Government revenues are used but also Central Government is giving funds liberally. Even the World Bank is also coming forward to support the programme of Jalayagnam.

At present the irrigated area in the State is 1,28,81,461 acres when the programme of Jalayagnam is going to be completed. Net irrigated area will increase to 2,31,62,511 almost it will be doubled. Probably it may lead to satisfy the people of all the regions in the process of development. When irrigation development take place agricultural output will increase industrial production will increase, employment will increase, purchasing power will increase and poverty will come down. Due to increasing in the levels of income of the people the literacy rate will increase and life expectancy will also increase. Therefore, there is every need to develop the irrigation infrastructure in the country in general and in backward irrigated areas in particular and in the State like Andhra Pradesh specifically.

It is opt to quote Prof. C.H. Hanumantha Rao regarding regional imbalances. "The inter-state disparities in the gross state domestic product, (GSDP) have been increasing, in particular, in the post-economic reform period. These disparities have been largely contributed by the large variabilities in the contributions made by the secondary and tertiary sectors. For reducing inter-state disparities, there is an urgent need for enhancing the levels of public investment for improving the social and economic infrastructure in the backward regions. There is also the urgency of speeding up social transformation through the empowerment of the common people and adoption of measures for good governance. Both the Finance Commission and the Planning

Commission have the responsibility of rising to the challenges of increasing disparities and adopting suitable corrective measures.

References

Dudley Dillord: Economics of John Maynard Keynes.

Statistical Outline of India, 2005-06, p. 260, published by Tata Services Ltd., Department of Economics and Statistics, Bombay House, Mumbai.

Centre for Monitoring Indian Economy (CMIE), 2006, Agriculture, pp. 26-27, March.

Yartha (2007), Daily Telugu News Paper, published from Hyderabad, dated 15 January, p. 13.

Prof. C.H. Hanumantha Rao (2006), "Growing Regional Disparities in Development in India Post-Reform Experience and Challenges Ahead", *The Indian Economic Journal*, Journal of Indian Economic Association, Vol. 54, No. 1, April-June.

2

Reforms and Regional Inequalities in India: An Analysis

R.V. DADIBHAVI AND S.T. BAGALKOTI

I. INTRODUCTION

Regional inequality continues to be a matter of grave concern among the policy makers and researchers. The unequal endowment of natural resources, historical factors and policy of the government have rendered the levels and trends in the development of regions dissimilar in India. This necessitates the study of the economic progress of the country to be taken down to the regional levels. Not only is the federal structure of polity a justification for such a study, the recently emerging coalition politics with regional parties having a stronger influence on the policy making also provides a greater fillip for such studies. A plethora of studies have analysed the levels, trends and causes of such inequalities in India (Das and Barua, 1996; Ghosh, Marjit and Neogi, 1998; Rao and Kalirajan, 1999; Dasgupta *et al.*, 2000; Rie Shand and Bhide, 2000; Nagaraj, Varadouski and Veganzones, 2000; Kalirajan and Takihiro, 2002; Shetty, 2003; Bhattacharya and Shaktivel, 2004; among others). The governments too have adopted proactive policies to achieve a balanced regional development, which has been an elusive goal. Additionally, the reform process underway in the country since 1991 seems to have disparately affected the states of India. The reforms have led to a spate of structural changes in the Indian economy, through deregulation of both domestic and foreign investment; liberalisation of trade; exchange rate, interest rate; capital flows and prices (Bhattacharya and Sakthivel, 2004).

Consequent to the reform, the public investment is expected to decline and that of private investment to increase. But the private investment naturally flows into already better-off regions that have better infrastructure and better overall congenial investment climate. The poorer regions, thus, are double constrained. Firstly, due to lack of own investible resources and compulsion of investing whatever they have in more pressing needs such as poverty alleviation or provision of minimum basic necessities. Secondly, their investment also suffers due to cut in the flow of grants and assistance from the enter. The evidence for India reveals that a major share of Foreign Direct Investment (FDI) flows into four to five developed states, so also the financial assistance by the all India development financial institutions. The less developed regions not only face scarcities of skilled labour, the market is neither deep nor wide to sustain the new investments. There is also a likelihood of migration of resource and skills to better-off regions leaving the poorer ones high and dry. The relative growth of the regions also depends upon the share of different sectors in the overall economic activity. The developed regions are naturally expected to possess a larger share of fast-growing sectors, that are attractive to private and foreign investors, and the poorer regions would continue to foster relatively slow growing sectors. Therefore, with reduced investment by the government and lifting of controls on private as well as foreign investment, more of it will flow to areas with a better investment climate. The advanced states with relatively better infrastructure and the fast growing activities in which they specialise would be the desired destination. This obviously leads to divergence in the level of inequality and would still worsen the situation. Elizondo and

Krugman (1992) argue that openness of an economy is an instrument to achieve both economic growth and geographical dispersion of economic activities. The present paper attempts to estimate the levels and trends in the regional inequalities for the major 17 states of India. Further, the impact of liberalisation leading to openness of the economy and its impact on regional disparities is studied. The period for 1980-81 to 2001-02 is the study period with 1991-92 to 2001-02 being the post-reforms period. The per capita net state domestic product (PCNSDP) is the major indicator employing which the analysis is made. The data on foreign trade and inflow of FDI has also been used. The secondary data as available in standard publications have been used. The paper is organized as follows: the next section discusses the method of obtaining comparable data series and the third section deals with the relative positions of the states in terms of their PCNSDP; the fourth one analyses the growth rates of NSOP as well as PCNSDP to identify the disparities in growth of the state economies; the fifth undertakes a statistical analysis of convergence/divergence; the sixth analyses the impact of liberalisation on the disparities; and the last summarises the findings of the study.

2. METHODOLOGY FOR ADJUSTMENT OF INCOME DATA

The present work mainly analyses the growth and disparity among major states of India in the pre-reform and post-reform period. Although a number of studies (for instance, Dholakia, 1985; Marjit and Mitra, 1996; Dasgupta, *et al.*, 2000) have already conducted the exercise and conclude that disparities have widened in the post-reform period. But the income figures, which they predominantly make use of, suffer from non-comparability as the CSO has revised the base year from 1980-81 to 1993-94 and the new system of national accounting is being used. Moreover, the new GDP and SDP series has changed base year in terms of price; production boundaries for many sectors (agriculture, real estate and finance) have been redesigned; the NSS occupational database is being used instead of that of the

Census; and certain new dynamic activities, like software, are included in the new series. This change has been effected from the year 1997-98. Hence, any comparison of income levels and growth rates based on the two series (1980-81 base series up to 1992-93 and 1993-94 base series there onwards) does not yield the correct trends (Bhattacharya and Sakthivel, 2004). Hence an important task before analysing the level and trends in income disparities is to evolve a comparable income series with single base year, preferably 1993-94. Whereas the CSO has published national accounts data for earlier years with the new base year (CSO, 2001) to develop the same the state level, an elaborate exercise was carried to evolve a single comparable series of SDP data. Since the techniques of base shifting or splicing to homogenize the series due to the issues, mentioned above—new price deflators, new sectors, change in the boundaries of certain sectors and changes in the weights—would be inadequate, an alternative methodology for extending the 1993-94 series backwards till 1980-81 and estimating revised SDP from 1980-81 to 1992-93 has been adopted.

Firstly, considering 1993-94 SDP (1980-81 series) as 100, the index of SDP was worked out backwards till 1980-81, for all states and sectors. And in the second step, the same indices were applied to the 1993-94 SDP of the new series—sectoral as well as state-wise. Thus, new revised series of SDP as 1993-94 the base year was worked out and linked to the series published by the CSO for later years making the series comparable from 1980-81 to 2000-01. Implicitly, it is assumed that sectoral composition, sectoral growth and the weighting pattern of the new series is applied to the old series, making it comparable. Further, the mid-year population estimates were used to compute per capita SDP-sector as well as state-wise, which is the main variable of analysis of the present study. However, the methodology is not completely foolproof as it blindly assigns weights and prices of the new series to the old one. Moreover, the limitations of the SDP data, as have been documented in the literature, (see *inter alia*, Bhattacharya and Sakthivel, 2004) are left undressed. These weaknesses of the data limit the exactness of the analysis. Nonetheless, it is a definite advancement of analysis over the earlier studies.

3. LEVELS OF PCNSDP

The level of regional development as measured through the level of PCNSDP (at 1993-94 prices) across the states is presented in Table 1. The per capita net domestic product has increased from Rs. 5352 in 1980-81 to Rs.7321 in 1990-91 to further Rs. 10254 by 2000-01. The average PCNSDP of the selected states has increased from Rs. 5555 to Rs. 7314 and to Rs. 9933 during the corresponding years. This is due to the fact that some of the high income regions like Delhi, Goa, Pondicherry and Chandigarh are outside our sample of states. Nonetheless, a steady increase in PCNSDP is discernible both at the national as well as that at the states.

Comparing with the all India PCNSDP, Punjab, Maharashtra, Haryana and Gujarat have had higher PCNSDP throughout indicating that they continue to retain their higher order in the development ladder. But Tamil Nadu (from 1990-91) and Himachal Pradesh (from 1991-92) have also performed better and raised their PCNSDP above the national level almost throughout the post-reform period. Similarly, Karnataka for the last three years and Kerala for the last two years under study were able to raise their PCNSDP above the national level. Hence looking at the level of PCNSDP we may consider Punjab, Maharashtra, Haryana, Gujarat, Tamil Nadu and Himachal Pradesh as advanced regions.

Similarly, comparing the individual state's PCNSDP with average PCNSDP of the corresponding year, a few more states emerge to be better performers in the group. Tamil Nadu and Himachal Pradesh had higher than average PCNSDP up to 1991-92. Karnataka too consistently recorded greater than average PCNSDP for the whole of the post-reform decade, Kerala which reported a higher than average PCNSDP intermittently upto 1991-92 has maintained its favourable position. On the other hand, Andhra Pradesh had a higher than the average PCNSDP for few years prior to 1991-92 but later on only for the year 2000-01 it had that favourable position. Jammu and Kashmir too reported a higher than average PCNSDP upto 1986-87, but could not retain the advantageous position later on. Thus, Kerala and Karnataka too can be included in the better-off or advanced

TABLE I

Levels of PCNDP Across Selected States (in Rs. at 1993-94 prices)

States	80-81	81-82	82-83	83-84	84-85	85-86	86-87	87-88	88-89	89-90	90-91	91-92	92-93	93-94	94-95	95-96	96-97	97-98	98-99	99-00	2000-01
A.P.	5470	6169	6104	6219	5896	6063	5701	6124	6926	7094	7050	7088	6881	7418	7704	8048	8467	8214	9162	4579	982
Assam	4611	5032	5159	5277	5195	5422	5157	5270	5192	5446	5543	5655	5588	5681	5694	5711	5734	5796	5664	5785	5867
Bihar	3363	3473	3429	3680	3939	3939	[illegible]	3850	4247	4092	4391	4055	3731	3738	3975	3552	3947	4114	4035	4123	4087
Gujarat	6607	7099	6840	7980	7811	7446	7753	6763	9323	9005	9022	8111	10529	9833	11603	11746	13307	12937	13493	13022	12975
Haryana	7549	7641	7921	7894	8003	9213	8999	8630	10475	10363	11175	11144	10895	11142	11706	11702	12827	12544	13003	13918	14331
H.P.	5760	5995	5674	5837	5408	6022	6347	6255	6918	7608	7578	7484	7665	7828	8431	8729	9140	9625	10131	10514	10942
J. & K.	6518	6503	6542	6586	6742	6724	6640	5766	6371	6349	6557	6515	6622	6726	6870	7052	6978	7128	7296	7384	7383
Karn.	5004	5211	5220	5472	5759	5411	5805	6099	6510	6764	6709	7444	7496	7895	8186	8497	9149	9218	10607	11254	11902
Kerala	5635	5491	5552	5256	5507	5634	5431	5539	6033	6374	6786	6826	7221	7904	8471	8694	8921	9079	9619	10178	10627
M.P.	4260	4278	4373	4499	4191	4468	4151	4611	4835	4821	5376	4882	5139	5552	5516	5688	5923	6023	6205	6368	5760
Mah.	8754	8752	8884	9227	9131	9623	9525	9927	10701	12163	12396	12082	13671	14590	14587	15893	16408	16479	16664	18048	18166
Orissa	4066	3993	3688	4355	4075	4463	4444	4227	5023	5258	4282	4736	4570	4776	4886	5021	4605	5272	5165	5265	5187
Punjab	8450	9085	9182	9178	9712	10267	10434	10777	11143	11786	11785	12088	12422	12710	12784	13008	13705	13758	14274	14980	15390
Rajasthan	4284	4508	4474	5349	4835	4692	5009	4542	6283	6016	6812	6155	6927	6228	7216	7335	8037	8850	8754	8707	7937
T.N.	5298	5800	5399	5595	6219	6360	6206	6498	7029	7406	7911	8028	9086	8997	10019	10276	10585	11312	11817	12348	12779
U.P.	3817	3814	4016	4077	4046	4108	4189	4281	4733	4759	4936	4861	4826	4869	5035	5111	5584	5497	5447	5682	5770
W.B.	4984	4748	4833	5293	5318	5421	5514	5682	5793	5862	6028	6372	6449	6800	7151	7562	7963	8408	8814	9330	9778
All In.	5352	5555	5555	5854	5956	6082	[illegible]	6260	6777	7087	7321	7212	7433	7698	8088	8498	9036	9288	9733	10067	10254
Mean	5555	5741	5723	5987	5988	6193	6204	6167	6914	7127	7314	7266	7630	7805	8226	8449	8899	9074	9421	9786	9933
CV (%) 17 states	28.32	28.87	29.64	27.99	29.42	31.05	30.92	31.74	31.60	33.64	33.76	33.79	36.94	37.29	36.66	38.27	39.29	37.58	38.08	39.28	40.43

Source: Computed from CSO, Various issues.

TABLE 2

Ranks of PCNDP of Selected States (in Rs. at 1993-94 prices)

Rank	80-81	81-82	82-83	83-84	84-85	85-86	86-87	87-88	88-89	89-90	90-91	91-92	92-93	93-94	94-95	95-96	96-97	97-98	98-99	99-00	2000-01
1	MAH	PUN	PUN	MAH	PUN	PUN	PUN	PUN	PUN	MAH	MAH	PUN	MAH	MAH	MAH	MAH	MAH	MAH	MAH	MAH	MAH
2.	UN	MAH	MAH	PUN	MAH	MAH	MAH	MAH	MAH	PUN	PUN	MAH	PUN	PUN	PUN	PUN	PUN	PUN	PUN	PUN	PUN
3.	AR	HAR	HAR	GUJ	HAR	HAR	HAR	HAR	HAR	HAR	HAR	HAR	HAR	HAR	HAR	GUJ	GUJ	GUJ	GUJ	HAR	HAR
4.	GUJ	GUJ	GUJ	HAR	GUJ	GUJ	GUJ	GUJ	GUJ	GUJ	GUJ	GUJ	GUJ	GUJ	GUJ	HAR	HAR	HAR	HAR	GUJ	GUJ
5.	JK	JK	JK	JK	JK	JK	JK	TN	TN	HP	TN	TN	TN	TN	TN	TN	TN	TN	TN	TN	TN
6.	P	AP	AP	AP	TN	TN	HP	HP	AP	TN	HP	HP	HP	KER	KER	HP	KAR	HP	KAR	KAR	KAR
7.	KER	HP	HP	HP	AP	AP	TN	AP	HP	AP	AP	KAR	KAR	KAR	HP	KER	HP	KAR	HP	HP	HP
8.	P	TN	KER	TN	KAR	HP	KAR	KAR	KAR	KAR	RAJ	AP	KER	HP	KAR	KAR	KER	KER	KER	KER	KER
9.	ITN	KER	TN	KAR	KER	KER	AP	JK	JK	KER	KER	KER	RAJ	AP	AP	AP	AP	RAJ	AP	AP	AP
10.	KAR	KAR	KAR	RAJ	HP	ASS	WB	WB	RAJ	JK	KAR	JK	AP	WB	RAJ	WB	RAJ	WB	WB	WB	WB
11.	WB	ASS	ASS	WB	WB	WB	KER	KER	KER	RAJ	JK	WB	JK	JK	WB	RAJ	WB	AP	RAJ	RAJ	RAJ
12.	SS	WB	WB	ASS	ASS	KAR	ASS	ASS	WB	WB	WB	RAJ	WB	RAJ	JK	JK	JK	JK	JK	JK	JK
13.	RAJ	RAJ	RAJ	KER	RAJ	RAJ	RAJ	MP	ASS	ASS	ASS	ASS	ASS	ASS	ASS	ASS	MP	MP	MP	MP	ASS
14.	MP	MP	MP	MP	MP	MP	ORI	RAJ	ORI	ORI	MP	MP	MP	MP	MP	MP	ASS	ASS	ASS	ASS	UP
15.	ORI	ORI	UP	ORI	ORI	ORI	UP	UP	MP	MP	UP	UP	UP	UP	UP	lup	UP	UP	UP	UP	MP
16.	P	UP	ORI	UP	UP	UP	BIH	ORI	UP	UP	BIH	ORI	ORI	OR!	ORI	ORI	ORI	ORI	ORI	ORI	ORI
17.	BIH	BIH	BIH	BIH	BIH	BIH	MP	BIH	BIH	BIH	ORI	BIH	BIH	BIH	BIH	BIH	BIH	BIH	BIH	BIH	BIH

Source: Computed from CSO, Various issues.

states along with Punjab, Maharashtra, Haryana, Gujarat, Tamil Nadu and Himachal Pradesh as mentioned earlier.

Of the remaining states, West Bengal and Rajasthan came nearer to the average PCNSDP but seldom crossed it. These two states along with Andhra Pradesh may be formed as the second or intermediate category of states. On the other hand, Assam, Bihar, Madhya Pradesh, Orissa and Uttar Pradesh, which have had consistently lower PCNSDP, can be said to form the third and the poorer category of states. Jammu and Kashmir may be included in this category as its performance has not been so good in the last 10 to 15 years due to frequent socio-political disturbances witnessed in the state.

These results are further confirmed in the analysis of the ranks (Table 2) of the states based on their PCNSDP. Maharashtra, Punjab, Haryana, Gujarat and Tamil Nadu have been the top five states throughout the twenty-one year period, with only minor movements. Similarly, Bihar, Orissa, Uttar Pradesh, Madhya Pradesh and Assam have been the bottom five states, again with minor movements. The co-efficient of concordance of the ranking across the states for the selected period, work out to be 0.836, which is highly significant. This indicates that the rankings have more or less remained unchanged as developed states have continued to move ahead and the backward states continue to lag behind.

4. GROWTH RATES IN NSDP AND PCNSDP

The growth rates of NSDP and PCNSDP for the chosen states are given in Table 3. Results in Table 3 reveal that average growth in NSDP of the selected states has jumped up from 4.71 per cent p.a. in the 1980s to more than 5 per cent p.a. in the 1990s but still for the overall period, growth rates remains to be less than 5 per cent mark. The Coefficient of variation (CV) of growth rates which was around 25 per cent in 1980s increased to about 30 per cent in the 1990s.

During 1980-81 to 1990-91, the first decade, it may be observed that Rajasthan witnessed the highest growth in NSDP at 6.57 per cent p.a. closely followed by Haryana at 6.55 per cent p.a. Except Andhra Pradesh (4.25% p.a.), Assam

TABLE 3

Growth Rates in NSDP and PCNSDP

(per cent per annum)

States/Period	*Growth of NSDP*			*Growth Rates of PCNSDP*		
	1980-81 to 1990-91	*1991-92 to 2000-2001*	*1980-81 to 2000-2001*	*1980-81 to 1990-91*	*1991-92 to 2000-2001*	*1980-81 to 2000-2001*
Andhra Pradesh	4.25	5.48	4.62	1.93	3.99	2.68
Assam	3.32	2.00	2.96	1.14'	0.34	0.90
Bihar	4.77	3.18	2.79	2.59	0.81	0.59
Gujarat	4.87	6.65	5.80	2.88	4.83	3.86
Haryana	6.55	5.15	5.66	4.01	3.07	3.27
Himachal Pradesh	4.88	6.29	5.40	2.96	4.53	3.52
Jammu and Kashmir	2.16	4.50	3.36	-0.36	1.67	0.60
Karnataka	5.20	7.40	6.15	3.12	5.64	4.27
Kerala	3.15	5.89	5.10	1. 71	4.69	3.77
Madhya Pradesh	4.18	4.51	4.44	1.80	2.78	2.34
Maharashtra	5.98	6.19	6.61	3.53	2.34	3.01
Orissa	3.95	2.78	3.12	2.14	1.39	1.43
Punjab	5.38	4.89	4.81	3.46	2.95	2.87
Rajasthan	6.57	6.56	6.32	3.94	3.87	3.77
Tamil Nadu	5.33	6.16	6.06	3.76	5.11	4.74
Uttar Pradesh	4.95	3.81	4.17	2.52	2.04	2.21
West Bengal	4.59	6.97	5.61	2.33	5.17	3.52
All India	5.52	6.31	568	3.79	4.22	3.46
Average	4.71	5.20	4.88	2.56	3.25	2.79
CV (%)17 states	24.68	29.91	25.43	44.05	50.48	45.78

Source: Computed from CSO, Various issues

(3.32% p.a.), Madhya Pradesh (4.18% p.a.) and Orissa (3.95% p.a.) have recorded growth lower than the average growth rate. Rajasthan, Haryana, Maharashtra, Punjab, Tamil Nadu and Karnataka were the states that performed above 5 per cent growth rate during the first decade.

In the second decade, i.e., 1991-92 to 2000-01, the average growth rate accelerated and majority of states experienced it. Karnataka with 7.40 per cent p.a. growth in

NSDP was the star performer. West Bengal (6.97% p.a.), Gujarat (6.65% p.a.), Rajasthan (6.56% p.a.), Himachal Pradesh (6.29% p.a.), Maharashtra (6.19% p.a.), Tamil Nadu (6.16% p.a.) Kerala (5.89% p.a.) and Andhra Pradesh (5.48% p.a.) are the states that exceeded the average growth rate. Thus, only 9 states grew faster than the average growth in the 90s, as compared to in the 80s. Andhra Pradesh, Kerala and West Bengal, which grew at below the average growth by the 90s improved their growth rates to above the average level. On the other hand, Bihar, Haryana, Punjab, and Uttar Pradesh whose growth rates were higher than the average growth in the first decade, fell below it during the second. Assam, Jammu and Kashmir and Orissa grew at less than the average growth during both the decades. Further, Rajasthan almost stagnated at 6.5 per cent per annum.

When we look at the overall performance the average growth rate is 4.88 per cent p.a. Maharashtra has been the fastest growing state with 6.61 per cent growth rate followed by Rajasthan (6.32% p.a.), Karnataka and Tamil Nadu with 6.15 per cent p.a. and 6.06 per cent p.a. rates of growth, respectively. These are the states that have crossed 6 per cent growth rate. Similarly, Gujarat (5.80% p.a.), Haryana (5.66% p.a.), Himachal Pradesh (5.40% p.a.) and Kerala (5.10% p.a.) are the states that grew at more than 5 per cent rate. Punjab's growth rate (4.81% p.a.) was almost comparable to the average growth rate. On the other hand, the poorer states, viz., Bihar (2.79% p.a.), Assam (2.96% p.a.), Orissa (3.12% p.a.), Jammu and Kashmir (3.56% p.a.) and Uttar Pradesh (4.16% p.a.) recorded lower growth rates. Andhra Pradesh too grew at 4.62 per cent per annum.

Thus, the overall growth has been quite impressive and has accelerated in the recent years. However, barring few exceptions like Haryana in the developed category and Rajasthan in the backward category, the growth rates in NSDP are such as to 10 perpetuate inter-state disparities. As observed, the CV of growth rates has increased. More so, the reforms seem to have favored better-off regions. It is also evident in the fact that the growth has decelerated in all the low-income states except Madhya Pradesh and Jammu and Kashmir. An interesting observation is the deceleration in the growth of Punjab and Haryana, which might be due to the higher share of agriculture in their NSDPs.

4.1. Growth of PCNSDP

Due to varying growth rates of population, the growth rates of PCNSDP need not coincide with those of NSDP. The data in Table 3 reveal that on an average PCI has grown at less than 3 per cent per annum for the period 1980-81 to 2000-01. The growth of PCNSDP too has accelerated from 2.56 per cent per annum in the first decade to 3.25 per cent per annum in the second decade. For the 21-year period, Tamil Nadu records the highest growth rate of 4.74 per cent per annum followed by Karnataka (4.27%). Other states to record higher growth are Gujarat (3.86%), Rajasthan and Kerala (3.77% each), Himachal Pradesh and West Bengal (3.52% each), Haryana (3.27%), and Punjab (2.87%). On the other hand, PCNSDP of Bihar, Jammu and Kashmir and Assam did not grow even at 1 per cent during the same period. While Orissa recorded 1.43 per cent growth in its PCNSDP, Uttar Pradesh (2.21%), Madhya Pradesh (2.34%) and Andhra Pradesh (2.68%) were the other states that did not grow at least at the average growth rate.

It is to be observed across the decades that 9 states, viz., Andhra Pradesh, Gujarat, Himachal Pradesh, Jammu and Kashmir, Karnataka, Kerala, Madhya Pradesh, Maharashtra, Tamil Nadu and West Bengal improved their growth in PCNSDP during 1991-92 to 2000-01, as compared to 1980-81 to 1990-91. However, the acceleration in Jammu and Kashmir is not only insignificant but it had experienced negative growth in the first decade.

In the first decade, Bihar, Gujarat, Haryana, Himachal Pradesh, Karnataka, Maharashtra, Punjab, Rajasthan and Tamil Nadu were the nine states to record higher than average growth in PCNSDP. But in the second decade due to reduced growth in NSDP, states like Bihar, Haryana, and Punjab experienced lower than average growth in PCNSDP. Jammu and Kashmir, Madhya Pradesh and Maharashtra, although experienced acceleration in NSDP, it was not enough to overcome the growth in population, hence the PCNSDP of these states increased at lower than the average level of growth. Interestingly enough, Assam, Bihar, Orissa and Uttar Pradesh have witnessed deceleration in PCNSDP growth owing to decelerated growth in NSDP and perhaps higher growth in population. Thus, it seems that Gujarat, Karnataka, Rajasthan and Tamil Nadu have surged ahead in terms of income growth; Punjab, Haryana and Maharashtra have lagged a little behind. The recovery of Andhra Pradesh, Kerala and West Bengal is clearly observed. The poorer states have not only grown slowly but have decelerated too. In fact, the CV of growth rates has increased from 43.94 per cent in 1980s to 50.43 per cent in 1990s. This points to the divergence of state incomes in the post-reform decades. Thus, the regional NSDP incomes have been diverging and the process has continued unabated in the reform period.

4.2. Levels and Trends in Inequalities

The regional inequalities are studied by considering the levels and trends in the co-efficient of variation (CV) of PCNSDP. The CV of PCNSDP has increased continuously from 28.31 per cent in 1980-81 to 40.43 per cent by 2000-01. The trend in inequalities is steadily rising.

Thus the inter-state disparities in economic development are increasing and these trends are confirmed in growth rates of CVs and CVs of growth rates across the pre and post-reform decades. The relevant information is furnished in Table 4.

TABLE 4

Trends in Disparities

Sector	1980-81 to 1990-91	1991-92 to 2000-01	1980-81 to 2000-01
Trends in CVs of PCNSDP (% p.a.)	2.58**	1.45ns	2.46*
CVs of Growth rates of PCNSDP (%)	44.05	50.48	45.78

Note: ** significant at 1% level; * significant at 5% level; ns—not significant
Source: Computed from CSO, Various issues

The CV of PCNSDP has grown at nearly 2.5 per cent p.a. during the study period.

The growth in CV of NSDP declined from 2.58 per cent in the first decade to 1.45 per cent in the second decade. Then, though the disparities in PCNSDP have increased, the increase has been somewhat subdued in the post-reforms decade. To supplement the analysis, the coefficients of variation (CV) of decadal growth rates of PCNSDP show that the growth rates in PCNSDP are very much divergent in the post-reform decades.

5. CONVERGENCE/DIVERGENCE: STATISTICAL EXERCISE

The usual tests adopted to verify the process of Convergence/Divergence are: a-convergence, α-convergence and β-convergence. The α-convergence hypothesis tests whether the inequalities have declined or not in terms of the standard deviation of the chosen variable. The trend rate of the log of standard deviation of PCNDP is estimated by fitting a log-linear time trend model. If the estimated beta-co-efficient is negative and significant, convergence is said to be taking place. On the other hand, if the co-efficient is positive, divergence occurs the selected regions. The α-convergence is tested by estimating the time trend of CV of PCNSDP during the study period. Similar to σ-convergence, if the beta coefficient is negative, convergence is the result, otherwise divergence. Lastly the β-convergence is tested by estimating the relationship between the trend growth the PCNSDP and the log of base year PCNSDP. Similar to the above, convergence is said to exist if the estimated beta coefficient is negative and significant. The results of the above exercises are presented as under:

5.1. σ–Convergence

The results reveal significant divergence in the levels of PCNSDP across the selected states.

The estimated beta-coefficients are positive and significant for all the three periods. Not only the R^2 value is high, the beta-coefficient has increased in value in the post-reform decade suggesting that economic reforms have resulted in widening of disparities.

5.2. α-Convergence

The α-convergence equations (4, 5 and 6) too report a non-decreasing tendency in the inequalities. The CV of PCNSDP is estimated to significantly increase overtime in both the pre and post-reform decades. Since the R^2 is high and beta-coefficients are positive divergence, instead of convergence is the trend in PCNSDP.

The model with a dummy time variable, δ (0 for pre-reform years) reveals that during the reform period also the disparity has increased—the coefficient for the dummy variable is positive but non-significant (equation 7).

Another model was tested to verify Kuznets' Inverted-U hypotheses, taking time squared as another explanatory variable. As expected, in equation 8, the estimated coefficient takes a negative sign but is non-significant. Thus the tendency of inequalities to decline overtime is suggested but not conclusively. Thus the α-convergence test also proves otherwise. However, 21 years is a relatively short time period to assess Kuznets type of changes to occur.

5.3. β-Convergence

The growth rates in PCNSDP of regions during the given period are regressed on their respective base year incomes in this exercise. The Neo-classical growth theory postulates that as income (capital stock) increases, the growth rate (productivity) of it declines. That is, the high income states tend to record lower rates of growth and *vice versa* or the beta-coefficient of the model has to be negative. However, to confirm the same, different approaches have been used in the study.

Firstly, the trend growth of PCNSDP has been regressed on log of PCNSDP of corresponding base year and the results are given as equations 9, 10 and 11.

The estimated beta co-efficients are positive but non-significant at 5 per cent level of significance. The goodness of fit is also not robust. These leads to conclude that there is no convergence but weak divergence.

Secondly, the growth rates for point-to-point triennial PCNSDP are regressed on base year triennium average PCNSDPs and the results are given as equations 12,13 and 14.

Log of SD of PCNSDP	= 0.244** + 0.0082** t	R^2 = 0.93**	...(1)
(1980-81 to 2000-01)	(0.007) (0.001)	F = 247.954	
Log of SD of PCNSDP	= 0.265** + 0.0041 ** t	R^2 = 0.77**	...(2)
(1980-81 to 1990-91)	(0.005) (0.001)	F =29.634	
Log of SD of PCNSDP	= 0.329** + 0.0096** t	R^2 = 0.86**	...(3)
(1991-92 to 2000-01)	(0.008) (0.001)	F = 50.637	

Note: **Significant at 1% level. Figures in brackets are standard errors of estimates.

The results of the statistical exercises presented in the equations indicate that divergence has occurred rather than convergence as the co-efficients are positive. Although the co-efficients for the 1980s and for the entire period are non-significant, it turns out to be significant for the post-reform period. This supports the argument that growth during reforms period resulted in divergence of incomes of the states in India.

Thus, unlike some studies (Barro R.J. and Sala-I-Martin, 1992 and 1995) in other countries that indicate convergence of incomes, the present study proves that in India, the divergence has taken place and hence supports the conclusions of many similar studies referred earlier.

CV of PCNSDP	= 26952** + 0.643**t	R^2 = 0.95**	...(4)
(1980-81 to 2000-01)	(0.4227) (0.034)	F = 3.57.34	
CV of PCNSDP	= 27.296** + 0.556**t	R^2 = 0.86**	...(5)
(1980-81 to 1090-1991)	(0.488) (0.072)	F = 59.623	
CV of PCNSDP	= 34.965* + 0.508*t	R^2 = 0.71**	...(6)
(1980-81 to 2000-01)	(1.925) (0.115)	F = 19.548	

Note: **Significant at 1% level. Figures in brackets are standard errors of estimates.

6. LIBERALISATION AND REGIONAL DISPARITIES

To examine the impact of liberalisation, we introduce two variables of openness i.e., volume of foreign trade as per cent of GDP (FT/GDP) and Foreign Direct Investment as per cent of GDP (FDI/GDP) and also a dummy variable (D), 0 for pre-reforms period and 1 for post-reforms period. However, the behaviour of inequalities is analysed on the basis of the sign and siginificance level of the estimated coefficients. The equations specified are as follows:

CV of PCNSDP	= 27.418 + 0.536** t + 1.506d	R^2 = 0.95**	...(7)
(1980-81 to 2000-01)	(0.464) (0.063) (0.770)	F = 207.175	
CV of PCNSDP	= 26.924 + 0.651** t - 0.003t2	R^2 = 0.95**	...(8)
(1980-81 to 2000-01)	(0.701) (0.147) (0.006)	F = 169.295	

Note: **Significant at 1% level. Figures in brackets are standard errors of estimates.

The results indicate that the indicators of openness, when considered individually, have diverged the inequalities. The coefficients have positive signs before them and also are found to be significant at 1 per cent level of significance for the post-reform period and overall study period. However, for the period 1980-81 to 1990-91 the coefficients were not found to be significant though they had positive signs before them. When all the indicators of openness were included, the value of R^2 has not shown any improvement but explains 86 per cent of variations in CVs of PCI across the states and only the volume of foreign trade as per cent of GDP was found to be significant at 1 per cent level of significance.

GR PCNSDP	= -10.27 + 1.504 $LnPCNSDP_{(1980-81)}$	R^2 = 0.10	...(9)
(1980-81 to 2000-01)	(9.773) (1.137)	F = 3.345	
GR PCNSDP	= -4.692 + 0.844 $LnPCNSDP_{(1980-81)}$	R^2 = 0.04	...(10)
(1980-81 to 1990-1991)	(8.915) (1.038)	F = 0.637	
GR PCNSDP	= -13.328 + 1.875 $LnPCNSDP_{(1991-92)}$	R^2 = 0.13	...(11)
(1991-1992 to 2000-01)	(10.851) (1.227)	F = 2.337	

Note: Figures in brackets are standard errors of estimates.

FDI as per cent of GDP and Dummy variables, though found to be non-significant, had positive signs before them. Thus, liberalisation has resulted increased divergence of

GR PCNSDP	= -8.494 + 1.283 $LnPCSDP_{(1980-83)}$	R^2=0.100	...(12)
(1980-83 to 1998-2001)	(8.559)(0.994)	F = 1.665	
GR PCNSDP	= -19.876 + 2.600 $LnPCSDP_{(1980-83)}$	R^2 = 0.258	...(13)
(1980-83 to 1990-93)	(10.103) (1.140)	F = 5.202	
GR PCNSDP	= -18.438** + 2.334** $LnPCSDP_{(1990-93)}$	R^2 = 0.61	...(14)
(1990-93 to 1998-2001)	(2.334) (0.479)	F = 23.674	

Note: **Significant at 1% level. Figures in brackets are standard errors of estimates.

disparities in the country. This calls for adoption of safety nets to prevent increased distance between rich and poor states in the country where, CVPCI is coefficient of variation of PCNSDP. If the coefficients for the variables of openness (i.e. FT/GDP, FDI/GDP) and dummy variable (D) are significant and positive, it can be said that liberalisation has resulted divergence of disparities and *vice-versa*. Multiple Regression results are given in the Table 5..

$$CV_{PCI} = a + bFT/GDP + e \quad ...(15)$$
$$CV_{PCI} = a + bFDI/GDP + e \quad ...(16)$$
$$CV_{PCI} = a + bD + e \quad ...(17)$$
$$CV_{PCI} = a + b1,\ FT/GDP + b_2\ FDI/GDP + b_3D + e \quad ...(18)$$

TABLE 5

Liberalisation and Disparities: Regression Results

Eq.	*Dependent Variable*	*Constant*	*FT/GDP* (*Independent Variables*)	*FD/GDP*	*Dummy*	*R^2*	*F-Value*
	CV of PCI (1980 -81 to 1990-91)	29.98	+0.054 (.634)	-	-	0.001	0.007
15.	CV of PCI (1990-91 to 2000-01)	22.59	+0.849** (0.118)	-	-	0.86**	51.70
	CV of PCI (1980-81 to 2000-01)	17.77	+1.100** (.117)	-	-	0.82**	88.10
	CV of PCI (1980-81 to 1990-91)	18.33	-	+191.02 (127.3)	-	0.20	2.25)
16.	CV of PCI (1990-91 to 2000-01)	34.33	-	+4.113** (1.023)	-	0.67**	16.10
	CV of PCI (1980-81 to 2000-01)	30.80	-	8.52** (1.12)		0.75**	57.4
17.	CV of PCI (1980-81 to 2000-01)	30.63	-	-	+7.129** (0.834)	0.79**	73.12
18.	CV of PCI (1980-81 to 20000-01)	25.85	+3.366*	+0.389	+2.258	0.86**	35.00

Notes: (i) ** significance at 1%; * significance at 5%.
(ii) Figures in brackets are standard error of co-efficient.

Source: Economic Survey 2003-04 and SIA Newsletter (Various issues).

7. CONCLUSIONS AND POLICY RECOMMENDATIONS

The income inequalities at aggregate as well as per capita level have diverged as is evident in the increasing of the co-efficient of variation (CVs). Growth and disparities seem to be positively correlated and the post-reform period is associated with increased disparities. The ranking of states in terms of their PCNSDP has changed very little overtime indicating that rich states have remained richer and poor ones poorer. The analysis of growth rates in incomes reveals that Gujarat, Himachal Pradesh and Tamil Nadu enjoy the high-income high growth status throughout, while Assam, Bihar, Madhya Pmdesh, Orissa and Uttar Pradesh remain as the low income, low growth states.

The convergence/divergence regressions support our earlier findings. The convergence tests prove otherwise. The divergence in income disparities is clearly indicated by the statistical exercise carried out. The Kuznets' U hypothesis is also proved but the coefficient is non-significant. So also is the dummy time coefficient, which indicates widening of disparities in the post-reform period. The indicators of openness of volume of trade and FDI as per cent of GDP have clearly contributed to divergence of state incomes in India. The estimated coefficients are found to be significant and carry expected signs, thereby, leading support to our hypothesis that liberalisation has resulted in divergence.

References

Barro, R.J. and Sala-I-Martin (1992), "Convergence", *Journal of Development Economics*, Vol. 100, pp. 223-51.

Barro, R.J. and Sala-I-Martin (1995), Economic Growth, Boston, MA, McGraw Hill.

Bhattacharya and Shaktivel (2004), "Regional Growth and Disparity in India—Comparison of Pre- and Post-reform Decades", *Economic and Political Weekly*, March 6, pp. 1071-77, Ministry of Planning, New Delhi.

Dasgupta, Dipankar; P. Maiti, R. Mukherjee, S. Sarkar and S. Chakrabarti (2000), "Growth and Inter-state Disparities in India", *Economic and Political Weekly*, 35(27), July 17, pp. 2413-22.

Das S.K. and A. Barua (1996), "Regional Inequalities, Economic Growth and Liberalisation: A Study of Indian Economy", *The Journal of Development Studies*, 32(3), February 1996.

Dholakia, R.H. (1985), Regional Disparities in Economic Growth in India, Himalaya Publishing House, Bombay.

Government of India (2004), Economic Survey, 2003-04, Ministry of Finance, New Delhi

Ghosh, Marjit and Neogi (1998), Economic Growth and Regional Divergence in India, 1960-1995", *Economic and Political Weekly*, June 27.

Kalirajan, K. and A. Takihiro (2002), "Institutions and Inter-regional Inequalities in India: Finding a Link Using Hayami Thesis and Convergence Hypothesis", *Indian Journal of Economics*, Vol. 49(4) April-June, pp. 47-57.

Marjit, S. and Mitra, A. (1996), "Convergence in Regional Growth Rates: Indian Research Agenda", *Economic and Political Weekly*, Vol. XXXI, No. 33.

Nagaraj, R., Varadouski, A. and M.A. Vegan Zones (2000), "Long Run Growth Trends and Convergence. Across Indian States", *Journal of International Development*, Vol. 12, pp. 45-70.

Rao, Govinda M., R.T Shand and K.P. Kalirajan (1999), "Convergence of Incomes Across Indian States—A Divergent View", *Economic and Political Weekly*, Vol. XXXIV, No. 13.

R.T. Shand and S. Bhide, 2000: "Sources of Economic Growth: Regional Dimension of Reforms", *Economic and Political Weekly*, October 14, pp. 3747-57.

Secretariat of Industrial Approvals (SIA): SIA Newsletter, (Various Issues), Ministry of Industrial Policy and Promotion, Government of India, New Delhi.

Shetty, S.L. (2003), "Growth of SDP and Structural Changes in State Economies Inter-Comparisons", *Economic and Political Weekly*, December 6, pp. 5189-99.

3

Regional Disparities and Variations in Monthly Per Capita Consumption Expenditure: Calorie Intake and Hunger

D.M. DIWAKAR

I. INTRODUCTION

Hunger and poverty have been widely deliberated among the cross-section of academics. Many more dimensions have been added in due course of time. Compounding presumptions have manoeuvred estimates and resultantly indirect estimates of poverty have been reduced considerably despite alarming prevalence of acute hunger. Hunger and poverty have now been seen at two different levels. Poverty deals with lesser acute situation than hunger adjusting through indirect estimates. The question arises here that if acute hunger is prevalent much above the level of estimates of poverty, is there much relevance of indirect estimates of poverty? Towards examining the status and dimension of hunger distribution of consumption pattern through different expenditure groups, community, regions may provide basis for analysis of the level of hunger and nutrition deficiency reflecting deprivation as direct estimates of poverty at the national and states level?

These questions are important for comprehending reality estimates of hunger and poverty reflecting living conditions of the society also. Living conditions of an individual or a household or a society depend mainly *inter-alia* on the level of access to and control over resources, and level of surplus (Bhardwaj, 1994:325) that one enjoys. Access to resources to ensure benefits of growth depends largely on growth process and accompanied distribution mechanism. Access to share in distribution of growth is reflected in consumption expenditure pattern that an individual household enjoys. Variation in consumption pattern through different groups of expenditure explains the variations in living conditions. This can further be delineated through distribution of calorie intake and deficiency therein which indicates level of hunger and reflects poverty as cumulative indicators of deprived living conditions of an individual household, society and state at large. This paper is intended to examine inter-state variation in quality of life in terms of regional distribution of consumption pattern, calorie intake reflecting consumption status and hunger and poverty in rural India. Besides introduction, this paper is divided into four parts. Part one discusses regional consumption pattern and part two examines regional distribution of calorie intake and hunger. Part three consolidates discussion for policy debates.

Disparities in Consumption Pattern

Latest data published by NSSO on distribution of households for monthly per capita consumption expenditure (MPCE) for rural and urban areas suggest that 55 per cent of consumption is directly of food items and 45 per cent items are non-food expenditure in rural areas (Table 1). Table also suggests that this consumption pattern in rural India has changed considerably from about 73 per cent on food items and remaining 27 per cent on non-food items in 27th Round and for urban area food consumption has fallen from 64 to 42

TABLE 1

Value of Consumption Per Person for a Period of 30 Days Over NSS Rounds

Rounds	*Average Monthly Expenditure (Rs.) at Current Prices—Rural*				
	Food	*Non-Food*	*Total*	*MPCE Index*	*CPIAL Index*
27th	32.16 (72.9)	12.01 (27.1)	44.17 (100)	100	100
32nd	44.33 (64.3)	24.56 (35.7)	68.89 (100)	156	144
38th	73.63 (65.6)	38.68 (34.4)	112.31 (100)	255	277
43rd	100.82 (64.0)	57.28 (36.0)	158.10 (100)	358	289
50th	177.80 (63.2)	103.60 (36.8)	281.40 (100)	637	520
55th	288.80 (59.4)	197.36 (40.6)	486.16 (100)	1100	833
61st	307.60 (55.0)	251.19 (45.0)	558.78 (100)	1265	922

Note: Figures in parentheses indicate percentage of total expenditure.
Source: NSS 61st Round, Report No. 508, p. 66.

per cent. Figure 1 suggests that average MPCE declines with increasing size of households significantly in urban areas. Difference in urban and rural MPCE is the obviously significant. However, distribution of MPCE with size of the household in rural areas does not have significant difference. Figure 2 indicates that more than 60 per cent of rural population survives below average MPCE level.

Inter-state variation suggests that Bihar, Jharkhand, Madhya Pradesh, Orissa, Chhattisgarh fall below average rural MPCE of Rs. 450 followed by Uttar Pradesh, Assam and Karnataka below 550. Urban average MPCE is the lowest for Bihar, Orissa and Manipur followed by Uttar Pradesh, Madhya Pradesh and Arunachal Pradesh.

Considering social groups for comprehending inter-group variations, if one examines further, data (Table 2)

FIGURE 2

Average MPCE in Different States and Union Territories

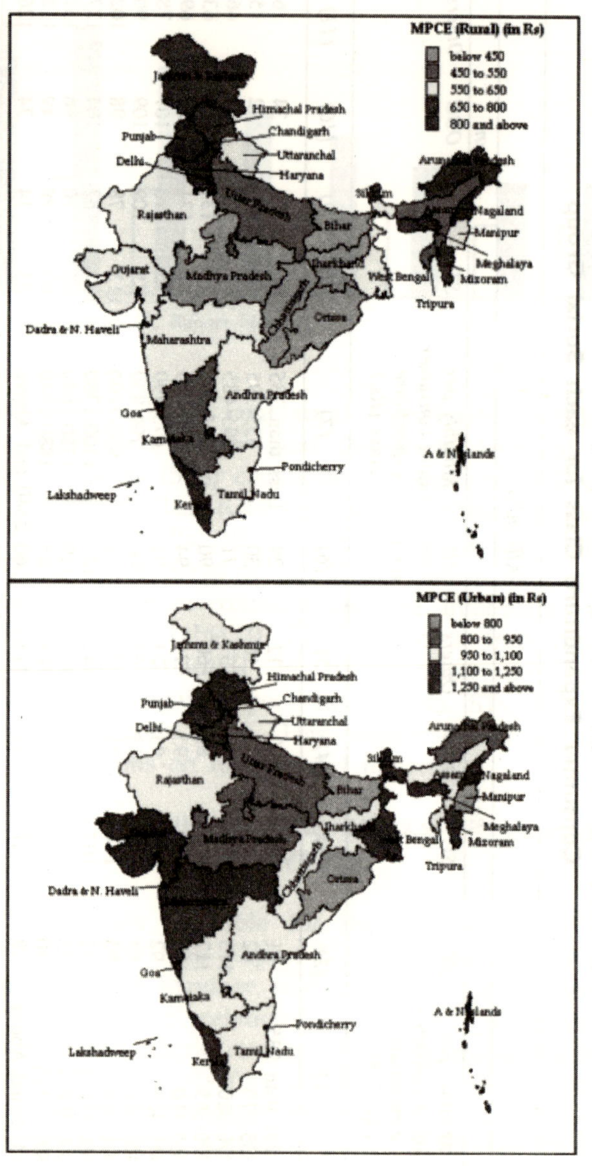

TABLE 3

Statewise Percentages of Rural and Urban Population Below Specified Levels of MPCE

State	*Percentage of rural population with MPCE*		*Percentage of urban population with MPCE below*		
	Below Rs. 365 (~Rs. 12/day)	*Below Rs. 270 (~Rs. 9/day)*	*State*	*Rs. 580 (~Rs. 19 per day)*	*below Rs. 395 (~Rs. 13 per day)*
Orissa	57	31	Bihar	55	28
Chhattisgarh	55	24	Orissa	50	25
Madhya Pradesh	47	21	Uttar Pradesh	44	17
Bihar	46	15	Chhattisgarh	44	20
Jharkhand	46	15	Madhya Pradesh	43	18
Uttar Pradesh	33	10	Rajasthan	36	10
Karnataka	32	7	Jharkhand	33	14
Maharashtra	30	11	Andhra Pradesh	33	8
Tamil Nadu	26	6	Karnataka	31	12
Andhra Pradesh	25	8	West Bengal	29	8
West Bengal	24	5	Tamil Nadu	26	7
Gujarat	21	5	Maharashtra	25	8
Assam	17	3	Assam	23	4
Rajasthan	17	3	Kerala	22	7
Haryana	7	1	Haryana	22	7
Kerala	7	2	Punjab	18	1
Punjab	4	1	Gujarat	16	3
All-India	30	10	All-India	30	10

Source: NSS Report No.508.

Medical Research (ICMR). In order to acquire these amounts of calorie intake for respective regions, data suggest that persons of the respective areas fall in expenditure group of rupees 525-615 and 575-665 respectively. In order to get exact figure if one draws ogive curve to find out cumulative percentage of the people up to this level. Rural area depicts 74.5 per cent of the people below 2400 calories intake. Similarly if one takes urban area for per capita monthly expenditure, and draws ogive curve, cumulative percentage crosses 50 per cent.

TABLE 4

Inter-state Official and Direct Estimates of Poverty in Rural India

State	HCR-Planning Commission (Indirect Estimates)				HCR-Direct Estimates		
	1993-94		1999-2000		1999-2000		
	%age	Implied of Poor	%age Calorie per diem per capita	Implied Poor	2400 Kcal Calorie per diem per capita	2200 Kcal per diem per capita	2000 Kcal per diem per capita
A.P.	15.92	1700	11.05(262.94)	1590	84 (595)	70.5 (490)	52 (405)
Assam	45.01	1960	40.04(365.43)	1790	91 (660)	81 (545)	57.5 (425)
Bihar	58.21	2275	44.30(333.07)	2010	77 (455)	64.5 (400)	39.5 (345)
Gujarat	22.18	1650	13.17(318.94)	1680	83 (735)	73.5 (635)	59.5 (540)
Haryana	28.02	1970	8.27(362.81)	1720	47.5 (615)	36 (540)	24 (470)
Karnataka	29.88	1800	17.38(309.59)	1600	82 (650)	69 (535)	45 (420)
Kerala	25.76	1630	9.38(374.79)	1440	82.5 (1105)	68.5(810)	52 (660)
M.P.	40.64	1970	37.06(311.34)	1850	78.5 (490)	69.5 (435)	46.5 (345)
Maharashtra	37.93	1780	23.72(318.63)	1760	92 (870)	76.5 (600)	46 (420)
Orissa	49.72	2150	48.01(323.92)	2120	80 (475)	60 (365)	39 (295)
Punjab	11.95	1810	6.35(362.68)	1710	58.5 (715)	45 (610)	28.5 (515)
Rajasthan	26.46	2130	13.74(344.03)	1925	53.5 (515)	36 (445)	16 (360)
Tamil Nadu	32.48	1650	20.55(307.64)	1510	94.5 (970)	82 (685)	68.5 (540)
U.P.	48.28	2220	31.22(336.88)	2040	61 (455)	47 (400)	27.5 (325)
W.Bengal	40.80	2080	31.85 (350.17)	1900	81 (575)	61 (455)	47 (400)
All India	37.27	1970	27.07(327.56)	1890	74.5 (565)	58 (455)	40 (380)

Note: Figures in parentheses indicate monthly per capita average expenditure in rupees.
Source: NSSO, 55th Round (1999-2000), Report Nos. 454 and 471.

Inter-state variation is more alarming than general at national level. Data of calorie distribution from 55th Round shown in Table 4 suggests that as high as 94.5 per cent people in Tamil Nadu could not avail 2400 k calorie intake for which they required Rs. 970 against which the calculation of per capita monthly expenditure of the Planning Commission was merely Rs. 307.64 and thereby only 20.55 per cent rural people were below the 2400 calorie intake norms.

Maharashtra being the second highest with 92 per cent people having less than per capita monthly expenditure of Rs. 870 to acquire 2400 calories against official estimates of Rs. 318.63 with which they could acquire merely 1760 calorie intake. Third highest calorie deficient state was rural Assam with 91 per cent people below 2400 calorie. Other states above 80 per cent rural people below 2400 kcal calorie norms were: Orissa (80 per cent: required average per capita monthly expenditure Rs. 475 against official estimates 323.92), West Bengal (81: 575 against 350.17), Karnataka (82:650 against 309.59), Gujarat (83:735 against 318.94), A.P. (84:595:262.94), Kerala (82.5:1105:374.79). Similarly if one takes the estimates of other states, Bihar (77% required Rs. 455 against official estimates of Rs 333.07), M.P. (78.5:490:311.34), U.P. (61:455:336.88), Rajasthan (53.5:515:344.03), Punjab (58.5 : 715:362.68) and Haryana (47.5:615:362.81). Thus, there was huge under estimation of hunger reflecting worst forms of poverty. So long calorie norms are accepted for determining estimates of poverty it, is difficult to set aside the alarming ground reality.

This underestimation can be seen further in latest estimates as well. Taking these expenditure and calorie intake for latest distribution of 2004-05 expenditure group by consumption basket schedule types 1 and 2 shown in Table 4 suggests that 53.9 per cent households are consuming less than 2400 k calorie in rural India (Table 5).

Official estimates of 1999-2000 suggest that Rs. 358 is the required level of calorie intake against Rs. 570 required for 2400 k calorie without adjusting inflationary effects. However, if one deflates adjusting growth rates of consumer price of agricultural labour which is 2.03 per cent for rural India the figures may escalate further. Moreover, official

TABLE 5

Percentage Inter-state Distribution of Households with Less than 2400 K Cal by Schedule Types I and 2, Growth Rate of CPIAL, Expenditure for Poverty Line and 2400 K Cal in Rural India

State	*Percentage of house-holds with less than 2400 kcal Sch. Type I per thousand hhs*	*Percentage of house-holds with less than 2400 kcal Sch. Type 2 per thousand hhs*	*Growth rates of consumer prices in per cent per annum 1990-00 to 2004-05 capital*	*State specific official poverty lines for 2004-05 Rural (Rs.)*	*Mid value of MPCE (Rs.) for 2400 kcal without price adjustment*
1	2	*3*	*4*	*5*	*6*
Andhra Pradesh	54.8	46.0	2.30	292.95	570
Assam	55.2	48.9	1.26	387.64	695
Bihar	61.4	41.4	1.54	356.36	445
Chhattisgarh	81.4	60.2*		–	497.5
Gujarat	59.8	51.0	2.46	353.93	695
Haryana	30.7	51.0	–	414.76	695
Jharkhand	65.5	47.8*	–	–	445
Karnataka	72.4	58.5	1.47	324.17	695
Kerala	56.9	49.1	2.27	429.07	1100
Madhya Pradesh	59.7	50.8	1.08	324.48	497.5
Maharashtra	79.3	66.4	2.88	362.25	862.5
Orissa	58.4	56.7	0.25	325.65	497.5
Punjab	29.4	21.1	2.60	410.38	695
Rajasthan	36.0	28.4	2.23	374.57	497.5
Tamil Nadu	88.2	69.3	2.84	351.86	862.5
Uttar Pradesh	35.2	29.1	2.28	369.76	445
West Bengal	52.0	52.0	1.87	382.82	570
All India—Rural	53.9	53.9	2.03	358.03	570

Source: NSS Report 505 for cols. 2 and 3, and for remaining coloums see Himanshu 2007.

estimates of poverty line per capita expenditure for 2004-05 shows significant difference and underestimation. Therefore this poverty line does not take care of hunger and nutrition deficiency, volume of which is much larger at the state level. Moreover, indirect estimates have been undermining hunger, i.e., acute form of poverty and destitution leading to deteriorating consumption level norms for poors. Except 1973-74, as data suggest in Table 6, consumption basket and calorie norms have not been followed and simple adjustment of prices did not take care of expanding consumption basket also.

TABLE 6

Rural Poor as percentage of Rural Population in India

	1973-74 %	*1994-94 %*	*1999-2000 %*	*MPCE (Rupees)*		
				1973-74	*1993-94*	*1999-2000*
MPCE for less than 2400 Kcal	56.4	74.5	74.5	49	325	570
Official Estimates	56.4	37.3	27.1	49	206	328
Corresponding Calorie Intake	2400	1970	1890			

Source: NSSO, 50th (1993-94) and 55th (1999-2000) Round.

If one adds deprivation and level of access to education, health, sanitation, productive infrastructure, etc. in the definition of poverty, figures may touch even a higher level. A careful analysis is required to reach a formidable conclusion in this regard. Latest estimates based on 61st Round data, which is comparable to 50th Round also, do not suggest much difference if one calculates through indirect methods. Official estimates of poverty comes to 29.18 per cent for rural area, 26.02 for urban area and over all 28.27 per cent. However, in view of direct estimates of MPCE along with distribution of calorie intake as per official norms of 2400 k calorie these estimates suffer underestimation.

Looking at the indicators for reducing poverty and hunger real wage and unemployment could be two important indicators among others. So fat rate of growth of unemployment is concerned out of 15 major states, 10 witnessed increasing rate of growth. States like Punjab witnessed highest unemployment rate (i.e., 25.7% per annum) during 1999-2005 on the base rate of 7.6 per cent during

1993-2000. M.P. stands second highest with 13.7 per cent followed by Karnataka 13.3, Rajasthan 12.8 and Haryana 12.2. However, Rajasthan has witnessed declining trend from 17.8 per cent. Bihar, and Kerala have shown declining growth rates in unemployment. And Gujarat indicated declining unemployment.

So far real wage rate is concerned, out of 15 major states, real wage rates for rural male workers have increased with declining rate in eleven states and Maharashtra witnessed declining wage rates during 1999-2000 to 2004-05. Real wage rates for casual workers in agriculture in India increased with substantiall declining rates for male females and combined. Situation of non-agriculture is not different rather it sounds worse. However, shift of workers to non-farm sector has been significant in 13 states out of 15 major states except Assam and Kerala which have witnessed negative and declining growth rates of real wage (Himanshu, 2007). On the basis of international poverty line the World Bank calculated $1 per day poor 34.7 per cent in India and $2 goes to the level of 80 per cent. (World Development Report, 2005). Ruddar Datt suggests to adopt basic needs approach for redefining povety to move upward from subsistence to a more human level of living condition (Datt, 2006)

III. CONCLUSION

Analysis suggests that there is disparity in distribution of MPCE patterns among the regions, states, social groups, and expenditure groups. MPCE patterns for relatively poor states indicate higher concentration of households towards less than 2400 k calorie intake. Discussion also suggests that indirect methods of official estimates of poverty underestimate the level of acute poverty, in terms of hunger and nutrition deficiency. Level of hunger and poverty is much beyond the level of official estimates. Such underestimation of poverty in the era of globalisation and market has significant implications on withdrawal of the state from its responsibilities (Saith, 2005) and surrendering to market for the benefit of corporate world. Needless to say that even the rate of reducing official poverty has been declining. With the second generation of reforms, there is every likelihood to undermine poor which will resultantly further accentuate the process of marginalisation.

Reference

Datt, Ruddar, (2006), Need for Redefining the Poverty Line, *Mainstream,* July 28-August 3.

Government of India (2001), Poverty Estimates for 1999-2000, Planning Commission, New Delhi, 22nd February.

Himanshu, (2007), Recent Trends in Poverty and Inequality: Some Preliminary Results, *Economic and Political Weekly,* Feb 10, 2007

NSSO, Reports of various Rounds.

Saith, A., (2005), Poverty Lines versus Poor: Method versus Meaning, *Economic and Political Weekly,* Vol. 40, No. 43, October 22-28.

Economic Development Expanding Slum Space and Vote Bank Politics —An Analysis

PARMANAND SINGH AND SHASHI BHUSHAN SINGH

I. INTRODUCTION

The issue of economic development is a complex one. The conceptual explanation of economic development is wider. This includes not only growth in income and the growth in net domestic product of a country but improvement in over all physical quality of life Index of the masses and of the weaker and poorer section in particular. Fifty years of planned economic development covers a very vast area. The issue is not easy to resolve. We all have intuitive notions of development, we speak of a developed society in which people are well fed, well clothed, and well possess and access to a variety of commodities, have the luxury of leisure and entertainment and live in a healthy environment. Such a society is free from violent discrimination and have tolerant levels of equality where sick receive proper medical care and people donot have to sleep on the side walls. In short most of us have in our mind that a minimum requirement of a developed nation is the physical quality of life be high, and be so uniformly rather than being restricted to an incongruously low minority.

Side by side with the developed nations go the notion of good society further. We might stress political rights and freedoms, intellectual and cultural development, stability of family, a low crime rate and so on. However a high and equally accessible level of material well being is probably a prerequisite for most of other kinds of environment, quite apart from being a worthy goal in itself.

Economists and policy makers, therefore do well by concentrating on physical quality life index aspect of development since it is the prerequisite of a good civil society, where there is no chance of deprivation and any one being ignored.

Quite contrast to economic development, the concept of slum originated as a product of rural urban differentiation, or because of adverse terms of trade between agriculture and industry. The productivity linked growth process stressed on economic growth via industrialisation where urbanisation is seen as an important growth indicator. The industry led growth process has set in motion a preference scale for technological improvement, upgradation of skill by technical know how and with a tilt towards better treatment to skilled works. This differentiation helps the managerial class to bifurcate the concept of work or design of work from the work itself and this leads to division of work between menials or physical work and technical work or mental work. Thus a dichotomy is being created among the working class via creating contradiction of knowledge in the work process. Those doing ardudous physical work gets a poor treatment with regard to their work place and environment. The process of industrialisation via urbanisation has enlarged the gap between workers in Industries and workers in the farm houses, between workers of technical core and physical workers.

The urbanisation in this process of differentiation is a settlement of the privileged people in their respective domain with better physical condition of living, decent job opportunities and a network of skill formation environment, information network, etc. It is this attractive living conditions, job opportunity and a cultural environment of exclusion i.e. exclusive settlement in colony life style that attract poor inhabitants in remote rural area and farm workers in absence of job opportunities to migrate to town and this influx of rural urban migration creates slum.

A slum is thus, an area where there is over crowding of houses on land and of persons in houses where houses are huddled together in an unplanned manner without provision for proper street layout, drainage, severage, electricity, community facilities and other basic necessaries of life resulting in insanitary and an healthy living conditions. Slum Area Improvement and Clearance Act 1956 defined slum as an area where (a) buildings in any respect are unfit for human habitation, or (b) by reasons of dilapidation, or over cowding faulty management design of buildings, narrowness and faulty arrangement of stress, lack of ventilation lights or sanitary facilities or by any combination of these factors, human habitation is detrimental to safety, health and morals.

The parameters to identify slum has been fixed by 1958 survey of Bombay which fixed threefold classification as slums Chawls, Patra Chowls and Zopadapattis. Chawls are permanent multistoreyed buildings built long ago and are today in deteriorated condition, Patra Chawls are semi permanent structure both authorized and unauthorised, often built with corrugated iron steels or some such hard materials (Patra means tin sheet).

Zopadapattis– Squatter settlement consisting of hovels made of a variety of hard materials including wood, rags, tin sheets, mud, bricks. Zopad means hutments.

It is these three types of slums that has increasing space in the present spate of economic development. While *chawls* are increasing in metropolitan cities, and *patrachals* and *zopadapatties* are increasing tremendously in mega urban centres and even in local towns. The state's share of slum thus is widening and the life conditions of the last man has worsened.

II. QUANTUM, MAGNTITUDE AND GENESIS OF SLUM IN INDIA AND ITS SOCIAL COMPOSITION.

According to current estimate, the total population in slums globally is approaching one billion mark and barring any intervention, will swell to three billion. One in every three people in less than fifty years is a slum-dweller. (UN Habital 2003) estimate. India, a home to more of world's income poor than any other country, has a slum population of 170 million a number that surpasses total population of all but five countries China, India, Indonesia, Brazil and united states (U.N. Population Fund 2004) India while boasting of its achievements on overall poverty reduction front during 1980's and 1990s it accounted for nearly one seventh of World's growth in slum-dwellers over the same period (Datta and Ravallion 2002, UN Habitat and Statistics Division 2001). It has, been pointed in a recent study that speaks of 56 to 65 per cent under reporting on BPL in developed states in Indian what to talk of poor states (2005-06 study). The slum population figure in India is of 158.4 million in 2001 and an average annual growth rate of 1.72 per cent for the year 2005 and for the period 2006-15 (U.N. Habitat and Statistic Division 2001 and U.N. Population Fund 2004). During 2006-15, the number of slum-dwellers in India is expected to increase at an average of nearly 3.2 million per year, a number exceeding total populations of 21 nations, Thus the question of restraining the growth of slums in India is important as it would improve the living conditions of the hundred of millions of the working class and working poors and unemployed Indians and would also have a significant impact in terms of the reduction in the global slum population.

As per U.N. Habitat and statistics division estimate of 2005, half of the residents of Mumbai, and two thirds of the residents of Delhi, India's financial hub and national capital respectively live in slum or squatter settlements.

N. Sridharan in 1995 in his article Indian Slums: Problems, Policies and Issues" highlighted that in spite of India's recent economic prowess the number of slums in the country continues to rise alarmingly which necessitates a closer analysis of the causes of slum formation. Report of the Government of India (2002) and National Territory of Delhi 2004 also corroborates the same point in the desired direction.

The Genesis of Slum

Economists and demographers have analysed the various theories of slum formation from various angles. The first is the over urbanisation" thesis—which emphasizes that developing countries urbanise much more quickly than their levels of industrialisation warrant primarily because of absence of job opportunities in rural areas and poor living conditions devoid of basic amenities of life.

Secondly through the phenomenon of rural urban migration this process of urbanisation gets speed up as a result of execessive unemployment, under employment and disquised unemployment in rural areas and shrinking job avenues on the farm.

Arup Mitra in (1994) demonstrated a different analysis of this formation of slum in India based on excessive supply and limited demand frame work. This framework attributes increasing informal sector employment in the wake of liberalisation regime and an interaction between phenomenal increases in urban population in absolute terms and limited demand for unskilled labour in urban economies. He has a lot of explanation in terms of research articles, reports, books, etc. Important among them are Growth and Poverty : The Urban Legend, *E.P.W.*, Vol. 37, No. 13, pp. 659-65 (1992). Quality, Employment Structure and Poverty Incidence : The Slum Perspective" (1990), *Indian Economic Review*, Vol. 25, No. 1, pp. 57-73. Urbanisation, Slums, Informal Sector Employment and Poverty : An Exploratory Study, B.R. Publishing Corporation, Delhi, (1994), "Agglomeration Economies as Manifested in Technical Efficiency at the Firm Level", *Journal of Urban Economics*, Vol. 45, pp. 490-500 (1999). Total Factor Productivity Growth and Urbanisation Economics: A Case of Indian industries, *Review of Urban and Regional Development Studies*, Vol. 12, No. 2, pp. 97-108 (2000). Occupational Choices, Network, and Transfer : An Exegesis Based on Micro Data from Delhi. Slums, Manohar, New Delhi (2003). Informal Sector, Networks and Intra City Variations in activities : Findings from Delhi Slum, *Review of Urban and Regional Development Studies,* Vol. 16, No. 2, pp. 154-69. (2003).

Arup Mitra demonstrated in 1994 in an article "Urbanisation, Slums, Informal Sector Employment and Poverty"—an exploratory study that excessive supply—limited demand framework better explains the growing urban poverty and concomitant growth of slum populations.

Hindu rate of growth that is growth from late 1940s until 1980, GDP grew at a rate of 3.8 per cent (Krueger, 2002 in Anne O Kruegor-led) Economic Policy Reform and the Indian Economy, Oxford University Press, New Delhi, pp. 1-6). It hardly outpaced population growth and in theory, accommodated India's slum growth. From 1993-94 to 1999-2000, India's aggregate GDP grew at the rate of 6.7 per cent per annum and it has its minimal impact on eradication of urban poverty which goes to prove the point that the present economic process of the Indian economy and its industrial growth has little impact on poors in improving their living conditions and thus has resulted in concentration of economic power in hands of few.

Another explanation of slum formation is increase in land values due to population pressure and growth of intensive infrastructure which has indivisible character. The concentration of population and Indivisibilities of infrastructure leads to congestion or slum formation.

Political Economy Aspect of Slum Formation

Public policy also plays its part in assisting urbanisation and consequently increasing land values and rents. Due to various measures that restrict the supply of land, including a ceiling on the amount of land one can hold, it prevents factories from shifting operations outside city limits and rent controls. Cities of Mumbai and Delhi have some of the highest house prices relative to income in the world. The Economies 2005 quoted that a recent survey which finds that Mumbai has higher office occupancy costs than Newyork, Sydney or Singapore and many other cities.

Further due to their desire to remit money to their family members in the countryside, urban poor often exhibit a strong bias against housing in individual's consumption

Bhattacharya, B.B. and S. Sakthivel pointed out (2004) that the regional growth disparity in India after the reform has increased and there exists an inverse relationship between population growth and income growth across states.

Both these findings have significant implications for the distribution of slums across states. This rise in coefficient of variation in states could also be due to the devolution of official decision making from the central to the state and municipal levels, which is likely to result in more divergent policies on slum removal/clearance/consolidation (Sridharan 1995).

Table 1 also makes clear the point that state higher on development ladder in term of per capita income and state

TABLE I

Poverty Among All Rural Persons and Farmers: 1999-2000 and 2003

States	*1999-00 Rural persons*	*2003 Rural persons*	*2003 Farmers*	*2003 Poverty line consumption level Rs./month*
A.P.	11.05	11.14	11.8	286.27
Assam	40.04	21.64	31.05	381.76
Bihar	44.3	37.56	39.90	337.69
Gujarat	13.17	14.62	22.47	346.76
Haryana	8.27	5.81	10.46	386.37
H.P.	7.94	6.39	12.45	393.24
J & K	3.97	7.06	6.15	393.24
Karnataka	17.38	11.04	19.21	326.72
Kerala	9.38	9.10	10.20	403.99
M.P.	37.06	24.48	35.30	316.65
Maharashtra	23.72	18.11	21.45	344.42
Orissa	48.01	43.24	53.51	315.62
Punjab	6.35	6.21	6.31	386.05
Rajasthan	13.74	19.08	21.89	359.94
T.N.	20.55	21.67	26.64	361.84
T.N.	20.55	21.67	26.64	361.84
U.P.	31.22	29.98	37.39	357.75
W.B.	31.85	20.87	27.17	360.66
All India	27.09	23.99	30.73	347.96

Source: NSSO, Consumption Expenditure all Households Consumption Exp. Farmers Households NSS 59th Round Reports Nos. 495 and 499.

net domestic product have large shares in slum and their slum areas has increased 11.44 per cent to 14.94 (A.P.) 19.90 to 32.22 per cent in (MHa) 13.90 to 15.72 (W.B.) in 1993-94 to 1999-2000. In these state sconsolidation of slums has also resulted because of the political contact of slum-dweller and use of slum as vote bank politics interms of increased percentage of notified slums A.P. 23.18 to 82.65. Maharashtra 43.10 to 61.15. Karnatka and Punjab and Gujarat has however have lower notified slums to total slums 77.99 to 59.40 (KAR) 41.75 to 33.33 Punjab in (19993-94 to 1999-2000) because of lower doses of poverty in there state Table 1 depict it.

It also gets strengthened the point that state with larger urban centres attract more slum-dwellers and with slum politics playing an increasing role in Indian politics. They wave large percentage of increased notified areas of slum say for example in Maharashtra and A.P. but in Karnataka, Gujarat and Punjab this is not the case. There the consolidation of slum has been at a slower rate and it is not affecting politics to that much level as states having large urban centres say Maharashtra, A.P., West Bengal, Tamil Nadu with exception of Delhi 52.89 to 9.15 where in place of slum consolidation slum clearance has taken place.

III. SLUMS IN BIHAR

Bihar is the most victim of slum on account of the largest proportion of workers (48.18%) followed by cultivators (29.17). The proportion of workers engaged in household industry is the lowest (3.87) while all other non-agricultural workers are clubbed as workers (18.78). They include workers in service sector, as well as factory, plantation, mining, construction, and political workers. It means more than 77 per cent workers are still engaged in agricultural activities in the state which provides the largest resource to many major industrial inputs. Percentage of workers engaged in non agricultural activities varies from 10.39 per cent in Madhepura district to 44.83 per cent in Patna district. Of the 37 districts only few have the presence of some industrial activity. These districts are Patna, Rohtas, Gaya, Katihar and Begusarai. Other 32 districts are industrially backward thereby explaining the prime cause of urban backwardness. So the state sans urbanisation. Agriculture represents 39 per cent of the SDP compared to 18 per cent for the country in 2003-04. In order to expedite growth of urbanisation it needs increase in industrialisation at a massive scale. Presently the industrial base of the state is agro-based industries and other industries. Among the other causes of industrial backwardness of the state the prime cause's shotage of investment flows from public and private sources. According to CMIE reports in Dec. 2003 private investment in Bihar allounted for 800 crore or 0.4 per cent of the total private investment in India as compared to U.P. (3.5%) Orissa (3.7%) M.P. (6.1%).

The industrial activities in the state is poor and very thinly spread over. An urbanised district should have more than 75 per cent of its male workers engaged in non agricultural activities. But even in most urbanised district of Patna this proportion is only 44.83 followed by Munger 42.21. No district is Bihar has crossed 50 per cent mark of workers engaged in non agricultural activities. Industrial scenario in Bihar is dominated by small scale industries. Here also with the exception of Patna, no other district account for any significant industrial activity in the state. So development scenario in the state is dominanted by low level of urbanisation and industrialination, each accounting for the other.

But still there is migration because of low income opportunity and lack of facilities compell people to leave villages. Bihar is also responsible for a negative growth in net migration rate as well. Rural to urban migration have been much higher than urban to urban migration. There's also large scale rural to rural migration which is a disturbing element which depicts poor state of agriculture in the state. Bihar stands next to U.P. in the number of out migrant from the state. In migration to Bihar has been very low compared to. Haryana, Gujarat, Karnataka and Maharashtra thereby reflecting strong push factor from rural areas rather than strong economic pull from urban areas. Patna city alone accounts for more than 50 per cent of total in migration in to state.

So the analysis of slum settlements in Patna most particularly is peculiar. Lack of diversified economic activities accounts for push migration from rural to urban areas. NSS data shows that the share of household heads working as casual wage labour actually increased in Bihar from 50 to 54 per cent during 1993-94 and 1999-00. So out migration has become a crucial survival strategy for the rural poor in Bihar. Both the Census and NSS data show that Bihar has the highest rate of gross inter-state out migration in India. North Bihar is poorer than South Bihar in terms of head count index, causing increasing flow of in migration to south.

Patna is the worst victim of that which attract maximum number of migrants who largely encroach upon public land as immediate solution to settlement. Two kinds of squatting settlements have been observed in Patna—residential and non-residential. A menacing types of non-residential squatting is the "Khatals" for cows and buffaloes which provide shelter to the owners and attendants as well. During social justice regime of Lalu Prasad, Patna was a city of Khatals all, Ran Basera meant for Rikshaw Pullers beside the Riskhaws and side become virtual Khatals converting the whole city, its main areas into slum.

Residential squatting in Patna usually consists of temporary and Kuteha hutments in public land.

Bihar has least notified slum area. A little over one-third of slum households live in notified slums in Bihar compared to around 65 per cent at the national level. At the national level 64 per cent of notified slums and 63 per cent of non notified slums are on public land, where as in Bihar more than 80 per cent of non notified slums are an public land, compared to 34 of notified slums. No slum household in Bihar has a pucca house and 88 per cent of these are non notified slums, live in Kutcha houses requiring urgent attention to housing condition. Though sour slum areas have consolidated their position with multi-storied houses for the slum settlers under Indira Awas Yojana by Lalu regime in Bihar. No slum household in Bihar has access to tap water for drinking. Similarly no slum enjoys street light facilities. But electricity connection is available to 66 per cent of households in notified slums and 37 per cent in non-notified slums in terms of access to most other amenities the position. In Bihar is quite disturbing.

Census 2001 has made it clear that 54.39 per cent houses in urban Bihar can be considered good while it is 68 per cent in Urban India. Nearly 8 per cent of urban houses in Bihar are in dilapidated condition against 3.63 per cent in urban India. More than one third urban household in Bihar live in one room houses (33%) Housing congestion at the national level is almost similar.

Census data on housing amenities show class III towns in India which have least access to three major facilities within premises while class one town enjoys maximum access to major facilities. Bihar does not have class VI town in 2001, While the number of class V towns only 6, showing weak hierarchy of linkage with rural areas. More than half of the class I towns have access to electricity. This figure does not reveal the fact that during most of the day, electricity is not available in citieis in Bihar. Access to latrine within premises is also available to almost half of the household on an average, though always connected to proper sewer system. Private initiatives like sulabh played significant role in providing and expanding latrine facilities. NSS figures spellout that quality of services require under more improvement. It requires significant expenditure in urban services for inhancing the quality of life in cities as well as to support economic productivity.

Table 2 attempts to correlate the relation of development indicators up ward hierarchy and its relation to slum.

While income, interms of SDP and urban population growth in terms of aggregate share in urban population urban consumption expenditure in relation to income have positive relation so far development is concerned but in case of their relation to states share of slum SDP moved positively from 0.19 to 0.27 below 1993-2002. Urban population share in all India aggregate and growth in per capita consumption expenditure showed a decreasing trend that is from 0.73 to 0.72 in 1993-2000 and from 0.65 to 0.48 in 1993-2000 respectively. It means life conditions of slum deweller with respect to their basic consumption needs have worsened over the years from 1993-2000.

TABLE 2

Estimates of Poverty

Year	*Poverty ratio (%)*		
	Rural	*Urban*	*Combined*
1973-74	56.4	49.0	54.9
1977-78	53.1	45.0	51.3
1983	45.7	40.8	44.5
1981-88	39.1	38.2	38.6
1993-94	37.3	32.4	36.0
1999-00	27.1	23.6	26.1
2007- (target)	21.1	15.1	19.3

Source: Economic Survey, 2003-04 and Planning Commission.

Public spending on education and health in slum area is negative since slum-dwellers require more public assistance thereby leading to a decrease in the resources devoted to education and health one would expect better education and health to result in improved employment prospects, higher incomes and lower slum population. Datta and Ravallion has made it a point that Indian States with lower literacy and lower health measues experience less poverty reduction through growth in non farm output.

A large majority of slum-dwellers have Kutcha or semi kutcha structures. Table 3 makes it clear that 35 per cent of slum households fell in this category in most states in 2002. Only states of A.P., Gujarat, Karnataka and Tamil Nadu indicate a rise in the percentage of pucca structures in the slums over the years. Orissa, Bihar, Rajasthan, Punjab and nearly 75 to 100 per cent slum-dwellers live in Kuchha structures and tenements made by Patna chauls and rags. N.S.S.O (2003) report severals that 58 per cent of the slums cover an area of less than a hectare each. This pattern is evident across most states leading too much houses in a particular areas and too much people in a house thus resulting in congestion and poor living and dusty environment. It thus, is the result of present development scenario what to say of quality life to the masses.

TABLE 3

Indian States Percentage of Aggregate Slums and Notified Slums in States.

State/UT	Shares of Slum all India aggregate per cent		Proportion of Notified slums total slums	
	1993	2002	1993	2002
A.P.	11.44	14.94	23.18	82.65
Bihar (Bh.)	4.27	2.57	5.82	26.32
Delhi (Del.)	8.31	3.57	52.89	9.15
Gujarat (Guj.)	4.60	2.97	47.93	26.94
Jammu and Kashmir (J & K)	0.00	0.70	-	60.16
Karnataka (Kar.)	10.67	3.84	77.99	59.40
Madhya Pradesh (M.P.)	4.98	6.71	51.62	58.62
Maharashtra (MAH.)	19.90	32.22	43.10	61.15
Orissa (Ori.)	3.08	0.78	7.67	2.74
Pondichery (PON)	0.02	0.41	-	19.43
Punjab (PUN)	0.94	0.31	41.75	33.33
Rajasthan (Raj.)	1.33	1.69	24.40	1.37
Tamil Nadu (T.N.)	7.22	6.12	14.61	29.39
Uttar Pradesh	5.47	5.11	34.81	29.32
W.B.	13.90	15.72	19.14	35.34
Other States/U.T.	3.88	3.04	16.22	44.72
Total/India wide	100	100	31.16	50.62
Co-efficient of variation	8113	133.52	62.63	64.10

Sources: 1. Slums in India, NSSO, 49th Round, Jan.-June 1993 figures, Draft Report No. 417, NSSO, 1997.

2. Condition of Urban Slums, National Sample Survey Organisation 58th Round, July-Dec. 2002, Report No. 486, NSSO, 2003.

IV. VOTE BANK POLITICS AND BASIC AMENITIES TO SLUM-DWELLERS

So far politics of vote bank and slum-dwellers are concerned, the conditions of slum-dwellers has worsened over the years. While cities are engine of growth, the slum concentration there have made them epi centres of major health catastrophies primarily because of over crowding and infrastructural shortcomings. The basic infrastructure seems to be heavily over burdened when viewd from the angle of availability of safe drinking water, sanitation, Sewerage facilities and Garbage disposal points are concerned. A large percentage of slums dwellers do not have access to these facilities employing vulnerability of these slum settlers to water born diseases and other epidemics and vote bank politics has not helped them much to amileorate their living condition. They are either being cheated or misled on emotional issues and on the basis of ethnic bondage. Due to proximity of slums to residential areas, outbreaks of epidemics and its after effect affects populations beyond their areas of slums. This possibility also implies a strong possibility of interactions among socio-economic groups. Thus constituting the overlaps between informal sector employment, slum-dwelling and poverty, and the other pertaining to formal sector employment, above poverty line level of living and residence outside slum. This interaction may be beneficial demonstrating the phenomenon of duality with interdependence which goes against Weibe's interdependence theory only and not duality which's being expressed in expanding slums pace in India. The implications of these interactions in terms of health hazards and environmental pollution could however be serious. Tables 4, 5 and 6 deals with these issues. It presents gloomy picture of Indian States with regard to these basic amenities to slum-dwellers. Majority of slum-dwellers are still without these

TABLE 4

Households having Access to Drinking Water Electricity, Latrine within Premises—2001 in Bihar

City size	*Town No.*	*Total household No.*	*Drinking water*	*Electricity*	*Latrins*
I	19	7,24,855	76.20	64.29	70.01
II	18	204,968	68.47	48.24	55.48
III	68	335,893	61.00	31.50	41.08
IV	19	51,150	63.17	31.83	42.18
V	6	5,913	68.61	40.44	53.56

Source: Census of India, 2001, Tables on House, Household Amenities and Assets.

basic amenities of tap water, latrine, severage and garbage dumping facilities even with the political contact and vote bank use of slum-dwellers. What has taken shape is the consolidation of slum space with meagre civic facilities. This is all gloomy side of our development efforts.

TABLE 5

State Level Development Indicators and State Share of Slum (Correlation and Coefficient) Variation Analysis

State level development indicator	*1993*	*2002*
Positive		
Per capita state domestic product (1991-92/1997-98)	0.19	0.27
Share of Urban population in all India aggregate (1991/2001)	0.72	0.72
Urban gini ratio for per capita consumption expenditure (1993-94 to 1999-2000)	0.65	0.48
Negative		
Public spending or education (1990-91/1998-97)	-0.35	-0.61
Public spending on Health (1990-91/1998-99)	-0.24	-0.23
Public spending on Education logged (1980-81/1990-91)	-0.32	-0.44
Public spending on health logged (1980-81/1990-91)	-0.31	-0.40
Negligible		
Share of Urban population below poverty line (1993-84/1999-2000)	0.03	0.10
Share of rural population below poverty line (1993-94/1999-2000)	0.02	0.15
Level of urbaniisation	0.07	0.01

Source: Calculated on the basis of information given in Table I and National Human Development Report, 2001 (Govt. of India, 2002).

TABLE 6

State Distributed Across Size Classes Formed by the Percentage of Slums with Kutcha and Semi-pucca Houses in 1993 and 2002

	Slums with Kutcha and Semi-pucca Houses (1993 per cent)		*Slums with Kutha and Semi-pucca Houses (2002 per cent)*	
	0.35	*35-55*	*55-75*	*75-100*
0-35			DEL.	J & K or RAJ.
35-55				
55-75		MAH. W.B.		
75-100	A.P.		U.P., GUJ., KAR., TN	PUN. BH, MP,

Source: Same as Table 1.

V. CONCLUSION

Thus, the present spate of development has led to concentration of population in slum in urban area via industrialisation urbanisation nexus. It has also intensified the inequitous process of income generation and this has led to concentration of income and employment opportunities to the few, leaving a large part of rural population and the poor working class to migrate to urban outfits and create congestion and slum. The politics of slum is not akin to knock the silence but it involves itself simply in local issues. Slum devellers want ration cards, water and a guaran tee that their shacks would not be demolished and politicians want to maximise vote with limited campaign funds and time at their disposal. High density slums with squatter settlements and vast population is curious about survivals not well being. They depend upon govt assistance in the form of land recognition, civic amenities, and with public works programme thus they present themselves with politicians easy pickings. Slum-dwellers lack in social networks and rely heavily on political networks for effecting improvements in their living conditions. These are their weakness. This helps the process of their marginalisation strengthened, the prospect of their political mobilisation thus become weakened and so Politicians easily tap such voters. This situation has helped the formation of a weak governance with a weak leadership and leading to increasing space for non-development syndrome. To improve this land tinny settlement for slum-dwellers is a must that will be helpful in slum upgradation move and that will benefit the poor even with this present growth scenario reducing role of government and their differences in education, caste and religious identity. It is because of this that the World Bank list land tenure as a necessary condition for slum upgradation. This will help expansion of growth process through social mobilisation, political involvement, and participation. Thus, it will lead to social action and social progress. We may conclude this, "The fate of Indian democracy is thus entrusted with vote banks, However, in the process of creation of new vote banks, it is true that narrow and parochial agendas are gaining upper and even as the broad all India vote banks lose ground. In the mushrooming of local regional political parties, some would see Indians discovering their political identity with local and regional considerations thus gaining ground and it is being harder to tie down voters as *monolith* Indians. The answer open up a big debate as India a nation or a nation of nations? Political development is the as result of present economic development scenario points to the latter. More specially concentrated and visible forms of Urban poverty are likely to generate new pressures on government to respond and in ways that may or may not be coincident with good policies for over all poverty reduction. In India their process of economic growth has contributed to the emergence of vote bank politics and these are linked with the political process which in tune with slum-dwellers and this justifies Ravallin's doubts regarding overall poverty reduction and questions the degree to which political contact benefits them as well.

NOTES

Census of India – 2001, Tables on Houses, Household Amenities and Assets. Classification of Towns as per Census Distribution Class I City? 100,000

II towns 50,000 and 99,999

III towns 20,000 and 49,999

IV towns 10,000 and 19,999

V towns 5,000 and 9,999

VI towns < 50000.

NSSO, 31st Round, July 1976-June 1977, first nation wide summary was restricted to class I cities each with a population at 1,00,000 and above. As per the 1971. NSSO 49th round survey (1999) covered rural as well as urban areas. It defined a "slum" as an area with a collection of poorly built tenements, mostly of temporary nature, over cowded by inhabitants and usually with inadequate sanitary and drinking water facilities. NSSO 58th Round (2002), third survey, focus on the urban slums.

"The fate of democracy is interlinked with vote banks. However, in the process of creation of new vote banks, it is also true that narrow and parochial agendas are gaining an upper hand even as the broad all India vote banks also get ground. In the mushrooming of local regional political parties, some would see Indians discovering their political identity, with local and regional considerations gaining ground and it being harder to tie down voters as "monolith Indians". The answers open up a big debate—is India a nation or a nation of nations ? Political developments via slum consideration points to the latter."

Amsterdam, pp. 2383-421. Urban political economists, however, considers a system of local governments providing collective goods to mobile residents who close between jurisdictions to maximise utility (Helsley, 2004, p. 2384).

"Physical segmentation of urban labour markets due to economic specialisation within cities, noting that even in expensive (intra city) transport for commutation need not eliminate their urban labour market barriers, especially in developing countries."

REFERENCES

Dreze Jean and Amartya Sen (2002), India, Development and Participation, Oxford Univ. Press, Oxford.

Growth and Poverty (1992), The Urban Legend, *Economic and Political Weekly*, Vol. 37, No. 13, pp. 659-65.

Gupta, Indrani and Arup Mitra (2002), "Rural Migrants and Labour Segmentation Micro Level Evidence from Delhi Slums" *Economic and Political Weekly*, Vol. 37, No. 2, pp. 163, 168.

Harris, J.R., M.P. Todaro (1970), Migration, Unemployment and Development. A Two Sector Analysis, *American Economic Review*, Vol. 60, No. 1, pp. 126-42.

Helsley, Robert W. (2004), "Urban Political Economics in J.V. Henderson and J.F. Thisse (eds.) Handbook of Regional and Urban Economics, Vol. 4, Elsevier.

Krueger, Anne O. (2002), "Introduction" in Anne, O. Kruger (ed.) Economic Policy Reforms and the Indian Economy, Oxford University Press, New Delhi, pp. 1-6.

Mishra, Girish K., Rakesh Gupta (1981), Resettlement Policies in Delhi, Centre for Urban Studies, Indian Institute of Public Administration, New Delhi.

Mitra, Arup (2003), Occupational Choices, Networks and Transfers : An Exegesis Based on Micro Data from Delhi Slums, Manohar, New Delhi.

National Sample Survey Organisation (2003), Condition of Urban Slums (2002), Salient Features, NSS 58th (Round July 2002, Dec. 2002) Report No. 486, Ministry of Statistics and Programme Implementation, Government of India, New Delhi.

Quality, Employment Structure and Poverty Invidence the Slum Perspective (1990), *Indian Economic Review*, Vol. 25, No. 1, pp. 57-73.

Ravallion and Martin (2002), "Why has Economic Growth been More Pro-Poor in Some States of India than others, *Journal of Economics Development*, Vol. 68, pp. 381-400.

Sridharan, N. (1995), "Indian Slums in Problems, Policies and Issues" in Brain, C. Aldrich and Ravinder, S. Sandhu (eds.), Housing the Urban Poor: Policy and Practice in Developing Countries, Vistaar Publications, New Delhi, pp. 385-400.

The Hindu (2005), "Slum-dwellers Storm", Shastri Bhawan, 16 March.

Urbanisation, Slums Informal Sector Employment Poverty—An Exploratory Study, B.R. Publishing Corporation, Delhi (1994).

Lord Mountbatten in his address to the Constituent Assembly, August 15, 1947 said, "India will now attain a position of strength and influence and take its right place in the comity of nations" but his dream still needs to be realized. No doubt, following 1947 India made significant strides in multiple areas as it made a change from a dependent colony to a free democratic nation and the immediate challenge for the first government of Independent India was to accelerate the growth rate and this formed the cornerstone of the economic policies of Independent India. It is hoped that accelerating economic growth would result in the creation of employment opportunities and this would yield greater incomes and higher standards of living but it is also recently felt that accelerated growth must be inclusive for enabling the benefits of development to be shared equitably by all segments of society.

5

Levels of Living and Health Indicators Across the Indian States

DALIP KUMAR AND SURENDRA KUMAR

INTRODUCTION

Health is very important in a person's level of livings. Level of living depends on personal income and consumption expenditure of a household. A level of income or expenditure higher than this means better conditions of living. The proportion of personal consumption expenditure is distributed among the various items of consumption. While comparing the levels of living of the people in terms of the level of expenditure as a whole and on individual items of expenditure, we are beset with the problem of price. We can also bypass the problem of prices, as also the problems connected with the supply of goods and services by the state, which is known to have an impact on the level of living. One important aspect of the indicator of the levels of living is their utility from the point of view of measurement of the degree of inequality in the levels of living in states.

The measurement of levels of living depends on several components like health, food consumption and nutrition, level sections of the Indian population remain disadvantaged in their quest for equitable treatment under the judicial system. Human right's violations are often generated by intense social tensions that disproportionately affect women, the poor, religious minorities, and other disadvantaged groups. Discrimination against women remains entrenched in India. Deep-rooted cultural and traditional practices deprive women of education, health care, and nutrition. Violence against women is widespread, and includes girl child foeticide/ infanticide, child abuse, and rapes, etc. India is a significant source and transit country for trafficked women and children. Compounding these serious problems in health is India's lack of financial viability in the power sector. Only one-third of households have electricity, and Indians have access to 30 times less water than individuals in the United States. Significant power shortages plague the country due to unsustainable subsidisation policies, a lack of cost-recovery by utilities, and the subsequent inability of utilities to provide reliable, high quality power. Widespread financial insolvency of the utilities, and the state governments that are forced to bail them out, significantly contribute to increasing levels of state fiscal deficits.

DISTRIBUTION OF HHs BY MONTHLY PER CAPITA EXPENDITURE (MPCE)

'Levels of living' is highly related with the good health of the household members as well as to the extent of medical care received by them. The distribution of Households and population by income level is useful information for health sector. NSSO collected data on consumption expenditure in its survey. Since monthly per capita expenditure (MPCE) provides the basis for ranking of the households according to level of living, the distributions of households by MPCE class for rural and urban India are presented below in diagram and Table 1 and Charts 1 and 2.

In urban India, about 20 per cent of households spend less than Rs. 500 per month per person. On the other hand, in rural India, about 65 per cent of the households spend less than Rs. 500.

CHART 1

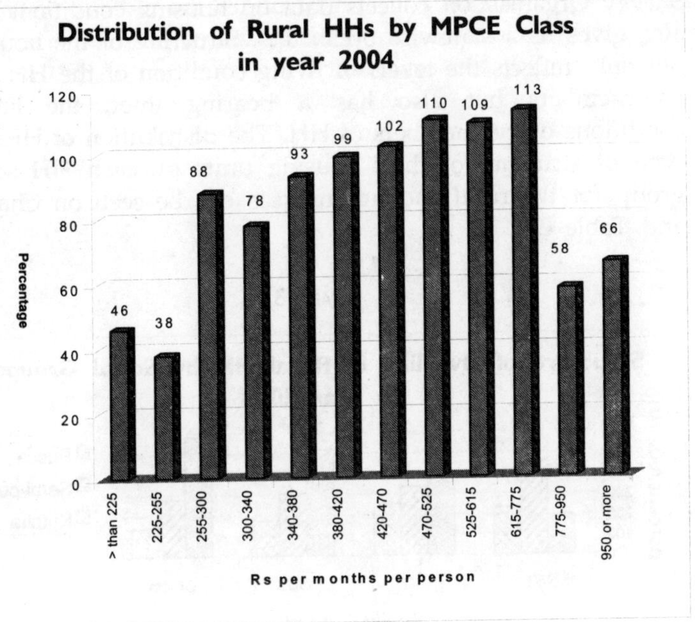

CHART 2

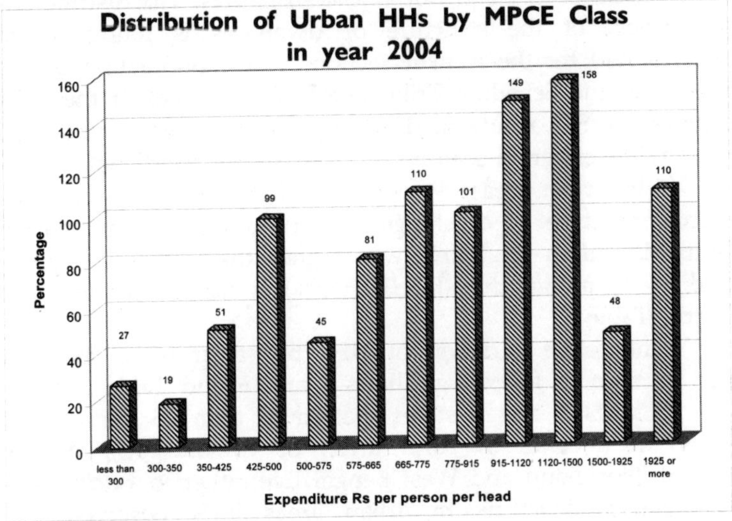

Type of Structure of Housing: The National Sample Survey Organisation collects data on housing conditions and also gives us a statewise break ups. Structure of the housing not only reflects the levels of living condition of the HH and its members but also has a bearing upon the health conditions of the members of HH. The distribution of HHs by type of structure of their housing units by each HH social group for the rural and urban areas can be seen on Chart 3 and Table 2.

CHART 3

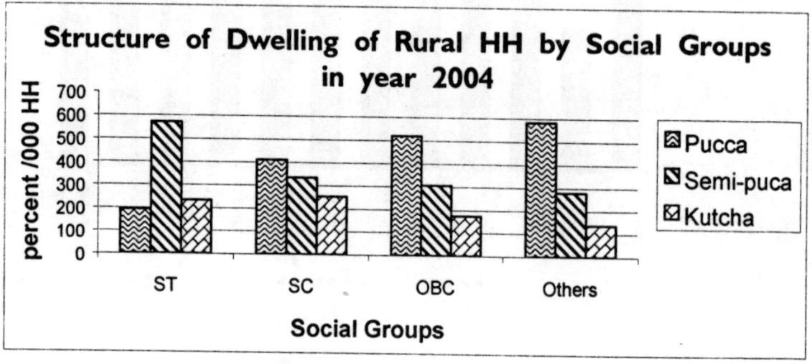

It can be seen in rural area that more than half of the HHs reside in *semi-pucca* or *kutcha* structures. The distribution in respect of the structure of dwellings is found to be deteriorated for the weaker sections of the population and is worst for the Schedule Tribes. Only 20 per cent of the HHs among the STs reside in dwellings made of *pucca* buildings, rest living either in *semi-pucca* or in *kutcha* dwellings.

In urban areas, 84 per cent of the HHs are reporting pucca structure of dwellings. The proportion of population living in pucca structures was higher than other categories and lowest among the STs HHs (65%). It can be seen in Chart 4 and Table 2

Inter-state variation of HHs by structure of dwelling can be seen in following Charts 5 and 6 and Table 3.

Charts 5 and 6 states that more than 75 per cent of HHs, in general, in rural areas of Chhattisgarh, Assam, Orissa, Jharkhand and West Bengal live either in *kutcha* or in semi-pucca structure. In urban areas it is observed that

CHART 4

Structure of Dwelling of Urban HH by Social Groups

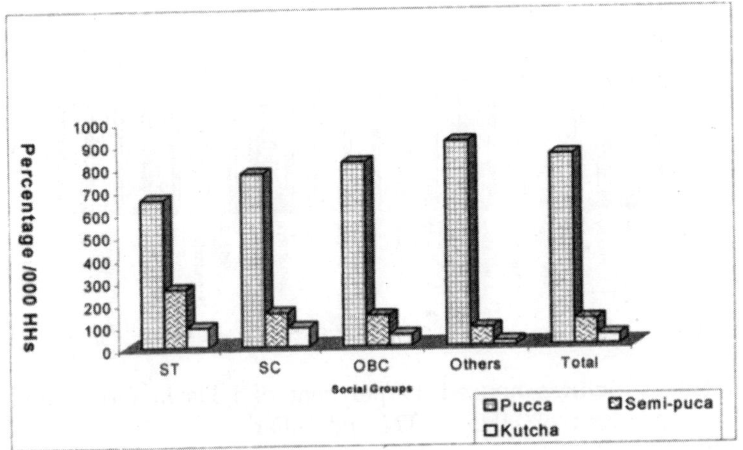

CHART 5

State-wise Rural HHs by Structure of the Dwelling

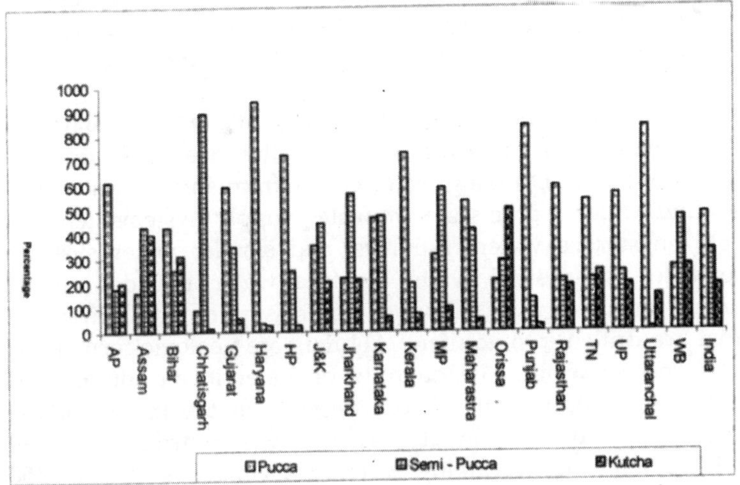

CHART 6

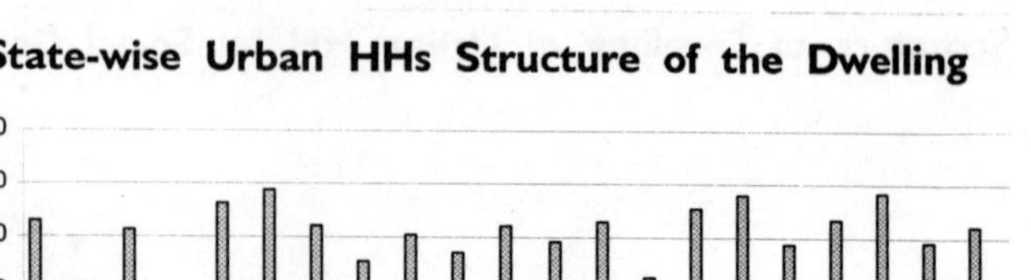
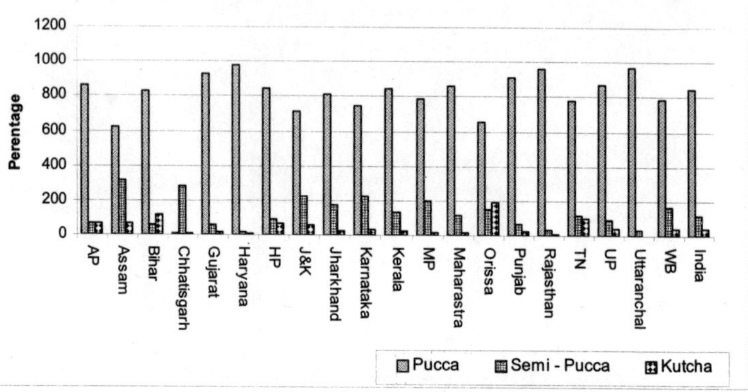

kutcha structures housed 19 per cent of HHs in Orissa and 10-11 per cent of HHs in TN and Bihar.

MPCE Class and Type of Structure of Dwelling

It is useful to find out the dwelling type in relation to the size of monthly per capita expenditure (MPCE). It can be seen in Table 4 and Charts 7 and 8 that in rural areas only 26 per cent of the poorest class (MPCE less than Rs. 225) reported living in *pucca* dwellings, as many as 84 per cent of the richest class of HHs (MPCE Rs 950 and above) live in *pucca* dwellings. The disparity between rich and poor is to be found less in urban areas as compared to rural areas.

Levels of Living and Source of Drinking Water and Sanitation

Sources of drinking water are the clear indicators of levels of living. Drinking water comes from surface water and ground water. Large-scale of water supply systems tend to rely on surface water resources, and smaller water systems tend to use ground water. Surface water includes rivers, lakes, and reservoirs. Ground water is pumped from wells that are drilled into aquifers. Aquifers are geologic formations that contain water. The quantity of water in an aquifer and the water produced by a well depend on the nature of the rock, sand, or soil in the aquifer where from the well withdraws water. Drinking water wells may be shallow (50 feet or less) or deep (more than 1,000 feet).

Chart 7

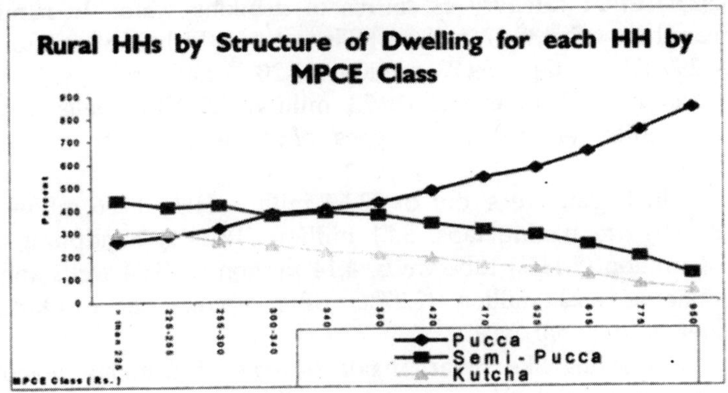

Chart 8

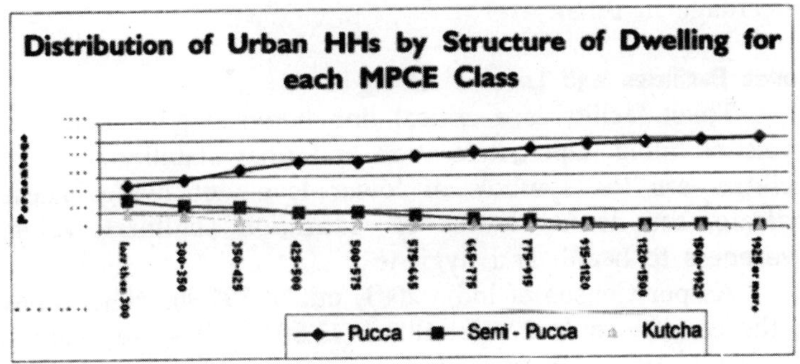

Water-related diseases include those due to micro-organisms and chemicals in water people drink. These diseases are like Malaria, Diarrhea, Hepatitis, Cholera, Fluorosis, Dengue, etc. They highly affect the levels of living in society.

Quality of Drinking water is also an important determinants of level of living to the HHs. Statewise source of drinking water can be seen in Table 5 and Charts 9A and 9B

As per Census 2001 out of 191.96 million HHs in the country, there are 70.44 million (36.70%) HHs having tap, 68.45 million (35.66%) hand pumps, 10.67 million (5.56%)

tube-wells, 34.87 million (18.17%) wells and 7.50 million (3.91%) other category as source of drinking water. In rural areas there are 138.27 million HHs out of which 33.58 million (24.29%) have taps, 59.73 million (43.20%) hand pumps, 7.93 million (5.74%) tubewells, 30.73 million (22.23%) wells and 6.28 million (4.55%) other types of drinking water in the country.

In Urban areas, out of 53.69 million HHs 36.86 million (68.66%) are having taps, 8.71 million (16.24%) handpumps, 2.74 million (5.11%) tube wells, 4.14 million (7.71%) wells and remaining 1.22 million (2.27%) other sources of drinking water at national level.

In states like Bihar, major sources of drinking water both in rural and urban areas are wells and tube wells which are considered not to be safe and hyegenic. Treated tap water, *pucca* wells and bottled water supply are very low percentage in Bihar.

Toilet Facilities and Level of Living

Toilet facility is a critical link between good and bad levels of living. Open defecation and unavailability of toilet facilities are the symbols of lower levels of living. These indicate the lower levels of education, cultural value, awareness to health and hygiene.

As per Census of India 2001, out of 191.96 million HHs in the country, only 22.07 million (11.50%) HHs are availing the facility of pit types of toilet within the house, whereas, 34.59 million (18.02%) and 13.21 million (6.88%) HHs have water closet and other types of latrine within the house. In rural areas14.23 million (10.30%) HHs, out of 138.27 million are using pit types of latrine within the house. 9.83 million (7.11%) are having water closet and 6.23 million (4.51%) other types of latrine facility within the house. Urban HHs counted for 53.69 million in the country 7.84 million (14.60%) re-using pit type of latrine within the house.

The highest percentage ranging from a 80.01 and above per cent HHs having no latrine facility within the house has been noticed in four states. Highest percentage is in Chhattisgarh (85.80%), followed by Orissa (85.11%), Bihar (80.81%) and Jharkhand (80.33%). In Bihar more than 80 per

CHART 9A

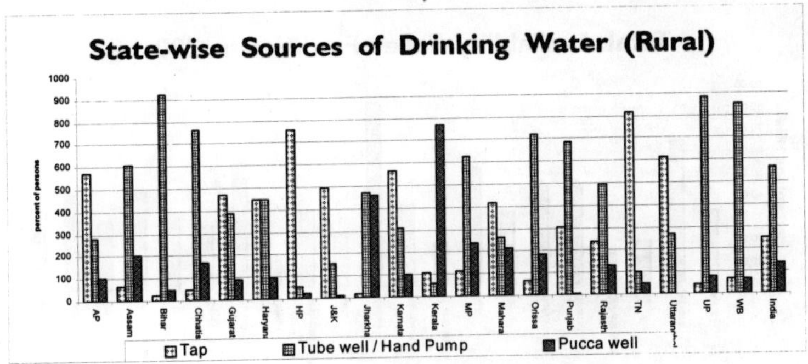

CHART 9B

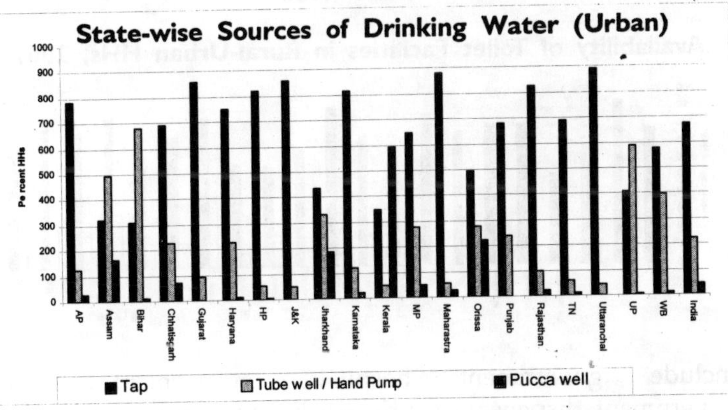

cent households do not have toilets. Nearly 86 per cent population in rural India ease out in the open. Even in urban areas more than 30 per cent population attends to the call of nature in the open. That creates health problems not only for them but also for those who have toilet facilities.

LEVELS OF LIVING AND HEALTH CARE

Improvement in health may also raise the level of living by releasing some of the gross national product which would otherwise be used for the care of the sick. (Philip and Stewart, 1962). Health care facilities are provided by public and private sectors. The public providers of health care

CHART 10A

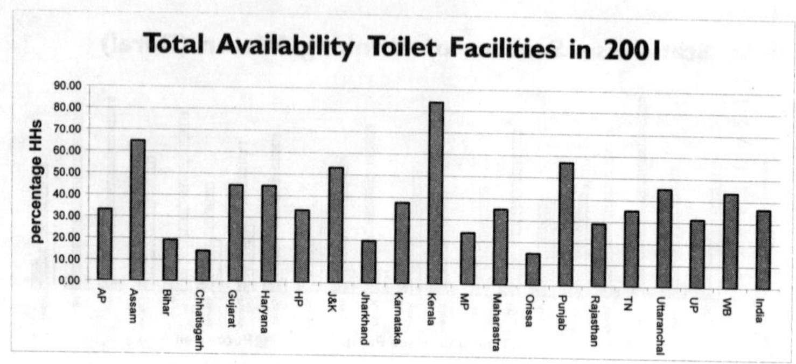

CHART 10B

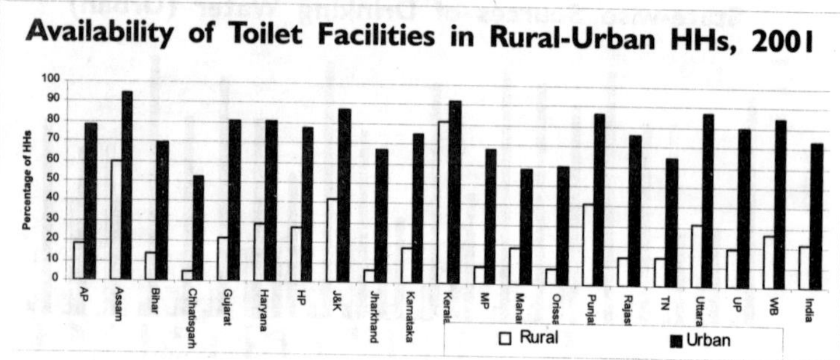

include government hospitals, government clinics, government dispensaries, primary health centres, community health centres and state and central government assisted ESI hospitals and dispensaries. The rest of the providers fall in the private sector. The private sectors include private doctors, nursing homes, private hospitals, charitable institutions, etc. Table 6 and Charts 11 and 12 shows how the share of public provider in treatment of ailments varies with monthly per capita expenditure (MPCE) class. It reveals that a large proportion of total ailments are treated at the private institutions including 78 per cent in rural areas and 81 per cent in urban areas.

In Table 6, the people in the lowest MPCE class less than Rs. 225 in the rural areas treatment was received from the Government Institutions about 30 per cent of the treated case, whereas the proportion was 18 per cent for the highest MPCE class (Rs. 950 and above). In the urban areas, this proportion was 26 per cent and 11 per cent.

Inter-State variation in proportion of ailments treated by Government institutions can be seen in Table 7. This table gives the estimated proportion (per 1000) of persons hospitalised during the reference period of 365 days in the rural and urban areas of major states. In Kerala, the proportion, in both rural and urban areas, was much higher than in the rest of major states. While as national average as whole out of every 1000 persons, 23 in rural areas and 31 in urban areas were hospitalised during a period of 365 days.

CHART 11

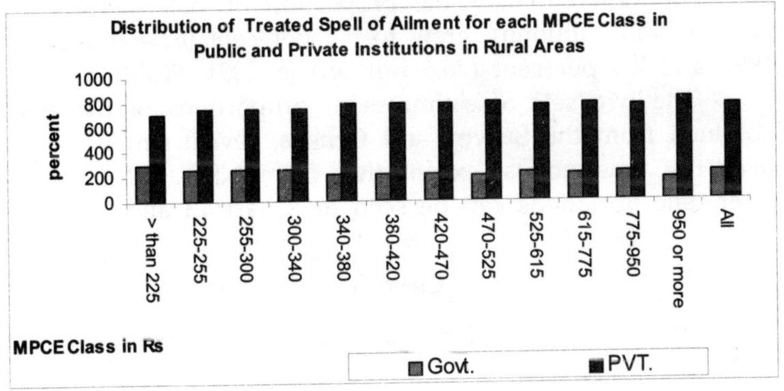

CHART 12

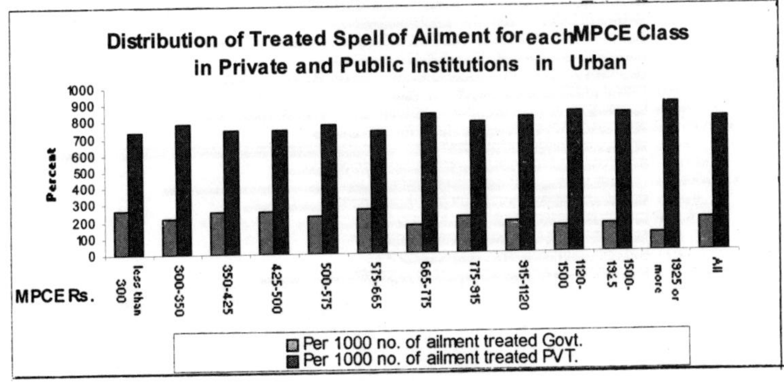

The corresponding estimates were as high as 101 and 90. The other states, reporting relatively high proportions of persons hospitalised through much less than Kerala were TN, Haryana, Maharashtra, and HP, Rural Punjab and urban areas of West Bengal and Gujarat.

Levels of living and health care of the aged persons: As per NSSO 60th Round persons 60 years and above are to be refereed as the aged persons. The main finding of NSSO 60th Round survey are presented under following heads:

A. *Demographic Burden*

As per NSSO survey results, an estimated 66.4 million aged persons in the country, about 75 per cent were residing in rural and remaining 25 per cent in the urban areas. As per 1981 Population Census the proportion of aged persons 6.5 per cent (43.5 million), grew to 6.8 per cent (61.4 million) in 1991 and 7.4 per cent (76.6 million) in 2001. (Table 8)

The two sets of estimates of proportions of the aged, obtained from the Survey and Census, reveal similar trends over the time points, except that from NSSO 52nd round. Inter-state variations can be seen on Chart 13 and Table 9.

CHART 13

Number of Aged Person per 1000 Population

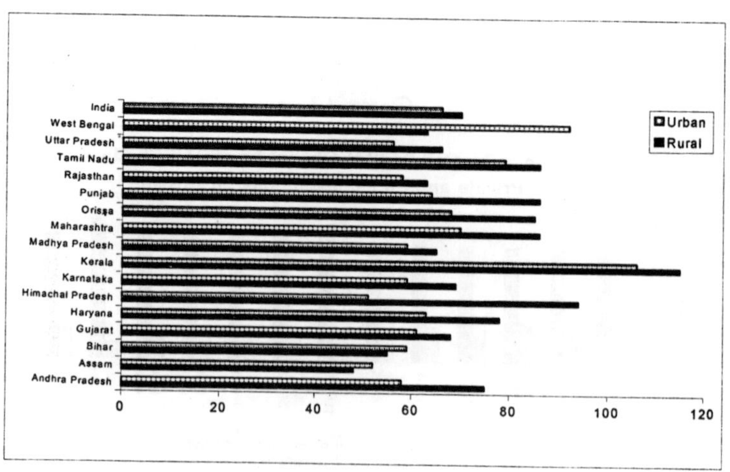

Inter-State Variations of the Levels of Living among Aged Persons

Male-female and rural-urban differences in the proportion of aged persons are found to exist and the differences are very significant. The share of the aged females was higher than that of the aged males in the urban areas and almost the same in the rural areas. This fact reflects the higher expectancy of life for females which is probably the outcome of migration of the males in the working age groups from the rural areas.

LEVELS OF LIVING AND STATUS OF HEALTH INDICATORS

The indicators of health status, the birth and death rates are more reflective of the demographic changes taking place in the country. The life expectancy rate and the infant mortality rates are better indicators of the health status of the population. A look at the relationship among these four indicators is sufficient enough to confirm that these indicators are inter-dependent over the time.

Crude Birth Rate

Birth rate is directly related to the economic development and levels of living. Poorer the family, larger its size, poverty breeds illiteracy and illiterate people do not understand the importance of small size of family. They are orthodox enough to adopt various birth control measures. Trends of crude birth rates in Bihar can be seen in Chart 14.

All India average birth rate was 24.10 per cent in 2004. The highest percentage of such rate being in UP (30.80%) followed by Bihar (30.20%), Rajasthan (29.00%), MP (29.80%) and Haryana and Assam (25.10%). Remaining 10 states of these 16 Major states had percentage lower than the National average.

Crude Death Rates

All India average death rate was 7.50 per cent in 2004. The highest percentage of such rate being in Orissa (9.60%) followed by MP (9.2%), UP and Assam (8.8%), and Bihar (8.1%). TN is equivalent to National Average. Remaining 11

CHART 14

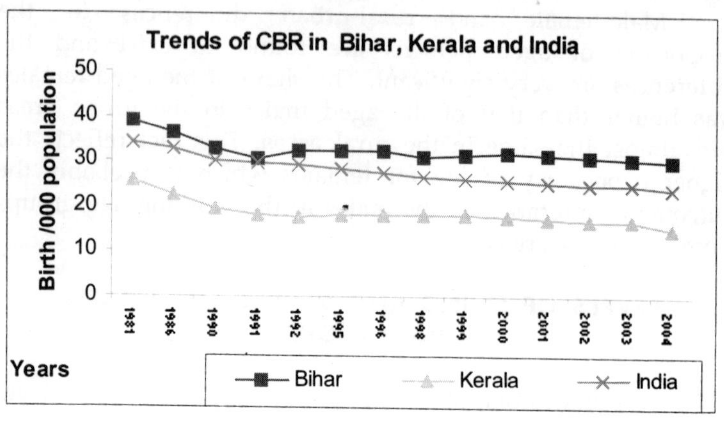

states of these 16 Major states had percentage lower than the National average. (Table 12) The inter-state variations are also noticeable. Comparatively richer states have CDR below than the national average. Again the figure in Kerala is the lowest at 6.1 per cent in 2004 whereas poorer states like Orissa, MP, UP, Assam and Bihar exceed the national average. Needless to say, these poorer states provide very poor health facilities to their population. Trends of crude death rates in Bihar can be seen in Chart 15.

In Bihar the crude birth rate is higher (8.1) in comparison to state of Kerala (6.1). This is due to prevalence and occurrence of disease, specially water born deceases and low body resistance as a result of nutritional deficiency in diets. This is also due to lack of medical facilities, inadequate child and women health care, and lack of awareness, etc.

Infant Mortality Rate

Infant Mortality Rate is an explicit indicator of health status and especially the women and child care which is the direct outcome of economic well-being of the people and success of government interventions. It is affected by factors like immunisation programmes, Pre-natal and post-natal care facilities for institutional delivery, etc. Poor people are more likely to live in massive over crowded areas without clean water and sanitation or in distant rural areas, also without

CHART 15

Trends of CDR in Bihar, Kerala and India

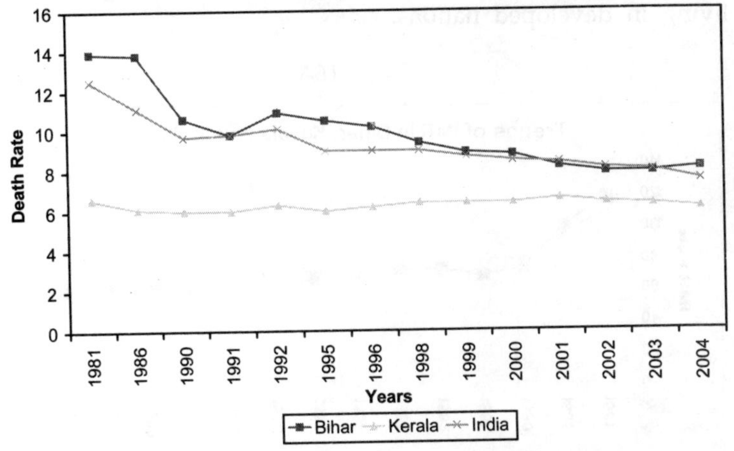

clean water and sanitation. As a result, they have a larger propensity to have diarrhoea, cholera, or typhoid fever, (Martine, 2005). According to UN's Children Funds, diarrhoea is one of the three main causes of child mortality (the other two are malnutrition and respiratory infections) (Sachs, 2001).

Kerala shows the lowest IMR at 12 in 2004, while Maharashtra, TN, Delhi, Uttranchal, Jharkhand, Punjab, Karnataka and HP have met the national goal of reducing the IMR to 58 by 2004. The major states such as MP (79), Orissa (77), UP (72) and Rajasthan (67) are still far behind the national average. Infant mortality rate (IMR) is used as a widely accepted measure of the general health of the population. Kerala performs rather marvellously on this front, with an IMR of 11 per 1,000 population, which is the lowest among all states in India. The state's performance is also above others when we look at figures on birth rates, proportion of institutional births, life expectancy, proportion of persons hospitalised, and so on. (Kurian and Kale, 2007). This trends can be seen in Table 12 and Chart 16.

Life Expectancy

Life expectancy reflects the level of economic and

health development and also levels of living. The staggering high life expectancy in countries like Japan and USA is testimony to the faster economic growth and raising levels of living in developed nations.

CHART 16A

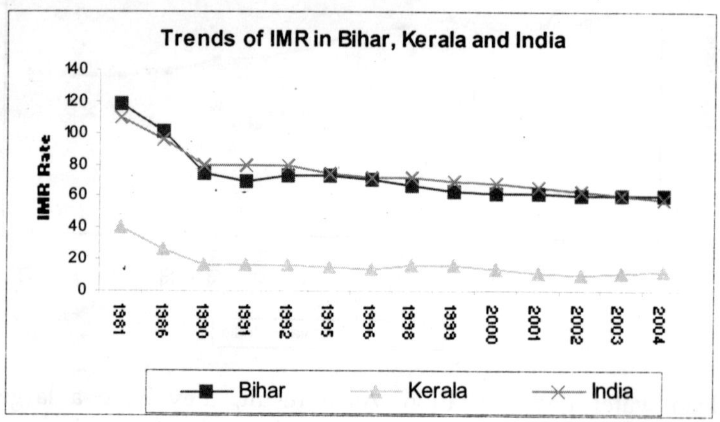

In 1950 life expectancy in developing countries was forty years; by 1990 it had increased to 63 years. In 1950 twenty-eight of every 100 children died before their fifth birthday; In year 1990 the numbers had fallen to 10. Smallpox, which killed more than 5 million annually in the early 1950s had been eradicated entirely. (World Bank, 2003). Now the life expectancy at birth is 64.7 years for both sexes in year 2006. To ensure the continued improvement in life expectancy, the health care delivery infrastructure is being expanded, MCH care is being improved, specific programmes such as the expanded programme on immunisation (EPI), introduction of oral dehydration therapy (ORT), etc. are being strengthened, and efforts are continuing to contain locally endemic diseases. There is also an increased thrust in other development and poverty alleviation programmes. The main constraints are the diverse population groups, low literacy and income levels, and socio-cultural beliefs and practices, which adversely affect health.

India has made substantial progress in the health indicators over the past few decades. Life expectancy increased from 54 year in 1980 to 64.7 years in 2006. This increase in life expectancy is the result of an overall decline in mortality. Japan has the highest life expectancy in the world and on an average a Japanese is expected to live 19 more years than a South Asian (Haq, 2004). Knowles and Owen (1997) and Jamison and Wang (1998) find that life expectancy contributes to economic growth more than education. For the first, differences in the life expectancy between the richest and poorest countries is over 40 years, says the World Health Organisation's World Health Reports-2008.Japan has the longest life expectancy at 81 years 6 months, while Zambia is the shortest at 32 years 8 months. Where as world's average life expectancy is 67 years.. In India average life expectancy is only 63 years, 62 for men and 63 for women (Sharma, 2008).

Regional Imbalance in life expectancy can be seen in Table 12. Kerala stands at 72 years which is the highest whereas economically backward states like MP, Assam, Orissa, UP, Bihar and Rajasthan have life expectancy lower than the national average of 65.20 years.

Expenditure on Health

According to the WHO definition, the health expenditure includes all expenditure whose primary purpose is to restore, improve and maintain health for nation and for individuals during a defined time period. (WHO, World Bank and USAID, 2003). The share of public expenditure as a percentage to GDP on health and education at higher level has been gradually declining (Panchmukhi, 2000; Dev and Mooji, 2002). Higher levels of health expenditure are generally associated with higher levels of health status. The demand for health services is bound to increase substantially in the next few decades with the rising share of old age groups in the country. Older people are usually prone to diseases and will require services for the specific needs of their age group. The rapid ageing of the population in the region, in particular the older population (more than 60 years) would increase expenditure on public health, for two reasons. First, older people and, in particular, those of advanced age, are more prone to diseases. The older

CHART 16B

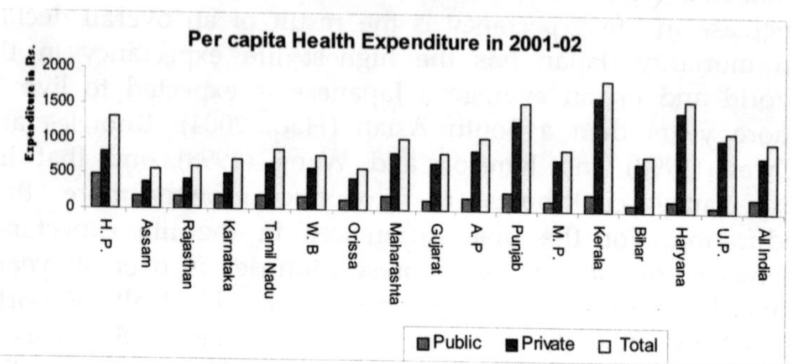

population group is expected to expand more during the coming years and is bound to increase the demand for health services at large scale. Second, health care for older persons is on average more expensive than the children and younger people. The public expenditures on health actually declined over the past decades. This declined from 3.12 per cent in 1992-93 to 2.99 per cent in 2003-04. Similarly, the combined expenditure (State and Central Government) on health as a percentage of GDP has also marginally declined from 1.01 per cent of GDP in 1992-93 to 0.99 per cent in 2003-04. (Table 13 and Charts 16B and 17).

The declining public expenditure, private expenditure and combined expenditure on health by the State and Central governments are both the causes and consequences of lowering down of levels of living. Expenditure on health is good investment which increases the productivity of labour force and hence the overall economic growth. The low expenditure on health is due to unaffordability and lack of resources both by the individual and government. It creates the vicious circle and results into the degrading levels of living. (Chart 16B)

Per capita health expenditure in India during 2001-02 was Rs. 997 of which public expenditure amounted to Rs. 207 and private expenditure to Rs 790. The per capita health expenditure of major states for the year 2001-02 indicated that the level of public health spending has been relatively higher in the states of HP, Punjab and Kerala while lower in UP, Bihar, MP, and Orissa. Private expenditure was higher in

Kerala, Punjab, Haryana and UP as compared to Assam, Rajasthan and Orissa (Table 13 and Graph 17). Per capita health spending in Kerala was the highest while in Assam it was the lowest.

CHART 17

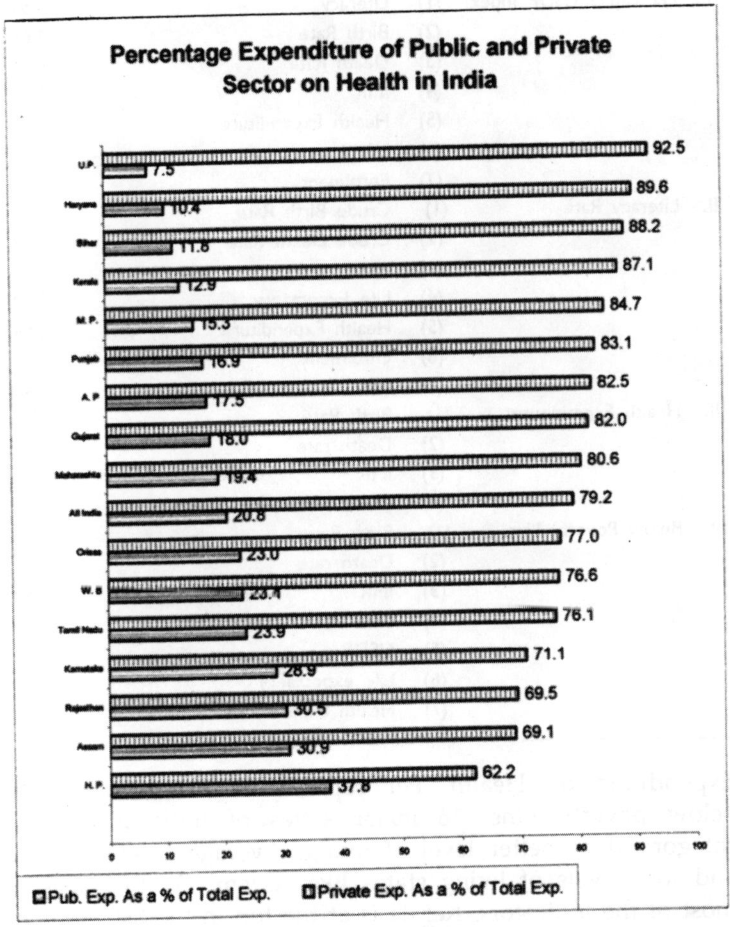

CONCLUSION

On the basis of various indicators, like Life Expectancy at Birth, CBR, CDR, IMR, Literacy Rate, Per capita

RANK CORRELATIONS, 2001

Rank Correlations

Correlation of		*With*	
I. Per capita GSDP Index	(1)	Literacy	0.54
	(2)	Birth Rate	-0.66
	(3)	Death Rate	-0.76
	(4)	IMR	-0.55
	(5)	Health Expenditure	-0.55
	(6)	Life expectancy	0.77
	(7)	Enrolment	0.74
II. Literacy Rate	(1)	Crude Birth Rate	-0.57
	(2)	Crude Death Rate	-0.47
	(3)	IMR	-0.54
	(4)	Life Expectancy	0.57
	(5)	Health Expenditure	0.55
	(6)	Enrolment	0.56
	(7)	BPL	-0.45
III. Health Expenditure	(1)	Birth Rate	-0.81
	(2)	Death rate	-0.77
	(3)	IMR	-0.69
	(4)	Life expectancy	0.82
IV. Below Poverty Line	(1)	Birth Rate	0.42
	(2)	Death rate	0.76
	(3)	IMR	0.54
	(4)	Enrolment	-0.14
	(5)	NSDP	-0.82
	(6)	Life expectancy	-0.73
	(7)	Health expenditure	-0.74

Expenditure on Health, Per capita GSDP and Population below poverty Line. 16 major states of India have been categorised as better level of living, Average level of living and low levels of living states like Assam. On the basis of most of the indicators, Kerala is at the top in the list of better performing states. In this category, HP, Punjab, TN, Maharashtra are included. West Bengal has done well in restricting the CBR and IMR. In few indicators AP and Gujarat have also done well. Bihar occupies place in the low performing states with poor states like Assam, Rajasthan,

LEVELS OF LIVING AND HEALTH RANKING OF MAJOR STATES

Summary Indicators: Ranking of Major States

Sr. No.	Life Expectancy at Birth Year	CBR/000 Population (1998-2002)	CDR/000 Population (2004)	IMR/000 Live Birth	Literacy Rates (2001)	Per capita Expenditure on Health in Rs. 2001-02 Public	Private (2004)	Per capita GSDP 2001-02	Population, BPL, (2000)
1	2	3	4	5	6	7	8	9	10
Better Performing States									
1.	Kerala	Kerala	Kerala	Kerala	Kerala	H.P.	Kerala	Punjab	Punjab
2.	Punjab	T.N.	W.B.	Maharashta	M.P.	Punjab	Haryana	Haryana	H.P.
3.	Maharashta	W.B.	H.P.	T.N.	H.P.	Kerala	Punjab	Maharashta	Haryana
4.	Haryana	Maharashta	Punjab	W.B.	T.N.	Karnataka	U.P.	H.P.	Kerala
5.	T.N.	A.P.	Gujarat	Punjab	Punjab	T.N.	A.P.	Gujarat	Gujarat
Average Performing States									
6.	H.P.	Punjab	Haryana	Karnataka	Gujarat	Maharashta	Maharashta	T.N.	Rajasthan
7.	Karnataka	Karnataka	Maharashta	H.P.	W.B.	A.P.	H.P.	Kerala	A.P.
8.	W.B.	H.P.	Karnataka	Bihar	Haryana	Rajasthan	M.P.	Karnataka	Karnataka

(Contd.)

(Contd.)

1	2	3	4	5	6	7	8	9	10
9.	A.P.	Orissa	T.N.	Gujarat	Karnataka	W.B.	Bihar	A.P.	T.N.
10.	Gujarat	Gujarat	A.P.	A.P.	Maharashta	Assam	Gujarat	W.B.	Maharastr
Low Performing States									
11.	Rajasthan	Assam	Rajasthan	Haryana	Assam	Haryana	T.N.	Rajasthan	W.B.
12.	Bihar	Haryana	Bihar	Assam	Orissa	Gujarat	W.B.	M.P.	U.P.
13.	U.P.	M.P.	Assam	Rajasthan	A.P.	Orissa	Karnataka	Assam	Assam
14.	Orissa	Rajasthan	M.P.	U.P.	Rajasthan	M.P.	Orissa	Orissa	M.P.
15.	Assam	Bihar	U.P.	M.P.	U.P.	Bihar	Rajasthan	U.P.	Bihar
16.	M.P.	U.P.	Orissa	Orissa	Bihar	U.P.	Assam	Bihar	Orissa

Orissa and UP. On some indicators a few better performing states are counted as low performing. For example, Haryana's record in controlling IMR, BPL population in WB and Per capita private expenditure on health in TN are like those of low performing states.

SUGGESTIONS AND WAY FORWARED

Important focus for policy makers is as under:

- Public expenditure in health sector has to be increased. Presently the public expenditure on health is only around one per cent of GDP. It has been stagnant since reform period.
- Government should promote health facilities and regulate the private sector. The share of private sector is in the total health care sector is high and has increased over time.
- Reduction of poverty should be the top priority
- Improve equity, efficiency and quality on education and health sectors.
- Investment in accesses to safe drinking water and improved sanitation facilities in both rural and urban sectors.
- Primary health facilities should focus more on preventive health measures rather than curative care only.
- Health education should be necessary for all women, adolescent girls and lactating/serving mothers.
- Government should implement health insurance schemes for the BPL people.
- Government should provide free health security to all elderly population (More than 60 years) specially in rural areas.
- Traditional and low cost Indian system of medicine like Ayurveda, Naturopathy and Unani should be encouraged and improvised to increase their acceptability by the masses.
- Yoga should be popularised with the help of trained and certified Yoga teachers.

References

Bajpai, N. 2004, India's Health Needs a Dose of Funds, Reforms, *Business Line*, April 09, 2004.

India in the Era of Economic Reforms, *The Hindu*, January 28, 2004.

Bhat, Ramesh and S.K. Babu (2004), "Health Insurance and Third Party Administrators: Issue and Challenges", *Economic and Political Weekly*, Vol. 39, No. 28, July 10-16.

Claeson M, Bos E.R., Mawji T., Pathmanathan I. (2000), Reducing child Mortality in India in the New Millennium., *Bull World Health Organisation*, 78-1192-99.

Chen L., Evans T., Anand S., Boufford J., Brown H., Chowdhury M., (*et. al.*), (2004), Human Resources for Health: Overcoming the Crisis, Lancet, 2004, 364:1984-1990.

Ganguli, B.N. and D.B. Gupta (1976), *Levels of Living in India : An Inter-State Profile*, S. Chand & Company Ltd, New Delhi.

GOI (2001), Census of India, *Housing Atlas of India, 2001*, Office of Registrar General, Government of India, New Delhi.

GOI (2003), Health Information of India, 2003, Government of India, Central Bureau of Health Intelligence, Directorate General of Health Services, Ministry of Health and Family Welfare, New Delhi.

GOI (2005), *National Health Accounts India 2001-02*, National Health Accounts Cell, Ministry of Health and Family Welfare, Government of India, New Delhi.

GOI (2006), Bulletin on Rural Health Statistics in India, 2006, Ministry of Health and Family Welfare, Government of India, New Delhi.

Haq (2004), Human Development in South Asia, 2004, The Health Challenge, Mahbub ul Haq Human Development Centre, Oxford University Press, Pakistan.

Kiros, G.E. and D.P. Hogan (2001), War, Famine, and Excess Child Mortality in Africa: The Role of Parental Education, *International Journal of Epidemiology*, 30; 447-455.

Martin, Xavier Sla-I (2005), On the Health—Poverty Trap, on Health and Economic Growth: Findings and Policy Implications (eds. by Gullien, Rivera and others), MIT Press, Cambridge, London.

Misra, R., Rachel Chatterjee, Sujatha Rao (2003), India Health Report, Oxford University Press, New Delhi.

Nath, Balkrishnan (2004), Health and Glow of Pharma, *Business Line*, January 28.

Park, K. (1997), Indicators of MCH care. In: *Park's Textbook of Preventive and Social Medicine*, 15th ed., Jabalpur: Banarsidas Bhanot, 370-80.

Philip E. Enterline, and William H. Stewart (1962), Health Program Requirements to Offset Effects on Levels of Living, *American Journal of Public Health*, Vol. 52, No. 3, pp. 401-409

Raaj Neelam (2007), Malnutrition Ails Indian Kids, *Times of India*, February 11, 2007.

Rivera, Berta and Luis Currais (2005), Individual Returns to Health in Brazil:

A Quintile Regeration Analysis, in Health and Economic Growth: Findings and Policy Implications (eds., al,) by Gullien, Rivera and others), MIT Press, Cambridge, London.

Sachs, J. (2001), Macroeconomics and Health: Investing in Health for Economic Development Report of Commission on Macroeconomics and Health, Geneva, World Health Organisation, pp. 1-213.

Sen, Amartya (1998), Mortality as an Indicator of Economic Success and Failure, *Economic Journal*, 108(446):1-25.

Sharma, Sanchita (2008), Rich Live Longer, Poor Die Younger, *Hindustan Times*, 15 October, 2008, Delhi Editions.

Silvi Kurian and Sumita Kale (2007), Neglecting God's own, *Business Standard*, February 7, 2007, New Delhi.

WHO (2003), The World Health Report: Shaping the Future, Washington, D.C., World Health Organisation.

WHO, World Bank and USAID (2003), *Guide to Producing National Health Accounts*, Geneva, World Health Organization.

WHO (2005), World Health Report, Making Every Child Count, 2005, Geneva, World Health Organisation.

WHO (2006), Working Together for Health, The World Health Report, 2006, World Health Organisation.

World Bank (1993), Investing in Health: World Development Report, 1993, Washington, D.C: The World Bank, p. 1.

Silvi Kurian and Sumita Kale (2007), Neglecting God's Own, *Business Standard*, February 7, 2007, New Delhi.

Wang and Jamison, Lau (1998), "Health's Contribution to Economic Growth, 1965-1990" in Health, *Health Policy and Health Outcomes*, Final Report, Health and Development Satellite, WHO Director-General Transition Team.

WHO (2003), The World Health Report: Shaping the Future, Washington, D.C., World Health Organisation.

WHO, World Bank and USAID (2003), *Guide to Producing National Health Accounts*, Geneva, World Health Organisation.

WHO (2005), World Health Report, Making Every Child Count, 2005, Geneva, World Health Organisation.

WHO (2006), Working Together for Health, The World Health Report, 2006, World Health Organisation.

World Bank (1993), Investing in Health: World Development Report, 1993, Washington, D.C: The World Bank, p. 1.

APPENDIX

TABLE 1

Per 1000 Distribution of Households by MPCE Class during January-June 2004

Rural		*Urban*	
MPCE class (Rs.)	*Households*	*MPCE class (Rs.)*	*Households*
Less than 225	46	less than 300	27
225-255	38	300-350	19
255-300	88	350-425	51
300-340	78	425-500	99
340-380	93	500-575	45
380-420	99	575-665	81
420-470	102	665-775	110
470-525	110	775-915	101
525-615	109	915-1120	149
615-775	113	1120-1500	158
775-950	58	1500-1925	48
950 or more	66	1925 or more	110
All	1000	All	1000

Source: NSSO 60th Round, Report No. 507, January-June 2004.

TABLE 2

Per 1000 Distribution of HHs by Structure of Dwelling for each HH By Social Group

Structure of Dwelling	*ST*	*SC*	*OBC*	*Others*	*Total*
			Rural		
Pucca	195	410	520	582	480
Semi-puca	570	335	306	280	332
Kutcha	235	255	173	138	188
All	1000	1000	1000	1000	1000
			Urban		
Pucca	653	765	813	902	842
Semi-pucca	259	150	136	79	115
Kutcha	88	85	50	19	43
All	1000	1000	1000	1000	1000

Source: NSSO 60th Round, Report No. 507, January-June 2004,

TABLE 3

Per 1000 Distribution of HHs by Structure of Dwelling for Major States: 2004

S. No.	States	Rural				Urban			
		Pucca	*Semi-Pucca*	*Kutcha*	*Total*	*Pucca*	*Semi-Pucca*	*Kutcha*	*Total*
1.	AP	616	181	203	1000	864	70	66	1000
2.	Assam	165	433	402	1000	622	311	64	1000
3.	Bihar	431	255	313	1000	825	60	114	1000
4.	Chhattisgarh	91	894	15	1000	7.6	281	8	1000
5.	Gujarat	594	349	57	1000	926	57	16	1000
6.	Haryana	940	34	26	1000	975	18	7	1000
7.	HP	723	251	26	1000	843	89	68	1000
8.	J & K	352	444	204	1000	714	227	59	1000
9.	Jharkhand	220	564	214	1000	809	170	21	1000
10.	Karnataka	466	473	60	1000	746	224	29	1000
11.	Kerala	730	198	72	1000	847	129	24	1000
12.	Madhya Pradesh	313	588	99	1000	788	196	15	1000
13.	Maharashtra	532	418	50	1000	864	117	19	1000
14.	Orissa	209	289	502	1000	651	153	189	1000
15.	Punjab	840	135	26	1000	913	63	24	1000
16.	Rajasthan	596	214	189	1000	961	29	9	1000
17.	TN	535	217	248	1000	779	119	102	1000
18.	UP	561	244	195	1000	868	88	44	1000
19.	Uttaranchal	837	14	149	1000	968	29	3	1000
20.	WB	262	469	269	1000	789	166	45	1000
	India	480	332	188	1000	842	115	43	1000

Source: NSSO 60th Round, Report No. 507, January-June 2004.

TABLE 4

Distribution of HHs by Structure of Dwelling as per Monthly Per Capita Expenditure Class

MPCE Class (Rs.)	Rural			
	Pucca	Semi-Pucca	Kutcha	Total
> than 225	259	441	299	1000
225-255	285	411	304	1000
255-300	319	421	261	1000
300-340	381	374	245	1000
340-380	400	385	215	1000
380-420	427	373	199	1000
420-470	477	335	188	1000
470-525	535	309	155	1000
525-615	575	286	139	1000
615-775	647	243	110	1000
775-950	740	190	70	1000
950 or more	839	115	47	1000
All	480	332	188	1000

MPCE Class (Rs.)	Urban			
	Pucca	Semi-Pucca	Kutcha	Total
less than 300	494	326	179	1000
300-350	561	274	165	1000
350-425	654	244	101	1000
425-500	746	187	68	1000
500-575	738	192	69	1000
575-665	810	145	45	1000
665-775	857	111	32	1000
775-915	897	82	20	1000
915-1120	938	50	12	1000
1120-1500	961	31	7	1000
1500-1925	976	18	3	1000
1925 or more	993	4	3	1000
All	842	115	43	1000

Source: NSSO 60th Round, Report No. 507, January-June 2004,

TABLE 5A

Distribution of HHs by Major Source of Drinking Water 2004

Sl. No.	*States*	*Per 1000 distribution of HHs by Major Sources of Drinking Water (Rural)*				*Per 1000 distribution of HHs by Major Sources of Drinking Water (Urban)*			
		Tap	*Tubewell/ Handpump*	*Pucca well*	*Others**	*Tap*	*Tubewell/ Handpump*	*Pucca well*	*Others**
1.	AP	572	279	99	50	783	127	25	65
2.	Assam	63	609	201	127	321	494	164	21
3.	Bihar	23	925	46	6	310	680	9	1
4.	Chhattisgarh	48	763	164	25	688	230	68	14
5.	Gujarat	470	386	88	56	859	91	2	48
6.	Haryana	445	446	94	15	752	229	11	8
7.	HP	758	56	25	161	819	53	4	124
8.	J&K	493	157	12	338	859	48	0	93
9.	Jharkhand	19	473	458	50	435	331	185	49
10.	Karnataka	563	307	104	26	815	117	20	48
11.	Kerala	107	62	766	65	347	49	591	13
12.	MP	116	625	237	22	648	278	48	26
13.	Maharashtra	415	259	213	113	879	55	27	39
14.	Orissa	64	718	183	35	492	278	221	9
15.	Punjab	302	687	4	7	682	239	0	79
16.	Rajasthan	236	493	133	138	828	99	23	50
17.	TN	815	100	48	37	691	58	13	238
18.	Uttaranchal	614	269	1	116	894	41	0	65
19.	UP	39	883	75	3	407	585	6	2
20.	WB	67	854	65	14	575	398	12	15
	India	248	564	139	49	676	224	44	56

Source: NSSO, Report No. 507, January-June 2004, pp. 38-39.

*Others included bottle water, tanker tank, pond, river, cannal, etc.

TABLE 5B

Distribution of HHs by Availability of Toilet within the House: 2001

Sl. No.	States	*Availability of Toilet* Total	Rural	Urban	*Not Availability of Toilet* Total	Rural	Urban
1.	AP	32.99	18.15	78.07	67.01	81.85	21.93
2.	Assam	64.64	59.57	94.6	35.36	40.43	5.4
3.	Bihar	19.19	13.91	69.69	80.81	86.09	30.31
4.	Chhattisgarh	14.20	5.18	52.59	85.8	94.82	47.41
5.	Gujarat	44.60	21.65	80.55	55.4	78.35	19.45
6.	Haryana	44.50	28.66	80.66	55.5	71.34	19.34
7.	HP	33.43	27.72	77.22	66.57	72.28	22.78
8.	J&K	53.14	41.8	86.87	46.86	58.2	13.13
9.	Jharkhand	19.67	6.57	66.68	80.33	93.43	33.32
10.	Karnataka	37.50	17.4	75.23	62.5	82.6	24.77
11.	Kerala	84.01	81.33	92.02	15.99	18.67	7.98
12.	MP	23.99	8.94	67.74	76.01	91.06	32.26
13.	Maharashtra	35.09	18.21	58.08	64.91	81.79	41.92
14.	Orissa	14.89	7.71	59.69	85.11	92.29	40.31
15.	Punjab	56.84	40.91	86.52	43.16	59.09	13.48
16.	Rajasthan	29.00	14.61	76.11	71	85.39	23.89
17.	TN	35.16	14.36	64.33	64.84	85.64	35.67
18.	Uttaranchal	45.20	31.6	86.88	54.8	68.4	13.12
19.	UP	31.43	19.23	80.01	68.57	80.77	19.99
20.	WB	43.71	26.93	84.85	56.29	73.07	15.15
	India	36.4	21.92	73.72	63.6	78.08	26.28

Source: Census of India, *Housing Atlas of India–2001*, Office of Registrar-General, Government of India, New Delhi.

TABLE 6

Per 1000 Distribution of Treated Spell of Ailment during 15 days by Source of Treatment for each MPCE Class

Rural			*Urban*		
MPCE Class (Rs.)	*Per 1000 No. of ailment treated*		*MPCE Class (Rs.)*	*Per 1000 No. of ailment treated*	
	Govt.	*Pvt.*		*Govt.*	*Pvt.*
> than 225	296	704	less than 300	260	740
225-255	262	738	300-350	214	786
255-300	257	743	350-425	255	745
300-340	262	738	425-500	253	747
340-380	214	786	500-575	230	770
380-420	220	780	575-665	261	739
420-470	222	778	665-775	171	829
470-525	202	798	775-915	215	785
525-615	227	773	915-1120	190	810
615-775	214	786	1120-1500	156	844
775-950	230	770	1500-1925	171	829
950 or more	179	821	1925 or more	109	891
All	224	776	All	192	808

Source: NSSO, Report No. 507, January-June 2004, p. 21.

TABLE 7

Inter-State Variation of Proportion (per 1000) of Persons Hospitalised in Rural and Urban Areas

Sl. No.	States	No. per 1000 hospitalised	
		Rural	Urban
1.	AP	22	28
2.	Assam	11	16
3.	Bihar	10	10
4.	Chhattisgarh	12	27
5.	Gujarat	29	36
6.	Haryana	32	31
7.	HP	32	31
8.	J&K	18	20
9.	Jharkhand	9	22
10.	Karnataka	23	26
11.	Kerala	101	90
12.	MP	18	29
13.	Maharashtra	30	36
14.	Orissa	23	30
15.	Punjab	30	30
16.	Rajasthan	18	25
17.	TN	37	37
18.	Uttaranchal	17	19
19.	UP	13	20
20.	WB	23	35
	India	23	31

TABLE 8

Share (per 1000) of the Age to Total Population from NSSO and Census

Source	*Rural*			*Urban*		
	Male	*Female*	*Person*	*Male*	*Female*	*Person*
Census 1981	68	68	68	51	58	54
NSS 43rd Round (1987-88)	65	66	65	54	61	57
Census 1991	78	74	76	62	66	63
NSS 50th Round (1993-94)	68	69	69	55	64	60
NSS 52nd Round (1995-96)	55	59	57	47	53	50
Census 2001	74	81	77	62	72	67
NSS 60th Round (Jan.-June, 2004)	70	71	70	62	71	66

Source: NSSO 60th Round, Report No. 507, January-June 2004, p. 54.

TABLE 9

Number of Aged Per 1000 for each Sex in Major States

Major State	*Rural*				*Urban*			
	No. of aged per 1000 persons			*Old age depend-ency ratio*	*No. of aged per 1000 persons*			*Old age depend-ency ratio*
	Male	*Female*	*Person*		*Male*	*Female*	*Person*	
Andhra Pradesh	73	77	75	110	53	64	58	83
Assam	53	43	48	76	54	50	52	76
Bihar	59	52	55	99	62	55	59	91
Gujarat	67	68	68	128	54	69	61	86
Haryana	72	84	78	103	51	77	63	92
Himachal Pradesh	92	95	94	119	50	52	51	79
Karnataka	71	66	69	100	58	61	59	84
Kerala	106	123	115	155	103	109	106	139
Madhya Pradesh	63	38	65	107	54	64	59	88
Maharashtra	83	88	86	129	65	76	70	96
Orissa	90	80	85	128	73	61	68	92
Punjab	85	88	86	128	62	67	64	92
Rajasthan	59	67	63	105	56	61	58	86
Tamil Nadu	87	85	86	122	73	85	79	108
Uttar Pradesh	64	67	66	116	51	60	56	88
West Bengal	62	64	63	95	90	95	92	122
India	70	71	70	111	62	71	66	94

Source: NSSO 60th Round, Report No. 507, January-June 2004, p. 61.

TABLE 10

Old-age Dependency Ratio (Per 1000) Population

Source	*Rural*	*Urban*	*Rural + Urban*
Census 1981	94	91	89
NSS 43rd Round (1987-88)	111	88	103
Census 1991	123	96	118
NSS 50th Round (1993-94)	108	90	104
NSS 52nd Round (1995-96)	92	74	87
Census 2001	141	107	131
NSS 60th Round (Jan.-June, 2004)	125	103	119

Source: NSSO 60th Round, Report No. 507, January-June 2004, p. 54.

TABLE 11

Trends of CBR, CDR and IMR in India

	CBR per 1000 population			*CDR per 1000 population*			*IMR per 1000 live birth*		
Years	*Rural*	*Urban*	*Combined*	*Rural*	*Urban*	*Combined*	*Rural*	*Urban*	*Combined*
1971	38.9	30.1	36.9	16.4	9.7	14.9	138	82	129
1976	35.8	28.4	34.9	16.3	9.5	15.0	139	80	129
1981	35.6	27.0	33.9	13.7	7.8	12.5	119	62	110
1986	34.2	27.1	32.6	12.2	7.6	11.1	105	62	96
1991	30.9	24.3	29.5	10.6	7.1	9.8	87	53	80
1996	29.3	21.6	27.5	9.7	6.5	9.0	77	46	72
2001	27.1	20.3	25.4	9.1	6.3	8.4	72	42	66
2002	26.6	19.9	25.0	8.7	6.1	8.1	69	40	64
2004	25.9	19	24.1	8.2	5.8	7.5	64	40	58

Source: SRS Bulletin, Various years.

TABLE 12

Inter-State Disparities in CBR, CDR, IMR and Life Expectancy

States	*CBR in 2004 Combined*	*CDR in 2004 Combined*	*IMR in 2004 Combined*	*Life Expectancy at Birth 1998-2002, Combined*
A.P.	19	7	59	63.5
Assam	25.1	8.8	66	57.9
Bihar	30.2	8.1	61	60.8
Gujarat	24.3	6.9	53	63.4
Haryana	25.1	6.6	61	65.2
H.P.	19.2	6.8	51	65.1
Karnataka	20.9	6.9	49	64.5
Kerala	15.2	6.1	12	73.5
M.P.	29.8	9.2	79	56.9
Maharashtra	19.1	6.2	36	66.2
Orissa	22.7	9.6	77	58.5
Punjab	18.7	6.4	45	68.5
Rajasthan	29	7	67	61.1
T.N.	17.1	7.5	41	65.2
U.P.	30.8	8.8	72	59.1
W.B.	19.3	6.3	40	63.9
All India	24.1	7.5	58	62.5

Source: SRS Bulletin, Various years

TABLE 13

Public and Private Expenditure on Health in Indian States, 2001-02

States	*Per Capita Expenditure in Rs.*			*Pub. Exp. as a % of Total. Exp.*	*Private Exp. as a % of Total Exp.*
	Public	*Private*	*Total*		
A.P.	182	857	1039	17.5	82.5
Assam	176	393	569	30.9	69.1
Bihar	92	687	779	11.8	88.2
Gujarat	147	670	816	18.0	82.0
Haryana	163	1408	1570	10.4	89.6
H.P.	493	812	1305	37.8	62.2
Karnataka	206	506	712	28.9	71.1
Kerala	240	1618	1858	12.9	87.1
M.P.	132	733	864	15.3	84.7
Maharashta	196	815	1011	19.4	80.6
Orissa	134	449	582	23.0	77.0
Punjab	258	1273	1530	16.9	83.1
Rajasthan	182	415	597	30.5	69.5
Tamil Nadu	202	644	846	23.9	76.1
U.P.	84	1040	1124	7.5	92.5
W.B.	181	593	775	23.4	76.6
All India	207	790	997	20.8	79.2

Source; National Health Account India, 2001-02, MOH&FW, GOI (2005).

6

Growth Competitiveness Index and Regional Inequality

MD. TARIQUE

I. INTRODUCTION

At the turn of the new century, Indian economy was 10 years into economic reforms during which the traditional "command and control" management of the economy and the "commanding heights" of the public sector were slowly and steadily replaced by market-oriented and business friendly economic structures and policies. In the process Indian economy became progressively synchronised with the global market. To its credit India successfully stood the contagion effects of South Asian meltdown of the late 1990s and also the currency crisis that hit many nations later. However, the global economic slowdown reached the Indian shores in 2001.

India has states like Maharashtra, Gujarat and Karnataka, which have grown as fast as Asia's tiger economies during the past 10 years. It also has Bihar, with a population size of Germany's and a living standard at par with Burundi's. The divisions among the states are widening because in the 1990s the guiding principle for resource sharing has shifted from entitlement to competition. Competition among the states is likely to increase regional disparities in future. In 1991, Bihar's per capita income was 4 times lower than Goa's. By 2002, the difference had grown more than 8 times. This however does not imply that inter-state disparities in performance are wholly a post-economic reform phenomenon.

Why do liberalisation and competition increase inequality? Because competition gives participants a chance to perform to their potential, even as it allows non-performers to drift. Private investment has shied away from the poorly governed states and has flowed almost entirely to better-managed richer states. Not all mechanisms of transferring funds from the rich (often also the better performing) to the poor (often also the non-performing) have been given up.

The Planning Commission and the Finance Commission still redistribute resources from the rich to the poor even now. Such redistribution has, however, shrunk a bit and private investment is free to go where it wants to.

While inequalities magnified, inter-state competition seemed to have been intensified in the nineties. Andhra Pradesh and Karnataka had been successfully hot selling themselves as alternatives and even better investment destinations than the established investment centres such as Gujarat, Maharashtra, and Tamil Nadu. To a lesser extent, Rajasthan, Madhya Pradesh, Himachal Pradesh and lately Chhattisgarh have been competing for increased shares in the investment pie with varying degree of success.

Following economic reforms the states are now empowered with increased autonomy in many key areas such as infrastructure. Slowly but surely there is increasing realisation among the states that they can shape their own destiny. This prompted the governments at the sub-national level to initiate measures to attract more financial resources into the states including foreign direct investments (FDIs). During the nineties some of the states emerged as the most happening places in India. Thus competition is a double-edged weapon. It can increase or decrease the inequalities in economic growth. Not all poor states are necessarily non-performers and competition allows the laggards the chance to catch up with the rich and thus bridge the inequality gap.

Several recent studies underlined the key role by the states in shaping the environment in which enterprises from both public and private sectors operate, despite globalisation and liberalisation. A significant part of the competitive advantage of states is believed to arise from far reaching incentive polices which are designed to attract foreign investment like tax breaks, subsidies, etc.

Competitiveness: The Concept

The word competitiveness ordinarily means 'ability to compete'. In economic terms it could be expressed at different levels such as the nation, industry and the company. In conventional economic theory a nations' growth prospects are governed by the principle of comparative advantage, derived from the factor endowments. The notion of national competitive advantage differs from the conventional comparative advantage in that, where as the latter is nature dictated and therefore unalterable, the former is policy driven, flexible and hence accommodates choices.

Competitiveness is one of the most powerful concepts in modern economic thinking and encompasses the economic consequences of non-economic aspects such as education, science, political stability or even culture and value systems. In a market economy, individual firms and industries play the critical role in building and sustaining national competitiveness. A nation's competitiveness depends on the capacity of its organisations to innovate and upgrade. At micro-levels, competitiveness is defined as the capacity to grow through market success or share, and improved profits based on its perceived superiority over the competitors, which depend on the macroeconomic environment in which firms operate and compete with each other.

World Economic Forum (WEF), which has been ranking the leading world nations on a number of competitiveness criteria, defines *Growth Competitiveness Index* (GCI) as "the ability of a country to achieve sustained high rates of growth in GDP per capita" (GCR, 2003). The *Business Confidence Index* (BCI), on the other hand, evaluates the underlying micro-economic conditions that define the current sustainable level of productivity in each country. The two specific areas evaluated by the BCI are "the sophistication of what the GCR called the operating practices and strategies of companies and the quality of the micro-economic business environment in which nations companies compete". In their World Competitiveness Yearbook, the Institute for Management Development (IMD) defines competitiveness as "the ability of a nation to create and maintain an environment that sustains more value creation for its enterprises and more prosperity for its people".

IMD's methodology is known for its simplicity and the direct approach while dealing with a large number (over 300) of diverse indicators. The fundamental principle, which underlies the distinction between notions of national competitiveness and enterprise competitiveness, focuses on where the creation of economic value takes place. A nation's environment hinders or supports the wealth creation process through its policies. The report *Competitiveness of Indian States, 2004* (CIS, 2004) extends this principle to the states in India. The competitiveness of economies and the competitiveness of firms are interdependent concepts. The CIS 2004 focuses on the first. It measures and compares how states are doing in providing an environment that sustains the domestic and global competitiveness of the firms operating within their borders.

State Competitiveness Studies

Experimental studies on competitiveness of Indian states have been pioneered by National Productivity Council (NPC) as early as in 1992 when fifteen major Indian states were ranked by it based on their performance in Human Development (HDI) (Productivity, 1992a). The four variables considered while ranking the states were life expectancy, literacy rate, per capita state domestic product (SDP) and population below poverty line. The study ranked Punjab at the top in terms of HDI followed by Kerala and Haryana. NPC followed this study with yet another study on the competitiveness of Indian States based on Infrastructure Development Index (IDI) (Productivity, 1992b). In this study also NPC considered the same list of fifteen major states for ranking purposes. Six variables related to infrastructure were taken in to account viz. road length, navigable waterways, railway route length, tele-density, electricity consumption and number of commercial bank branches. Based on IDI, Punjab was ranked at number one followed by Gujarat and Haryana. Bihar ranked last in both the studies.

In their recent study on the state competitiveness by the *India Today*, 2004 (August 16), 35 Indian States and Union Territories have been considered in three different categories such as Big States (20), Small States (10) and Union Territories (5). The bigger states are identified as the ones having more than 35000 sq.kms and with a population of over five million. Among the bigger states Punjab was ranked first, while Kerala got second rank and Himachal Pradesh got third rank while Bihar was ranked the last. Among the smaller states category Pondicherry was ranked first followed by Delhi while Meghalaya got the last rank. Among the Union Territories, Chandigarh was ranked first and Dadar and Nagar Haveli got the last rank. One major finding of the study is that the smaller states are relatively more competitive as compared to their bigger counter parts. This study considered 49 measures across eight broad macro-economic performance parameters. Principal Components Analysis was used to generate weights for each of the measure.

It is in this backdrop that the present study focuses on the impact of interaction by the five factors like Economic strength, Business efficiency, Governance quality, Human resource and infrastructure on the state's local environment. The entire study is divided into four sections. The first section is related to the introduction which defines the relation of competition with inequality and the concept of competitiveness index. The second part is related to methodology which assumes that healthy performance in these dimensions creates the environment that sustains the state's competitiveness. The third part is associated with the data analysis and mainly deals with the factor Economic Strength at the different standard under this criterion for detailed study to know the comparative strength of different states and thus the prevalence of level of regional inequality among these states. The states on the basis of population have been divided into two categories, viz. Bigger states and Smaller states. The last and the fourth part of the study gives the concluding observations giving some special references to Bihar.

II. METHODOLOGY

Innumerably a large number of micro and macro level aspects govern the competitiveness dynamics of anyone economy. It was found almost impossible to track all of them in a single study especially because of the non-availability of reliable indicators in the case of a developing country like India with inadequate data infrastructure, more so at the disaggregated levels of the states. A study by the NPC identified about 95 socio-economic and technological criteria through extensive research of economic literature and feedback from the business community, government agencies and academia. The 95 criteria were grouped under the following *five competitiveness factors*:

1.	Economic Strength	11 Criteria	Macro-economic evaluation of the state economy: Economy, Investment and Prices
2.	Business Efficiency	12 Criteria	Extent to which enterprises are performing in an innovative, profitable and responsible manner: Productivity, Labour costs, management practices and entrepreneurial resources
3.	Governance Quality	18 Criteria	Extent to which government policies are conducive to competitiveness: Fiscal Policy and health, transparency and outlook of the government towards business
4.	Human Resources	32 Criteria	Extent to which human resources meet the needs of business: Quality of manpower, employment scenario and work culture
5.	Infrastructure	22 Criteria	Extent to which basic infrastructure meets the needs of business: Basic infrastructure—Physical and Social

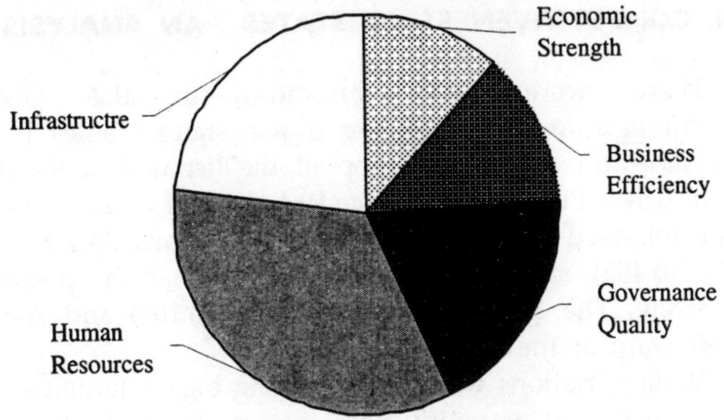

Standard Value

As the criteria are scaled differently, a comparable standard scale is used to compute the overall factor results. The relative performance of each state in the final rankings is measured through the Standard Deviation Method (SDM). First, for each criterion, we compute the average value for all the states. Then the standard deviation is calculated using the following formula:

$$S=\sqrt{\frac{\sum(x-\bar{x})}{N}}$$

Finally, we compute each of the 29 states *Standard Values* (STD) for the 95 ranked criteria by subtracting the average value of each criterion from the state's original value and then dividing the result by the standard deviation.

$$\textit{Standard Value} = \frac{(x-\bar{x})}{S}$$

where:

x = original value
$\bar{x}$ = average value of all the states
N = number of states
S = Standard Deviation

III. COMPETITIVENESS OF STATES : AN ANALYSIS

There were wide variations in the *Overall Competitiveness* among the bigger Indian states (Tables 1 and 2). Maharashtra came to the top of the list with a *Standard Value* of 0.543. Punjab with a *Standard Value* of 0.524 came the second followed by Gujarat (0.511). Karnataka (0.478) and Kerala (0.452) came to the fourth and fifth positions respectively. The *Standard Values* of UP (-0.106) and Assam (–0.238) were at the bottom.

Wide variations were noted among bigger Indian states in the case of Competitiveness Factor *Economic Strength*. Maharashtra on the top of the list recorded a *Standard Value* as high as 0.750. The next in the list, Tamil Nadu, achieved a *Standard Value* significantly lower, 0.197, closely followed by Karnataka (0.189). Assam (–0.623) and Orissa (–0.674) were at the bottom of the list.

As in the case of bigger states significant inter-state variations were observed among the smaller states in regard to *Overall Competitiveness* (Tables 3 and 4). Goa with a *Standard Value* of 0.776 came to the top followed very closely by Delhi (0.775). Himachal Pradesh (0.291) and Mizoram (0.172) at the third and fourth places respectively achieved significantly lower *Standard Values*. Nagaland at the bottom of the list recorded a *Standard Value* of –0.332.

Vast variations were seen among the smaller states in the case of *Economic Strength*. First in the list, Delhi with a *Standard Value* of 2.028 was far ahead of Goa (0.888) in the second and Uttaranchal (0.606) in the third. At the bottom of the list was Jharkhand with a *Standard Value* –0.504 followed by Arunachal Pradesh (–0.744).

If we look at the criterion-wise ranking of states to show the Economic Strengths of different states (Table 5), we find that among the bigger states Punjab is at the top to be followed by Maharashtra and Haryana. At the lowest ebb are MP (11), UP (13), Orissa (14) and Bihar (15). However, there is a silver lining for Bihar in terms of SDP growth and Per Capita SDP growth and it ranks 1 and 2 respectively on these two criteria. In terms of consumer prices and per capita consumption expenditure which is a direct reflection of cost

TABLE 1

Overall Competitiveness Ranking of Indian States

Bigger States	*STD Values*	*Rank*
Maharashtra	0.543	1
Punjab	0.524	2
Gujarat	0.511	3
Karnataka	0.478	4
Kerala	0.452	5
Tamil Nadu	0.440	6
AP	0.233	7
Haryana	0.090	8
WB	-0.023	9
MP	-0.066	10
Orissa	-0.091	11
Rajasthan	-0.091	12
Bihar	-0.100	13
UP	-0.106	14
Assam	-0.238	15

TABLE 2

Factor Competitiveness Ranking of Indian States—Economic Strength

Bigger States	*STD Values*	*Rank*
Maharashtra	0.750	1
Tamil Nadu	0.197	2
Karnataka	0.189	3
Gujarat	0.142	4
Punjab	0.140	5
Kerala	0.130	6
WB	0.099	7
AP	0.040	8
Haryana	-0.091	9
UP	-0.242	10
Bihar	-0.271	11
Rajasthan	-0.353	12
MP	-0.413	13
Assam	-0.623	14
Orissa	-0.674	15

TABLE 3

Overall Competitiveness Ranking of Indian States

Smaller States	*STD Values*	*Rank*
Goa	0.776	1
Delhi	0.775	2
HP	0.291	3
Mizoram	0.172	4
Uttaranchal Pradesh	0.144	5
Jharkhand	0.110	6
Arunachal	0.079	7
Sikkim	0.064	8
Chhattisgarh	-0.011	9
J&K	-0.109	10
Tripura	-0.166	11
Manipur	-0.211	12
Meghalaya	-0.220	13
Nagaland	-0.332	14
–	–	–

TABLE 4

Factor Competitiveness Ranking of Indian States—Economic Strength

Smaller States	*STD Values*	*Rank*
Delhi	2.028	1
Goa	0.888	2
Uttaranchal	0.606	3
Tripura	0.091	4
HP	-0.048	5
J&K	-0.057	6
Chhattisgarh	-0.124	7
Mizoram	-0.133	8
Sikkim	-0.199	9
Manipur	-0.271	10
Nagaland	-0.377	11
Meghalaya	-0.416	12
Jharkhand	-0.504	13
Arunachal Pradesh	-0.744	14
–	–	–

TABLE 5

Criterion-wise Ranking of States—Economic Strength Bigger States

States	Per capita SDP	SDP Growth	Per capita SDP Growth	Share of Service	Consumer Price (Capital Cities)	Per capita Consumption Expenditure
AP	8	8	5	6	12	10
Assam	12	13	12	10	NA	13
Bihar	15	1	2	4	3	14
Gujarat	4	14	14	9	2	6
Haryana	3	4	4	14	14	3
Karnataka	7	3	1	7	11	7
Kerala	6	5	6	1	10	1
MP	11	12	13	11	5	12
Maharashtra	2	11	10	2	9	4
Orissa	14	15	15	13	7	15
Punjab	1	6	8	15	1	2
Rajasthan	10	10	11	12	8	8
Tamil Nadu	5	7	7	3	13	5
UP	13	9	9	8	6	11
WB	9	2	3	5	4	9

TABLE 5 (CONTD.)

States	Total Investment	FDI Inflow	Commercial Banks Deposit	Credit Disburse-ment by Commercial Banks	Commercial Bank Offices
AP	3	5	9	7	11
Assam	14	15	15	14	12
Bihar	15	14	13	15	7
Gujarat	2	4	4	6	10
Haryana	11	10	7	8	5
Karnataka	7	3	6	4	8
Kerala	13	13	3	5	1
MP	9	6	11	10	15
Maharashtra	1	1	1	1	9
Orissa	12	8	14	12	13
Punjab	6	12	2	3	2
Rajasthan	10	11	12	11	14
Tamil Nadu	5	2	5	2	4
UP	4	9	10	13	6
WB	8	7	8	9	3

TABLE 6

Smaller States

States	*Per capita SDP*	*SDP Growth*	*Per capita SDP Growth*	*Share of Service*	*Consumer Price (Capital Cities)*	*Per capita Consumption Expenditure*
Arunachal	6	14	13	11	NA	7
Chhattisgarh	13	10	12	12	NA	NA
Delhi	2	4	7	1	2	1
Goa	1	3	3	5	NA	2
HP	3	5	6	10	3	6
J&K	11	6	9	8	1	5
Jharkhand	14	9	10	13	NA	NA
Manipur	12	8	4	9	NA	9
Meghalaya	10	11	8	4	4	8
Mizoram	4	12	11	2	NA	4
Nagaland	7	13	14	3	NA	3
Sikkim	5	7	5	7	NA	11
Tripura	9	2	1	6	NA	10
Uttaranchal	8	1	2	NA	NA	NA

TABLE 6 (CONTD.)

States	*Total Investment*	*FDI Inflow*	*Commercial Banks Deposit*	*Credit Disbursement by Banks*	*Commercial Bank Offices*
Arunachal	11	NA	8	12	11
Chhattisgarh	1	NA	10	6	NA
Delhi	5	1	1	1	1
Goa	4	3	2	2	2
HP	3	2	3	5	4
J&K	8	5	5	3	10
Jharkhand	2	NA	6	7	NA
Manipur	13	7	13	13	8
Meghalaya	9	4	7	10	5
Mizoram	NA	NA	12	11	9
Nagaland	10	6	11	14	7
Sikkim	12	NA	4	8	6
Tripura	7	8	9	9	3
Uttaranchal	6	NA	NA	4	NA

TABLE 6 (CONTD.)

States	Growth in Employment (Mfg.)	Number of New Industries/ Enterprises	Profits (Mfg.)	Number of Small Scale Industries	Problem-Solving Attitude of Managers	Competent Senior Managers
Arunnachal	NA	NA	NA	5	NA	NA
Chhattisgarh	5	NA	4	NA	5	5
Delhi	6	1	2	1	1	1
Goa	3	5	3	4	2	2
HP	7	2	5	2	4	3
J&K	4	NA	8	6	NA	NA
Jharkhand	8	NA	1	NA	3	4
Manipur	11	3	10	7	NA	NA
Meghalaya	10	6	9	8	NA	NA
Mizoram	NA	8	NA	3	NA	NA
Nagaland	9	7	11	9	NA	NA
Sikkim	NA	9	NA	11	NA	NA
Tripura	1	4	6	10	NA	NA
Uttaranchal	2	NA	7	NA	NA	NA

IV. CONCLUDING OBSERVATIONS

The above analysis shows that there exists a wide regional disparity among different states and it is obvious from the standard values of overall competitiveness index of different states. In terms of various criteria showing economic strength of the economy, among bigger states Orissa, Assam and Bihar is at the lowest level whereas the position of Maharashtra, Gujarat, AP, Karnataka and Tamil Nadu is very promising. Among smaller states the position of Delhi and Goa is very good whereas the hilly states like Nagaland, Tripura and Arunanchal Pradesh are worst effected states.

Though Bihar is at the lowest level in terms of most of the criteria except SDP growth, per capita SDP growth and problem solving attitude of the managers (showing hidden entrepreneurial ability of the people in the state) where it ranks at the top, everything has not gone away for the poor, deprived and neglected state. If we look at the strengths and weaknesses (Table 7) of the state in terms of broad parameters like economic strength, business efficiency, governance quality, human resource and infrastructure, there seems to be a silver lining in the tunnel. What actually we need to do is to reap the benefits of the approaching opportunities by utilising our strengths and improving at the level of weaknesses.

TABLE 7

Strengths and Weaknesses: Bihar

Factors	*Strong Criteria*	*Weak Criteria*
Economic Strength	SDP Growth Consumer Prices	Per Capita SDP Total Investment FDI Inflow Commercial Bank Credit Disbursement
Business Efficiency	Average Hours Worked Problem-solving Attitude of Managers	Registered Factories Employment Growth (Mfg.) Profits of Manufacturing Industries
Governance Quality	Government Expenditure Government's Procedures Transparency Government's Finances in Next Two Years	Revenue Receipts Per Capita Plan Expenditure Transport and Communication Spending
Human Resource	Public Education Expenditure Labour Relations IT Literates	Birth Rate Health Expenditure Pupil-Teacher Ratio (Primary Schools) Female Literacy
Infrastructure	Rail Route kms Electricity Connected Villages Population Covered by Primary Expenditure Health Centres	Degree Colleges (Nos.) Technical Institutes (Nos.) Infrastructure

References

Business Today (1995), Competitive Advantage of Indian States, June 7-21.

—— (1997), *Best States to Invest in,* Dec. 22, 1997-Jan. 6, 1998.

—— (B 1999), *Best States to Invest in,* Dec. 22, 1999-Jan. 6, 2000.

Confederation of Indian Industries and Rajiv Gandhi Institute for Contemporary Studies (2000), *Performance of the Indian States.*

Global Competitiveness Report (2004), World Economic Forum (WEF), Geneva, Switzerland.

Goldman Sachs (2003), *Dreaming with BRICs: The Path to 2050,* by Dominic Wilson and Roopa Purushotaman, Global Economics Paper No. 99.

India Today (2003), Small is Beautiful – India's Best and Worst States: The State of the States, May 19.

—— (2004), North South Lead—India's Best and Worst States: The State of the States, August 16.

Kearney, A.T. (2004), *FDI Confidence Index,* Global Management Consulting Firm, Chicago, US.

National Productivity Council (1992a), Human Development in Indian States, *Productivity,* Vol. 33, No. 2, July-September.

—— (1992b), Infrastructure Development in Indian States, *Productivity,* Vol. 33, No. 3, October-December.

National Productivity Council (1994), Competitiveness Ranking of Indian States, *Productivity,* Vol. 35, No. 2, July-September.

National Council of Applied Economic Research (2000), Policy Competitiveness of Indian States in Attracting Direct Investment.

World Competitiveness Yearbook (2004), Institute for Management Development (IMD), Lausanne, Switzerland.

7

Regional Development and Disparity in Levels of Living in India

H.C.L. Das

India is a vast country having different regions with different natural resources and socio-economic structure. Its political and economic map has been characterised by disparities and divergencies among the potential of the performance of the various states. The states in India are differing from one another not only in being bigger or smaller in area or population, but also in terms of social and economic development in such areas like levels of living, progress of agriculture, industrialisation, development of transport and commercialisation, public health services, spread of literacy, human development, quality of life and work, etc. Hence, it is necessary to measure the degree of development of different sectors in different regions and find out the different factors which have accelerated or retarded the growth of different sectors in different regions.

In economic literature, the problem of regionalism has developed from the theory of location of industries which took its birth in Germany where the works of Von Thunen and Weber were among the most important contributions.

In India the convention of dividing the country into some sorts of regions seems to have started with the preparation of the Census reports. After the Independence, the first major attempt at regionalisation of the country was made at the time of 1951 Census (Paper No. 2 of 1952). Daniel Thorner, M.S. Randhawa, O.H.K. Spate, Ashok Mitra, P.S. Sengupta, P.S. Sharma, Abel and Easter, M.N. Pal, and Hemlata Rao, made significant contributions towards the development of economic/agricultural regionalisation of the Indian economy. In almost all the studies mentioned above, the terms 'region' and 'state' have been used interchangeably.

In the present study and attempt has been made to identify the degree of inter-state disparity in respect of levels of living mainly in the context of quality of life and work in India.

LEVELS OF LIVING

'Level of Living' is the American version of 'Standard of Living'. Standard of living with reference to a person, family or a body of people means the extent to which they can satisfy their wants. Thus, if they can afford only the minimum of food, clothing and shelter, their standard of living is very low. If, on the other hand, they are able to enjoy a great variety of food, a good supply of clothing and live in well furnished house, and in addition, are able to satisfy wide variety of other wants, then clearly such people are said to be enjoying high standard of living.

The standard of living of people depends, in the first place, on the size of national income, and secondly on the manners of distribution of the national income. People in a developing regions of the World are poor, because the national income as an average per head is low; wide differences in the standard of living of people in the same countries are the result of unequal distribution of the national income. The higher standard of living of the people in the advanced economies is due to these countries having large stocks of up-to-date capital and well-trained labour, and the willingness of the people themselves to work for a higher standard of living. Today there is also less inequality of income in the economically more advanced countries than that in many of the underdeveloped parts of the world. A great deal is being done to raise the standard of living in the economically less developed countries, since the accumulation of capital proceeds more rapidly the more a country has of it, and this, therefore, otherwise tends to widen the gap between the developed and the underdeveloped nations.

The problem of measuring the level or standard of living has been engaging the attention of research institutions, universities, governments and the specialised agencies of the United Nations for a fairly long time. The U.N. Committee of Experts under the Chairmanship of Professor V.K.R.V. Rao released in 1954 its pioneering report on the 'International Definition and Measurement of Standards and levels of Living' which discussed the fundamental problems of methodology facing researchers in this field. Since then the U.N. agencies have tried 20 to operationalise the concepts and suggested certain standard procedures.

METHODOLOGY

The present paper is based purely on secondary data available from the Government and non-government publications. First, Ginni's coefficient of concentration in respect of net state domestic product has been calculated on the basis of the following formula:

$$1.\ \frac{1}{100}\ \text{G.C.C.} = [(X_1 \times X_2 - X_2 \times Y_1) + (X_2 \times Y_3 - X_3 \times Y_2) + \ldots + (X_n \times 100 - 100 \times Y_n)]$$

where G.C.C. = Ginni's coefficient of concentration,

$X_1, X_2, \ldots X_n$ = Subsequent cumulative percentage of populaltion distributed over states in India,

$Y_1, Y_2, \ldots Y_n$ = Subsequent cumulative percentage of net state domestic product distributed over states in India.

The Ginni's coefficient of concentration has been calculated for 1991 and 2001 mainly to find out the trend in concentration of net state domestic product.

The weighted index of regional inequality in respect of different variables have been calculated on the basis of the following formula:

$$2.\ Vw = \sqrt{\frac{\Sigma(si - N) \cdot \frac{Pi}{P}}{N}}$$

where Vw = Weighted index of regional inequality in respect of a variable,

Si Per capita value of variable for the ith state,

N = Per capita value of a variable for the nation as a whole,

Pi = Population of the ith state,

P = Population of the nation.

The weighted indices of regional inequality have been calculated in respect of per capita net state domestic product for 1991 and 2001, per capita availability of k calorie (rural and urban) for 1993-94 and 1990-00, per capita availability of foodgrains (rural and urban) for 1988 and 2002, per capita consumption expenditure for 1993-94 and 1999-00, and per capita domestic consumption of electricity.

INDICATORS OF ECONOMIC DEVELOPMENT

Economic development is a process a quantitative change between two levels of development or levels of development at two points of time. Development is basically an inter-temporal comparison. It is a well-know fact that development is process and the process is multi-dimensional. When any process is conneived as multi-dimensional, it becomes difficult to adequately capture its character through any index. However, some attempts have been made to measure the level of index. However, some attempts have been made to measure the level of development, namely Per capita Income, Physical Quality of Life Index, Human Development Index, and quality of life index.

Per Capita Income

Net national income at factor cost divided by population is popularly known as per capita income of a country. Similarly, net state domestic product divided by population is known as per capita net state domestic product which is an important. Indicator for measuring and comparing the development of regional units of an economy.

Physical Quality of Life Index

Morris David persuing the variables adopted by several U.N. Committees, United Nations Research Institute for Social Development (UNRISD) and the Origanisation for Economic Co-operation and Development (OECD) had developed the Physical Quality of Life Index (PQLI) based on the three variables life expectancy at age of one year, infant mortality rate per thousand, and basic literacy. In the case of positive indicators of life expectancy and basic literacy the best is demonstrated by the maximum and the worst is demonstrated by the minimum. But in the case of negative indicator of infant mortality, the best is represented by the minimum and the worst by the maximum. By the use of the following formula, the achievement levels of positive variable, negative variable and the physical quality of life are calculated.

3. $$AL\ (+) = \frac{\text{Actual Value} - \text{Maximum Value}}{\text{Maximum Value} - \text{Minimum Value}}$$

4. $$Al\ (-) = \frac{\text{Maximum Value} - \text{Actual Value}}{\text{Maximum Value} - \text{Minimum Value}}$$

5. $$PQLI = \frac{1}{3}(LEI + IMI + BLI)$$, where AL (+)

= Achievements level for a positive indicator,

AL (–) = Achievements level for a negative indicator,
PQLI = Physical quality of life index,
LEI = Life expectancy index,
IMI = Infant mortality index, and
BLI = Basic literacy index.

In the present paper the state-wise PQLI has been calculated for 1991 and 2001.

Human Development Index (HDI)

Since 1990 an agency of the United Nations, viz., the United Nations Development Programmes (UNDP) has been publishing every year a Human Development Report (HDR). This report, besides discussing various aspects of human development, has been ranking the different countries according to the level of human development index.

In India, the Planning Commission has published in 2002 the National Human Development Report (2001) in which the human development index has been calculated for 1981, 1991, and 2001 for India as well as for the major states of the country.

Quality of Life Index

Dasgupta and Weals 1985, have computed the quality of life index (QLI) based on six parameters what they have called 'living standard' indicators or 'constituent of well-being'. These parameters are: (a) per capita income, (b) life expectancy at birth in years, (c) infant mortality rate in per thousand live births, (d) adult literacy rate in per cent of adult population, (e) index of political rights, and (f) index of civil rights. It may be noted that while political rights are citizens' rights to play a part in governance of their country, civil rights are rights of individual *vis-à-vis* the state.

In the present paper, the quality of life index has been calculated for 1991 and 2001 for the 15 major states in India based on the first four indicators.

Further, the final index of development for the 15 major states have been computed for 2001 on the basis of seven indicators namely—life expectancy at age of one year, infant mortality rate per thousand live births, percentage of literacy, per capita net state domestic product, motor vehicles per lakh of population, daily circulation of newspapers per thousand of population, and coverage of televisions (% of population).

Again, the correlation coefficients of rank differences (developed by Charles Spearman) among the ranking of final index of development, ranking of human development index and ranking of quality of life andwork index (computed by *India Today:* 2003 and 2004) have been computed. The

Student's t-distribution has been applied to test the significance of correlation coefficients.

Analysis

The state-wise distribution of net state domestic product for 1991 and 2001 has been presented in the Table 1. It is evident from the table that in 1991 Maharashtra and the highest net state domestic product (Rs. 15163 crore). On the other hand, Assam had the lowest net state domestic product (Rs. 2298 crore), followed by Haryana (Rs. 3032 crore) and Orissa (Rs. 3443 crore)

TABLE I

State-wise Distribution of Net State Domestic Product (1991 and 2001)

(Rs. Crore at current price)

State	*Net State Domestic Product*			
	1991		*2001*	
	Amount	*Rank*	*Amount*	*Rank*
Andhra Pradesh	7324	4	126321	4
Assam	2298	5	28262	15
Bihar	6349	8	42224	13
Gujarat	6547	7	89877	7
Haryana	3032	14	48381	12
Karnataka	5287	9	93386	6
Kerala	3823	12	63737	10
Madhya Pradesh	7012	6	64553	9
Maharashtra	15163	1	210193	1
Orissa	3443	13	33906	14
Punjab	4449	10	58787	11
Rajasthan	4126	11	69898	8
Tamil Nadu	7218	5	125970	5
Uttar Pradesh	14012	2	150676	2
West Bengal	9594	3	128975	3
India	450280		1704719	

Source: Of basic data: Economic Surveys (2000-01 and 2005-06).

Almost the same trend emerges for 2001. Again Maharashtra is found to have the highest net state domestic product (Rs. 210193 crore), followed by Uttar Pradesh (Rs. 190676 crore) and West Bengal (Rs. 128975 crore). Assam, on the other hand, has been found with the lowest amount of net state domestic product (Rs. 28262 crore), followed by Orissa (Rs. 33906 crore) and Bihar (Rs. 42224 crore).

The Ginni's coefficient of concentration has been found to be 74.16 in 1991 which feel down to 13.79 in 2001. This significant decline in the coefficient of concentration may be regarded as the result of the planned efforts for the balanced regional development of the country.

Table 2 presents some important weighted indices of regional inequalities in India at two points of time. The table

TABLE 2

Weighted Indices of Regional Inequalities in India

	Weighted Indices of Regional Inequalities	*Year*	
1.	Weighted index of regional inequalities in respect of per capita net state domestic product	1991	2001
		23274.89	11297.54
2.	Weighted index of regional inequalities in respect of per capita availability of k-calorie—	1993-94	1999–00
	Rural	350.61	52.77
	Urban	6.45	9.52
3.	Weighted index of regional inequalities in respect of per capita availability of foodgrains—	1988	2002
	Rural	0.5079	0.2301
	Urban	0.0224	0.0121
4.	Weighted index of regional inequalities in respect of per capita consumption expenditure	1993-94	1999–02
		4.18	13.56
5.	Weighted index of regional inequalities in respect of domestic consumption of electricity	1992-93	1999-02
		293.09	17.28

Source: 1. Government of India, Economic Surveys, (2000-01 and 2005-06).
2. Tata Services Ltd., Mumbai, Statistical Outline of India, (2001-01, 2001-02 and 2002-03).

reveals that the weighted index in respect of per capita net state domestic product in 1991 was 23274.89 which came down to 11297.54 in 2001.

The weighted index of regional inequality in respect of per capita availability of k-calorie in 1993-94 for rural area was 350.61 and for urban area it was 6.45. while the index for rural area declined to 52.77 in 1999-00, the same for urban area increased to 9.52 in 1999-00.

The weighted index of regional inequality in respect of per capita availability of food grains in 1988 was observed to be 0.5079 for rural area and it was 0.0224 for urban area. The corresponding figures declined to 0.2301 and 0.0121 respectively in 2002.

The weighted index of regional inequality in respect of per capita consumption expenditure were found to be 4.18 and 13.50 in 1993-94 and 1999-00.

The weighted index of regional inequality in respect of per capita domestic consumption of electricity declined from 293.09 in 1992-93 to 17.28 in 1999-00.

There has been a marked decline in the consumption of all the cereals over the period 1987-88 through 2001-2002 in almost all the states in both rural as well as urban areas with the reduction being particularly sharp in the case of smaller cereal items, that is, barley, maize and cereal substitutes such as tapioca. There has been a switch over in preference towards non-cereal items such as meat/fish/eggs and fruits/ vegetables. Whatever the underlying actors causing these changes, these have led to a significant decline in calorie consumption due to the switch over from calorie intative cereal items to non-cereals which are more expensive sources of calorie.

However, malnutrition occurs also in many families which are not poor, because people do not always know what food or feeding practices are best for their children or for themselves, and, because people cannot easily tell when their children are becoming malnourished, since faltering growth rates and micronutrients defficiency are not easily visible to the untrained eyes. The need to correct these informational asymmetrics suggests intervention on the part of the government. Such interventions through specific channel can help improving nutrition and reduce the spread of contagious diseases. With respect to the public distribution system, it is suggested that the system of dual prices which encourages leakages, may be replaced by a uniform price policy along with a system of food coupons for the below poverty line families.

Considering the standard calorie requirements of 2400 and 2100 respectively for rural and urban people, the estimates of available calorie are well within the prescribed limit of balanced diet, which emphasises 50 per cent of calories to be derived from carbohydrates and the remaining from the protein and fat with 25 per cent each. But all the monthly per capita consumption expenditure (MPCE) classes may not be able to get 50 per cent of calories from the consumed cereals. Fifty per cent of the required calorie means 1200 out of 2400 and 1050 out of 2100 calories. To get 1200 calories 10.44 kg cerea; per capita per 30 days or 348 gm per capita per day are required by the rural people. Similarly, 9.12 kg cereal per capita per 30 days or 304 gm per capita per day are required by the urban people to get 1050 calories in when areas be able to get the required calorie from their consumed cereals, the similar percentage for urban areas were 5 and 2.5 per cent respectively. Of course how far the remaining calories to be estimated from food items containing protein and fat by different MPCE classes is yet to be estimated. But the quantitative data for such items are not readily available from NSS reports. Pulses data although available, the quantum of pulse consumption was insignificant. Net production and availability of pulses were not increasing, but decreasing over time.

The state-wise distribution of per capita net state domestic product at current prices for 1991 and 2001 has been presented in the Table 3. It is evident from the table that in 1991 the per capita net state domestic product was the highest (Rs. 8318) in Punjab, followed by Haryana (Rs. 7508) and Maharashtra (Rs. 7439). The corresponding figure was the lowest (Rs. 2600) in Bihar, followed by Orissa (Rs. 3077) and Uttar Pradesh (Rs. 3590).

Almost the same trend reveals for 2001 in respect of the distribution of per capita net state domestic, product.

TABLE 3

State-wise Distribution of per capita Net State Domestic Product (1991 and 2001)

State	Per capita Net State Domestic Product in Rupees at Current Prices) 1991		2001	
	Amount	Rank	Amount	Rank
1. Andhra Pradesh	4531	7	16708	9
2. Assam	4261	9	10718	12
3. Bihar	2600	15	5157	15
4. Gujarat	5891	14	17938	6
5. Haryana	7508	2	23194	2
6. Karnataka	4508	8	17816	7
7. Kerala	4200	10	20107	5
8. Madhya Pradesh	4049	12	10777	11
9. Maharashtra	7439	3	21883	3
10. Orissa	3077	4	9281	13
11. Punjab	8318	1	24183	1
12. Rajasthan	4191	5	12514	10
13. Tamil Nadu	4983	5	20346	4
14. Uttar Pradesh	3590	13	9162	14
15. West Bengal	4673	6	17499	8
India	7323		16223	

Source: Government of India, *Economic Surveys* (2001-01 and 2005-06).

Again Punjab has been found having the highest amount of per capita out state domestic product (Rs. 23194), and Maharashtra (Rs. 21883). Further, the per capita net state domestic product has been observed to be the lowest (Rs. 5157), in Bihar, followed by Uttar Pradesh (Rs. 9162) and Orissa (Rs. 9281).

The state-wise distribution of physical quality of life index (PQLI) for 1991 and 2001 has been presented in the Table 4 which reveals that the value of PQLI was the highest (1) for Kerala in 1991, followed by Punjab (0.6095) and Maharashtra (0.5611). On the other hand, the lowest value of PQLI was found to be in Orissa (0.1115), followed by Uttar

TABLE 4

State-wise Distribution of Physical Quality of Life Index (1991 and 2001)

State	*1991*		*2001*	
	Index	*Rank*	*Index*	*Rank*
1. Andhra Pradesh	0.3138	9	0.3522	9
2. Assam	0.2263	13	0.2144	11
3. Bihar	0.2311	12	0.2069	12
4. Gujarat	0.4303	7	0.4341	8
5. Haryana	0.4396	6	0.4726	6
6. Karnataka	0.4161	8	0.4588	7
7. Kerala	1.0000	1	0.0000	1
8. Madhya Pradesh	0.2544	10	0.1801	13
9. Maharashtra	0.5611	3	0.6233	2
10. Orissa	0.1115	15	0.1767	14
11. Punjab	0.6095	2	0.6183	3
12. Rajasthan	0.2329	11	0.2785	10
13. Tamil Nadu	0.5000	4	0.5286	4
14. Uttar Pradesh	0.1721	14	0.1681	15
15. West Bengal	0.4680	5	0.4873	5

Sources: 1. Planning Commission (2002), National Human Development Report, (2001).
2. Tata Economic Services Ltd., Mumbai, *Statistical Outline of India* (2000-01, 2001-02, and 2002-03).

Pradesh (0.1721) and Assam (0.2263). Almost the same trend reveals for 2001. Kerala has been observed as having the highest value (1) of the PQLI, followed by Maharashtra (0.6223) and Punjab (0.6163), followed by Orissa (0.1767) and Madhya Pradesh (0.1801).

The state-wise distribution of quality of life index (QLI) has been given in the Table 5. It is very much evident from the table that the highest value of the QLI (53) was found in Punjab, followed by Kerala (51) and Maharashtra (50) in 1991. The lowest value of the QLI, on the other hand, was seen to be with Orissa (12), followed by Uttar Pradesh (13) and Rajasthan (16).

In 2001, Kerala was observed to have the highest value of QLI (56), followed by Maharashtra (54) and Tamil Nadu

TABLE 5

State-wise Distribution of Quality of Life Index in India (1991 and 2001)

State	*1991*		*2001*	
	Index	*Rank*	*Index*	*Rank*
1. Andhra Pradesh	27	9	26	9
2. Assam	19	11	18	11
3. Bihar	16	12	15	12
4. Gujarat	40	6	37	7
5. Haryana	39	7	42	5
6. Karnataka	33	8	36	8
7. Kerala	51	2	56	1
8. Madhya Pradesh	24	10	14	13
9. Maharashtra	50	13	54	2
10. Orissa	12	15	12	14
11. Punjab	53	1	43	4
12. Rajasthan	16	13	19	10
13. Tamil Nadu	46	4	48	4
14. Uttar Pradesh	13	14	11	15
15. West Bengal	41	5	39	6

Sources: 1. Government of India, (2001 and 2006), *Economic Surveys*, (2000-01 and 2005-06).

2. Tata Economic Services Ltd. Mumbai, *Statistical Outline of India* (2000-01, 2001-02, and 2002-03).

(48). In contrast, Uttar Pradesh was observed with the lowest value of QLI (11), followed by Orissa (12) and Madhya Pradesh (14).

Table 6 presents the state-wise distribution of human development index (HDI) for 1991 and 2001. In 1991. Kerala was observed to have the highest value of HDI (0.591), followed by Punjab (0.475) and Tamil Nadu (0.466). Bihar, on the other hand, has been found with the lowest value of HDI (0.308), followed by Uttar Pradesh (0.314) and Madhya Pradesh (0.328) in 1991,

In 2001, the highest value of HDI was observed with Kerala (0.638), followed by Punjab (0.537) and Tamil Nadu (0.531). Again, on the other hand, Bihar has been found to have the lowest value (0.361) of HDI, followed by Assam (0.386) and Uttar Pradesh (0.388).

TABLE 6

India Today's Index of Quality of Life and Work (2003 and 2004 Combined)

State		2003 and 2004 Combined	
		Index	*Rank*
1.	Andhra Pradesh	2.78	8
2.	Assam	1.55	12
3.	Bihar	0.65	15
4.	Gujarat	3.62	5
5.	Haryana	3.77	4
6.	Karnataka	3.06	7
7.	Kerala	4.57	2
8.	Madhya Pradesh	1.94	11
9.	Maharashtra	3.55	6
10.	Orissa	1.17	14
11.	Punjab	4.98	1
12.	Rajasthan	2.14	9
13.	Tamil Nadu	4.02	3
14.	Uttar Pradesh	1.37	13
15.	West Bengal	1.95	10

Source: Living Media Ltd., (2004, *India Today*, New Delhi, Table 6.

The quality of life and work index (QLQI) as estimated by *India Today* (2003 and 2004 combined) has been presented in the Table 7. This table clearly shows that Punjab has got the first rank with 4.98 value of QLQI, followed by Kerala (4.57) and Tamil Nadu (4.02). On the other extreme, Bihar has got the last (15th) rank with 0.65 value of QLWI, followed by Orissa (1.17) and Uttar Pradesh (1.37).

The final index of development (FDI) which may be regarded as the level of living as well, prepared on the line of Morris David Morris has been presented in the Table 7. It is apparently clear from the table that Kerala has obtained the first rank with 0.8185 value of FDI, followed by Punjab (0.8031) and Maharashtra (0.6156). Orissa, on the other hand, has been observed with the lowest value of FDI (0.2040), followed by Bihar (0.2137) and Madhya Pradesh (0.2185).

TABLE 7

State-wise Distribution of Human Development Index in India (1991 and 2001)

State	*1991*		*2001*	
	HDI	*Rank*	*HDI*	*Rank*
1. Andhra Pradesh	0.377	9	0.416	10
2. Assam	0.348	10	0.386	14
3. Bihar	0.308	15	0.367	15
4. Gujarat	0.431	6	0.479	6
5. Haryana	0.443	5	0.509	5
6. Karnataka	0.412	7	0.478	7
7. Kerala	1.591	2	0.638	1
8. Madhya Pradesh	0.328	13	0.394	12
9. Maharashtra	0.452	4	0.523	4
10. Orissa	0.345	12	0.404	11
11. Punjab	0.475	2	0.537	2
12. Rajasthan	0.307	11	0.424	9
13. Tamil Nadu	0.466	3	0.531	3
14. Uttar Pradesh	0.314	14	0.388	13
15. West Bengal	0.404	8	0.472	8
All India	0.381		0.472	

Source: Planning Commission (2002), National Human Development Report (2001), p. 25.

From the analysis of the table from 1 to 7, it is clear that Kerala, Punjab, Maharashtra, Tamil Nadu and Gujarat and Haryana have emerged as the advanced six states holding first to sixth ranks. On the other hand, Uttar Pradesh, Bihar, Madhya Pradesh, Assam, Orissa, and Rajasthan have emerged as six backward states holding 10th to 15th ranks,

The correlation coefficients of rank differences amount the three indices namely—final development index, human development index (prepared by the Planning Commission, Government of India), and quality of life and work index (prepared by India Today) have been computed. Further, Student's t-distribution has been applied to test the significance of correlation coefficients among these indices.

TABLE 8

State-wise Distribution of Final Index of Development in India (2001)

State	*Index*	*Rank*
1. Andhra Pradesh	0.3710	9
2. Assam	0.2137	14
3. Bihar	0.2287	12
4. Gujarat	0.5210	6
5. Haryana	0.5575	5
6. Karnataka	0.4119	8
7. Kerala	0.8185	1
8. Madhya Pradesh	0.21.85	13
9. Maharashtra	0.6156	3
10. Orissa	0.2040	15
11. Punjab	0.8031	2
12. Rajasthan	0.4121	10
13. Tamil Nadu	0.5671	4
14. Uttar Pradesh	0.2746	11
15. West Bengal	0.5032	7

The result of the correlation analysis has been presented in the Table 9.

The correlation coefficient between final development index and human development index has been found to be +0.936 which is significant at 0.001 level of probability. The correlation coefficient between final development index and quality of life and work index has been found to be +0914 which is significant at 0.001 level of probability. Again, the correlation coefficient between human development index and quality of life and work index has been observed to be +0.944 which has been found significant at 0.001 level of probability. Thus, all the three correlation coefficients among these indices have been found highly significant.

All the six backward states are termed as BIMARU stares Madhya Pradesh, Bihar, Assam, Rajashthan, Orissa and Uttar Pradesh. State-specific development strategy is required for the development of the BIMARU states.

The basic weakness of the steps taken so far under the various plans to tackle the problems of inter-state/region

TABLE 9

Correlation Coefficients of Rank Differences among Different Indices of Development

State	FDI Rank	HDI Rank	ITI Rank
1. Andhra Pradesh	9	10	8
2. Assam	14	14	12
3. Bihar	12	15	15
4. Gujarat	6	6	5
5. Haryana	5	5	4
6. Karnataka	8	7	7
7. Kerala	1	1	2
8. Madhya Pradesh	13	12	11
9. Maharashtra	3	4	6
10. Orissa	15	11	14
11. Punjab	2	2	1
12. Rajasthan	10	9	9
13. Tamil Nadu	4	3	3
14. Uttar Pradesh	11	13	13
15. West Bengal	7	8	10

Sources: 1. Rank Correlation Coefficient between FDI and HDI = 0.936 t = 9.5867 (Significant at 0.001 level of probability).

2. Rank Correlation Coefficient between FDI and ITI = +0.914 t = 0.3623 Significant at 0.001 level of probability).

3. Rank Correlation Coefficient between HDI and ITI = +0.944 (Significant at 0.001 level of probability).

disparities is that they have been largely in financial terms, e.g., additional finance and location of heavy investment projects in the backward regions. Central assistance should, however, be linked with specific programmes for the development of relatively backward states. Besides, the financial approach should be replaced as far as possible, by the planning approach, under which the backward regions should be clearly identified along with their capabilities and potentialities so that separate strategies may be adopted for each type of backward region/state. In view of the peculiar nature of some backward district as drought-prone, industrial development in some areas of the districts cannot spread to the rest of the districts due to the inbuilt constraints.

Naturally, incentives alone are not adequate to bring about dispersal of industrial development. In stead, agricultural development becomes significant in the growth process. There is therefore, the necessity to co-ordinate the dispersal process and the development of agriculture through a scheme of agro-based industries.

References

Thunen, Von J.N. (1966), *Isolated States*, (Translated from German into English by C.M. Wentenberg, Penguin Books Ltd, London).

Weber, Alfred. (1965), *Theories of Industries*, (Translated from French into English by C-J. Fredrich) Fifth Edition, Chicago University Press, Chicago.

Census of India (1952), *Poopulation Zones, National Regions, Sub-Regions, and Divisions*, (paper No. 2 of 1952).

Thorner, Daniel. (1957), Demarcation of Agricultural Regions in India, Indian Society of Agricultural Economics, Bombay.

Randhawa, M.S. (1969), *Farmers in India*, (quoted by C.B. Mamoria in *Agricultural Problems of India*, Kitab Mahal, Allahabad.

Spate, O.H.K. (1964), *India and Pakistan*, Oxford University Press, London.

Mitra, Ashok (1964), *Levels of Regional Development in India*, Census of India, New Delhi.

Sengupta, P. (1964), *"Planning Regions for Resource Development in India"*, Paper contributed to the 20th International Geographers' Union Congress, *New Castle*, Upon TYNE.

Sharma, P.S. (1964), "Regional Approach to Agricultural Development in India," *Indian Society of Agricultural Economics*, Vol. 19, No. 1.

Sharma, P.S. (1968), "Quantitative Delimitation of Agricultural Regions in India", *Indian Journal of Agricultural Economics*, Vol. 23 No. 1.

Abel, Martin E. and K.W. Easter (1971), "Agricultural Planning Programme Evaluation: Focus on Regional Restraints", *Economic and Political Weekly*, Special No. 30, 31 and 32, July.

Pal, M.N. (1968), *Regional Analysis of National Development: Technique and Case Study*, Doctoral Dissertation, University of Delhi, Delhi.

Rao, Hemlata. (1977), "Identification of Backward Regions and the Trends in Regional Disparities", *Arthavijnan*, Vol. 19.

Gupta, B.N. (1990), *Statistics*, Sahitya Bhawan, Agra

Williamson, J.G. (1965), "Regional Inequality and Process of National Development: A Description of Change", *Economic Development and Cultural Change*, Vol. 13.

Chaubey, P.K. (2002), Indian Economic Development, National Council of Educational Research and Training, Delhi.

Dasgupta, P. and Martin Weal (1985), Measuring the Quality of Life, Oxford University, London.

India Today, May 19, 2003, and *Indian Today*, August 16, 2004.

Golait, Ramesh and N.C. Pradhan (2006), "Changing Food Consumption Pattern in Rural India: Implications on Food and Nutrition Security *Indian Journal of Agricultural Economics*, Vol. 61, No. 3, p. 86.

Giri, A.K. (2006), "Cereal Consumption Over Time in the Country and Across the States", *Indian Journal of Agricultural Economics*, Vol. 61, No. 3, p. 397.

Ganguli, B.N. and D.B. Gupta (1976), *Levels of Leving in India*, S. Chand and Co., Delhi, p. (v).

Planning Commission (2002), *National Human Development Report (2001)*, Government of India, Delhi, p. 25.

Level of Living of Industrial Workers in India

A Study of their Family Budget Surveys and Consumer Price Index Numbers

MRITYUNJAY KUMAR, KUMAR RATNESH AND BINAY KUMAR SINGH

INTRODUCTION

The origin of family living studies dates back to seventeenth century when surveys of poverty were conducted by Frederic Le Play. Many other Sociologists or Statisticians, such as Quetelet, Engel, Wright and Mayhew, undertook similar other surveys in the second half of the nineteenth century; the most outstanding of which was the monumental enquiry on living conditions of the London Working Class conducted by Charles Booth in 1886. The techniques, however, improved greatly with the use of interviewers by Rowntree in 1901 and introduction of sampling by Bowley in 1912. The enquiries conducted by Sociologists concerning the living conditions created great interest and by the outbreak of the First World War many such studies were conducted by the Government Administration. Though originally started to study and disseminate information regarding the distressing living conditions of the poorer sections of the community, the family living studies became a method of collecting data for many other purposes especially during and after the First World War. In course of time the family living studies assumed international importance. The Third International Conference of Labour Statisticians (1926) made detailed recommendations relating to the conduct of the family living studies. The ILO and the League of Nations prepared comprehensive reports on national projects in the field of food consumption levels and nutrient requirements. A significant milestone was the report of the ILO 'Methods of Family Living Studies,' 1940. Among other things, the Second World War resulted in a radical change in the consumption habits and this necessitated the construction of new consumer price indices. Postwar conditions also focussed attention on the problems of the underdeveloped countries and it was realised that multi-subject household surveys offered the best means of collecting information on various aspects of the level of living such as nutrition, health, education, employment, etc. The whole subject of family living came up for consideration in the Seventh International Conference of Labour Statisticians in 1949. This Conference adopted a resolution defining the objectives of family living studies and setting new internatiional standards. The Committee on International Definition and Measurement of Standards and Levels of Living (1954) formed by the United Nations in joint collaboration with the ILO, UNESCO, FAO and WHO made further improvements in this field and laid great stress on the desirability of planning and conducting family living studies to obtain a direct and comprehensive measurement of actual family living conditions. The ILO also brought out a Symposium on the subject discussing types of family living studies, their methods, problems, etc. in different countries. The ILO compiled a 'Bulletin on Family Budget Surveys', 1959-60 and the UN a 'Handbook of Household Surveys.'

An attempt is made in this paper to analyse the level of living of industrial workers in India with special reference to their Family Budget Surveys and Consumer Price Index Numbers on the basic of data as obtained from the Indian

Labour Year Book, 2004, Labour Bureau, Ministry of Labour and Employment, Government of India. The paper is divided into four sections. Section I is the conceptral framework for the study. Section II deals with family budget surveys of industrial workers in India. Section III analyses the consumer price index number of industrial workers in India. Finally, Section IV presents the concluding observations of the study.

I

THE CONCEPT OF 'LEVEL OF LIVING'

The concept of the 'level of living' is implied to indicate actual conditions of life and work. In other words, 'level of living' means plan of living or content of living which would take into consideration the composite of goods and services actually consumed, which may or may not be identical with what the individual or family regards as necessary or desirable. Thus 'level of living' is an organic unit embracing both 'material' and 'non-material' aspects of existence. While 'material' aspects include income and expenditure of the population covered 'non-material' aspects express in a large measure, a state of mind as a result of patricipation in non-material aspects of life as well as the level of consumption of material goods and services. With regard to a given population, it involves questions of distribution. Moreover, the evaluation of a level of living is necessarily the function of a given set of values. From this it follows inevitably that the level of living as a whole, or the level of any of the components of elements into which it may be sub-divided, will have different meanings in the context of varying cultures. The term 'standard of living', on the other hand, relates to the aspirations or expectations of the people, that is, the living conditions which they seek to attain or regain or which they regard as be fitting and proper for themselves to enjoy. The consumption considered proper may be either that which is habitual or customary to the individual or family or that to which they aspire and for which they strive as their legitimate and reasonably attainable goal. The third concept, namely, 'norm of living' represents a combination of goods and services recommended by experts who base their judgments on certain objective criteria.

Thus, as distinct from 'standard of living' and 'norm of living' which are concerned with what ought to be the concept of 'level of living' serves as a means of evaluating the adequacy of what is the 'level'. It is thus more than a mere description of the way of living and hence is being widely used in preference to other terms.

The widely accepted concept of 'level of living' was adopted while conducting the survey by the Labour Bureau during 1958-59. As outlined in the Report of United Nation on Internatioinal Definition and Measurement of Standards and Levels of Living (1954), sub-division of level of living into components necessarily involves arbitrary classification. Several such classifications of components, or elements of living, have been proposed, some by the United Nations and the specialised agencies. The main components recommended by the Committee on International Definition and Measurement of Standards and Levels of Living are as follows :

(i) Health, including demographic conditions;
(ii) Food and nutrition;
(iii) Educatioin, including literacy and skills;
(iv) Conditions of work;
(v) Employment situation;
(vi) Aggregate consumption and saving;
(vii) Transportation;
(viii) Housing, including household facilities;
(ix) Clothing;
(x) Recreation and entertainment;
(xi) Social security; and
(xii) Human freedoms.

In conducting the family living surveys 1958-59, the Labour Bureau included all the major components of level of living along with the useful family budgets required for deriving the weighting diagram for the construction of consumer price index numbers.

Types of Family Living Studies

Experts have classified the household surveys, multi-subject surveys and continuous surveys. Family budget surveys, food consumption surveys, health surveys, labour force sample surveys, demographic surveys, education surveys, etc. are some of the specialised surveys in the course of which special data are obtained for special types of studies. Although in each case the survey covers a particular problem, some general information is also covered in order to facilitate objective analysis of the special information collected.

Multi-subject surveys generally also at a broad spectrum of data combining many aspects of the level of living. This type of surveys are generally conducted where there is immediate requirement of data on different aspects and the cost to be kept to the minimum. Multi-subject surveys also help to study the different aspects of level of living in relation to each other. While specialised surveys and multi-subject surveys are *ad-hoc* in nature, continuous surveys continue over a period of time. The intention is to secure all the desired information over a period of time which could not be collected in one single survey.

A family is defined in terms of sociological and economic cosiderations as consisting of persons :

(a) generally related by blood and marriage of adoption;
(b) usually living together and/or served from the same kitchen; and
(c) pooling the major part of their income and/or depending on a common pool of income for a major part of their expenditures.

Thus, even relatives and friends, besides wife and children, living with the family and depending on the common family pool for their expenditure were covered as members of the family. But paying-guests and domestic servants who constituted separate families within the household were excluded. Temporary absentees, such as, family members on tours or on visits to relatives or friends or in hospital were, however, included in the family. Casual guests, even though they might have stayed with the family for a long period were not considered to be family members. Where members pooled only a part of their income for messing, each member was taken to constitute a separate family.

A Working Class Family

Since the present study deals with industrial workers, a definition of working class family is very necessary. A working class family may be defind as one which derives 50 per cent or more of its income during the last calendar month through manual work in a factory, plantation or mine covered by the Factories Act, 1948, the Plantation Labour Act, 1957 or the Mines Act, 1952, as the case may be jobs involving physical labour but at the same time not also requiring much of educational (general, scientific, technical or otherwise) background were treated as 'manual'. On the other hand, a job though essentially involving physical labour but requiring a certain level of general, professional, scientific or technical education was classified as 'non-manual'.

II

FAMILY BUDGET SURVEYS OF INDUSTRIAL WORKER

In India family budget enquires date back to the beginning of the 20th century when family living enquiries were conducted in industrial centers in Bihar. Standardised statistical type of family budget enquiry was however, conducted for the first time in 1921 at Bombay by G.F. Shiras. This was followed by enquiries at Sholapur, Ahmedabad and Bihar. The recommendations of the Royal Commission of Labour in India (1931) gave an impetus to the conduct of family budget enquiries among working classes on more scientific lines mainly for the construction of consumer price indices. The Rau Court of Enquiry constituted under the Trade Disputes Act, 1929 recommended the construction of consumer price indices by the Central Government. Accordingly, family budget enquiries among working classes were conducted by the Central Government during 1944-46 for the first time on more or less uniform lines. These were followed by the rapid family budget enquiries among plantation workers in north and south India, which were conducted by the Labour Bureau, Ministry of Labour and Employment, Government of India. The enactment of the Minimum Wages Act, 1948, gave further impetus to the conduct of family budget surveys as the Act made it necessary for the Central and State Governments to maintain consumer price indices for the employees in unorganized industries. As a result of this Act, some of the State Governments and the Government of India conducted family budget enquiries among workers employed in the scheduled employments.

Most of the enquiries mentioned above were conducted to derive weighting diagram for consumer price indices, though the results of some enquiries were also used to study nutritive contents of diets or for fixation of wages on the basis of consumption requirements. Moreover, many of the surveys were not conducted on scientific lines.

The need for fresh surveys on a scientific basis and on uniform lines was being pressingly felt as the weighting pattern which formed the basis of the consumer price indices on base 1944 had become outdated and this affected the usefulness of the indices based on these weighting diagrams. A conferences of Central and State Statisticians was held in October 1953, which recommended the conduct of fresh family living surveys to obtain fresh weighting diagrams for replacing the old consumer price indices by a new series. This was followed by similar recommendations in the Second Five Year Plan. In pursuance of these recommendations, the Government of India decided to conduct fresh family living surveys among industrial workers. Fifty important industrial centers representing factory, mine and plantation industries were selected for survey in consultation with the State Governments, and Employees and Employees Organisation. The scope of these surveys were extended so as to cover not only the material aspects of the level of living such as income and expenditure but also the non-material aspects such as education, health, housing, etc. The surveys were therefore, termed as the family living surveys rather than family budget surveys where the objective almost always used to the derivation of a weighting diagram for consumer price indices. This development with regard to the enlargement of the scope of the surveys are in line with the current thinking in the international sphere in the field of household surveys. The Seventh International Conference of Labour Statisticians held in 1949 adopted a resolution defining the objectives of family living studies and setting new international standards. The Committee of Experts on International Definition and Measurement of Standards and Levels of Living jointly convened by the United Nations, the International Labour Organisation and UNESCO with the co-operation of the FAO and the WHO made further improvements in the field and laid great stress on the desirability of planning and conducting family living studies for comprehensive measurement of actual family living conditions.

Accordingly, several State Governments as well as the Labour Bureau of Government of India Conduct Family Budget Surveys in various centers with a view to compile Consumer Price Index Numbers. In order to introduce a uniform and scientific procedure for conduct of such surveys throughout the country, the Labour Bureau conducted, during 1958-59, Family Living Surveys at 50 Centres spread over length and breadth of the country. The weighting diagram derived from the results of these surveys was adopted for the compilation of Consumer Price Index Numbers for Industrial Workers on base 1960=100 for each of the 50 centers. An All-India Index was also complied as a weighted average of these centre indices.

During 1981-82, the Labour Bureau conducted fresh Working Class Family Income and Expenditure Surveys at 70 important industrial centres in order to derive a new set of weighting diagrams for compilation of Consumer Price Index Numbers for individual centers as well as an average All-India Index based on latest consumption pattern of the Working Class. In addition to the three sectors of employment (viz., Factories, Mines and Plantations) covered during the preceding survey, four more sectors viz., (i) Railways (ii) Public Motor Transport Undertakings,

(iii) Electricity generating and distributing establishment, and (iv) Ports and Docks were covered during the course of the 1981-82 survey. The Technical details of the survey were finalised by the Labour Bureau under the guidance of the Technical Advisory Committee on Statistics of Prices and Cost of Living (TAC on SPCL) constituted by the Government of India to render guidance on all such matters. In addition to 70 centres, the survey was also conducted in 6 additional centers with a view to updated the old series of Consumer Price Index Numbers of the centres on base 1982=100.

As per the recommendations of the International Labour Organisation, Family Living Surveys should be conducted at frequent intervals generally not exceeding 10 years. So as to revise the base of the Consumer Price Index Numbers. However, due to some administrative reasons, the scheme for updating the base of existing series (1982=100) could be made operational in 1997. There has been an increase of about 20 per cent in the sample size under the new series *vis-à-vis* the existing series. Similarly the number of markets and centres which are 226 and 70 in the existing series were increased to 291 and 78, respectively under the new series. The calendar year 2001 was proposed to be the base under the new series.

The main survey for collection of income and expenditure date from all the 78 selected centres and its computerized processing and tabulation has been completed. On the basis of these results, the centre specific weighting diagrams for all the 78 centres have been derived. Besides, the retails price date from all the 291 markets at all the 78 centres, is being collected, posted, analyzed and finalized on a regular basis and is being used for compilation of provisional indices on month to month basis. Simultaneously collection of house rent data for compilation of house rent indices through six monthly rounds is also being undertaken. Technical aspects relating to the updating of the existing series and currently being examined by the Technical Advisory Committee on SPCL and subsequent to its approval, the consultation process with the index user's would be initiated prior to the release of the index.

Urban Non-Manual Employees

A Family Living Survey among the middle class employees was conducted by the C.S.O at 45 centres during 1958-59. Based on the results of the survey, it has brought out a General Report and released Consumer Price Index Numbers for middle class on base 1960=100 for different centres as also an average All-India Index.

The consumption pattern of middle class having undergone a change over 1958-59 when the last survey was conducted, the Central Statistical Organisation, Govt. of India launched a fresh Middle Class Family Living Survey at 59 centres during 1982-83 with the objective of updating the base and weighting diagram of the Consumer Price Index Numbers for Middle Class on base 1960=100. It has since released the new series of Consumer Price Index Numbers for urban Non-manual employees on base 1984-85=100 w.e.f. November 1987 Index.

III

CONSUMER PRICE INDEX NUMBERS FOR INDUSTRIAL WORKERS

The Consumer Price Index Numbers for Industrial Workers which measure the rate of change in prices of fixed basket of goods and services consumed by the defined population are being compiled and maintained by the Labour Bureau since its inception in October, 1946. The Consumer Price Index Numbers are one of the most widely used statistical product which is being put to numerous uses, such as: (i) revision of wages and determination of Variable Dearness Allowance to lakhs of workers/employees in the Government and Corporate Sector, (ii) revision of minimum wages of workers in Unorganized Sector, (iii) measuring inflationary trend in the country, (iv) for policy formulation by the Government, and (v) for analytical purposes by the researchers. These index numbers are being compiled on scientific lines by following the standard methodology approved by the Technical Advisory Committee on Statistics and Prices and Cost of Living (TAC on SPCL).

The three essential ingredients of Consumer Price Index Numbers, are: (i) the percentage share of expenditure on each item in relation to the total consumption expenditure known as the "Weighting Diagram", (ii) base year price which are average prices of 12 month of the year, and (iii) current prices. The average consumption expenditure per family as revealed by the Working Class Family Income and Expenditure Survey (1981-82) forms the basis for deriving the weighting diagram of the existing series, i.e. 1982=100. The non-consumption expenditure such as taxes, interest, remittances and litigation expenses were excluded. A uniform base year was adopted for all the Central Series so the All-India Index could be obtained directly from the constituent centre indices without resorting to any arithmetical shifting of base in any series. The retail prices firstly for the base period and subsequently for the current period are collected on continuous basis in respect of all the items on a fixed day every week/month, from two selected shops of the selected markets of a centre. These prices are inclusive of taxes and levies payable by the consumer. As the Consumer Price Index Numbers are designed to measure the changes of prices alone, all other elements such as specifications, units, shops, markets and price collection day/time are kept fixed during the lifetime of the series so as to exclude spurious changes in prices. All these elements are settled in advance before launching the main survey when the organisations of price collection machinery and other details are worked out. The guiding factor for deciding these elements is their popularity with the working class families in the base year. The number of markets in a given centre depends on the sixes of the centre, the concentration of working class population, the variability in prices, etc.

Prices are collected for different items and services included in the index basket by personal interview method from the shopkeepers/vendors of the selected shops by the State Government Employees. Prices are collected on weekly basis for price sensitive items. For a few standard items such as tea, cigarette, cinema ticket, barber charges, utensils, toilet soap, clothing and footwear, etc. prices are collected on monthly basis which are not expected to fluctuate at short intervals. In case of items distributed through the Public Distribution Systems, the average price is calculated as the weighted average of the fair price and the open market price, the weights being the proportion of the quantity available through Public Distribution System and the quantity produced from the open market in relation to the base year requirement of an average family. The prices of some items such as house rent, school, college fee and books are collected once in six months.

Indices are compiled directly at the central level by using Laspeyre's formula. The All-India Index is computed as weighted average of the index numbers of 70 centres, weights being the ratio of total consumption expenditure of estimated number of families allocated to a centre in the state to the sum total of all such expenditure over all centres in the country. The All-India Index can be linked to the earlier series on base 1960=100 by using conversion factors of 4.93 and 4.98 for General and Food Indices respectively.

A detailed note on the scope and method of compilation of All-India Consumer Price Index Numbers for Industrial Workers (Base: 1982=100) was published in January 1989 issue of the Bureau's monthly publication the "Indian Labour Journal". Annual average of Consumer Price Index Numbers for Industrial Workers of all the 70 centres for the year 1996 to 2003 are presented in Table 1. During 2003 all the 70 centres recorded an increase in the Index. The degree of rise, however, varies from centre to centre. Quilon centre has experienced the highest rise of 7.41 per cent whereas; Vadodra centre has experienced minimum increase of 0.64 per cent when compared to 2002.

Table 2 present annual average of All-India Consumer Price Index Numbers (General and Food) on base: 1982=100 for the year 1992 to 2003 along with the month-wise figures for the year 2003. The annual average of All-India Index (General) for 2003 works out to 496 which is about 3.98% higher over the 2002 level of 477. The annual average of All-India Index (Food Group) for 2003 increased to 490 showing a rise of 3.38 per cent over the 2002 level of 474. The movement of the month-wise indices (General) for the year 2003 shows a fluctuating trend. It showed an increasing trend till July, 2003 followed by a declining trend during August and September 2003. It again showed an increasing trend during the months of October and November 2003. However, the index, finally, fell by two points to stand at 502 in December, 2003.

IV

CONCLUDING OBSERVATIONS

Family Budget Surveys of industrial workers in India provide material for study into this living conditions and behaviour patterns of working class people. In less developed countries, where basic and primary data are often lacking, family living surveys are the most direct way of knowing the essential news and resources of the population for planning a future. The basic objective is, however, the derivation of a weighing diagram on the basis of the pattern of expenditure shown by the survey results for the construction of index numbers which would mean the changes in the retail price level. At present three terms viz. cost of living index, retail price index and consumer price index are generally used in appropriate circumstances in different countries with practically no difference in their connotations. The family living survey data also provide material for the compilation of retail prices comparison between different regions or areas of the index of 'comparative costliness'. This index measures the relation between the price levels of two places as indicated by basket of foods and service of the kind purchased by different regions or areas.

The Consumer Price Index Number for industrial workers measure the rate of change in prices of goods and services consumed by the working class people, which are one of the widely used statistical product, being used for revision of wages and variable dearness allowances: (i) revision of wages and variable dearness allowances, (ii) revision of minimum wages for workers in unorganized sector, (iii) measuring inflationary trend in the country, and finally (iv) policy formulation by the government.

TABLE 1

Consumer Price Index Numbers for Industrial Workers on Base 1982=100
(General Index—Annual Averages)

Sl. No.	*State/ U.T./Centre*	*Centre Weight in All India*	*1996*	*1997*	*1998*	*1999*	*2000*	*2001*	*2002*	*2003*
1	*2*	*3*	*4*	*5*	*6*	*7*	*8*	*9*	*10*	*11*
Andhra Pradesh										
1.	Gudur	0.75	342	360	416	435	438	443	451	469
2.	Guntur	1.11	332	356	394	414	431	438	473	504
3.	Hyderabad	1.63	308	331	377	395	419	438	468	496
4.	Visakhapatnam	1.63	319	343	388	410	436	444	469	484
5.	Warangal	1.54	324	344	399	415	440	461	501	526
Assam										
6.	D.D. Tinsukia	0.57	309	320	362	386	389	384	398	416
7.	Guwahati	0.66	341	357	405	436	460	471	480	496
8.	Labac-Silchar	0.44	295	312	345	375	370	372	374	383
9.	Mariani-Jorhat	0.51	324	339	389	416	418	411	411	432
10.	Tezpur Rangapra	0.63	323	340	390	412	408	419	417	427

Bihar									
11. Monghyr	1.10	316	331	379	415	416	416	435	459
Chhattisgarh									
12. Bhilai	1.91	302	323	361	373	390	407	413	439
Gujarat									
13. Ahmedabad	3.74	333	357	399	422	441	460	476	488
14. Bhavnagar	0.99	350	373	425	447	466	483	492	504
15. Rajkot	1.17	332	350	393	409	430	433	447	457
16. Surat	0.86	356	373	417	432	446	474	484	490
17. Vadodra	0.88	332	350	385	405	430	453	467	470
Haryana									
18. Faridabad	1.17	326	359	426	435	443	469	480	499
19. Yamunanagar	1.05	315	335	378	392	412	428	443	462
Jammu and Kashmir									
20. Srinagar	0.22	321	347	414	471	480	520	547	574
Jharkand									
21. Jamshedpur	1.63	321	340	385	397	405	419	431	456
22. Jharia	2.39	286	301	353	363	363	365	374	393
23. Kodarma	0.59	290	310	359	379	368	373	388	402
24. Noamundi	1.22	310	336	371	377	395	410	411	436
25. Ranchi Hatia	1.35	320	340	402	414	418	426	433	438

(Contd.)

TABLE 1 (Contd.)

1	2	3	4	5	6	7	8	9	10	11
Karnataka										
26.	Bangalore	3.27	331	361	391	405	425	438	452	476
27.	Belgaum	1.33	353	380	423	457	473	486	514	535
28.	Hubli-Dharwar	1.29	337	362	409	430	434	451	471	494
29.	Mercara	1.16	339	375	418	444	458	457	458	474
Kerala										
30.	Alwaye	1.58	348	371	404	423	442	458	478	490
31.	Mundakayam	1.01	355	384	419	443	453	451	469	489
32.	Quilon	0.58	362	391	395	428	449	457	486	522
33.	Thiruvananthapuram	1.02	371	397	430	468	499	504	541	563
Madhya Pradesh										
34.	Balahgat	1.37	324	342	375	382	385	409	424	443
35.	Bhopal	1.51	344	356	406	425	445	488	510	525
36.	Indore	1.28	339	356	409	435	446	470	448	511
37.	Jabalpur	1.32	339	356	409	435	446	458	468	488
Maharashtra										
38.	Mumbai	7.87	363	400	453	468	505	528	558	583
39.	Nagpur	1.56	342	370	427	438	461	483	495	503
40.	Nasik	2.04	353	377	423	432	465	498	514	532
41.	Pune	1.94	359	388	448	466	493	516	528	554
42.	Solapur	1.24	357	371	431	450	467	471	486	501

Orissa									
43. Barbil	0.80	324	336	371	390	411	420	429	434
44. Rourkela	0.80	303	341	390	396	406	407	416	432
Punjab									
45. Amritsar	1.86	298	314	369	379	388	403	418	431
46. Ludhiana	1.17	301	320	374	381	396	413	431	441
Rajasthan									
47. Ajmer	1.59	332	357	392	411	433	452	472	487
48. Jaipur	1.25	321	346	387	390	403	423	442	452
Tamil Nadu									
49. Chennai	3.47	356	382	425	446	475	487	513	533
50. Coimbatore	1.89	330	354	383	402	432	441	472	495
51. Coonoor	1.54	348	377	404	414	433	445	473	497
52. Madurai	1.51	346	366	401	423	440	446	459	482
53. Salem	1.16	348	364	394	414	432	443	464	483
54. Tiruchirapally	1.35	364	406	435	463	481	488	533	568
Uttar Pradesh									
55. Agra	1.09	313	334	384	398	403	418	435	455
56. Ghaziabad	1.27	321	347	406	440	448	467	475	493
57. Kanpur	1.30	328	351	411	428	428	447	459	471

(Contd.)

TABLE 1 (Contd.)

1	2	3	4	5	6	7	8	9	10	11
58.	Saharanpur	1.68	306	322	369	388	402	420	436	454
59.	Varanasi	1.42	347	371	450	473	466	477	486	504
60.	Asansol	1.00	307	322	381	400	412	431	456	472
61.	Darjeeling	0.59	292	304	355	384	382	393	399	423
62.	Durgapur	0.98	346	368	430	443	472	509	553	564
63.	Haldia	0.83	359	385	433	464	481	533	582	590
64.	Howrah	1.78	346	364	439	482	499	519	542	556
65.	Jalpaiguri	0.94	299	312	379	399	400	492	417	421
66.	Kolkata	4.24	340	359	316	437	451	407	530	541
67.	Raniganj	1.31	398	314	357	373	380	399	416	426
Chandigarh										
68.	Chandigarh	0.16	315	345	401	447	460	488	514	526
Delhi										
69.	Delhi	1.79	346	380	447	480	514	529	550	570
Pondicherry										
70.	Pondicherry	0.25	387	428	464	467	477	482	510	543
	All-India	100.00	334	358	405	424	441	458	477	496

Source: Indian Labour Year Book, 2004, pp. 95-96.

TABLE 2

All India Consumer Price Numbers for Industrial Workers on base 1982=100

Year/Month	*General*	*Food*
1992	237	251
1993	252	265
1994	278	296
1995	306	331
1996	334	359
1997	358	380
1998	405	437
1999	424	444
2000	441	452
2001	458	462
2002	477	474
2002	496	490
2003		
January	483	474
February	484	475
March	487	479
April	493	488
May	494	490
June	497	494
July	501	499
August	499	494
September	499	493
October	503	500
November	504	501
December	502	496

Note: The Linking Factors between 1960 and 1982 series are 4.93 and 4.98 for General and Food Index respectively.

Source: Indian Labour Year Book, 2004, p. 97.

References

Family Living Studies—A Symposium, ILO, 1961.

The Workers' Standard of Living, ILO, 1938.

Comments of Goverment on the Report on International Definition and Measurement of Standards and Levels of Living, UN E./CN/3/213, 1956.

Report of the Committee on International Definition and Measurement of Standards and Levels of Living, UN, 1954.

Family Living Studies—A Symposium, ILO, 1961 and Hand-book of Household Surveys, U.N., F. 10, 1964.

Royal Commission on Labour.

Indian Labour Year Book, 2004, GOI, Labour Bureau, Shimla/Chandigarh.

B.P. Guha and J.N. Sharma, 1971, Level of Living, Indian Publication, Calcutta.

Report of the National Commission on Labour, 1969.

Report of the Second National Commission on Labour, 2002.

Level of Living of Child Labour: A Case Study

M.S. Gupta

I. INTRODUCTION

The problem of child labour does not exist with the third world countries only. It has been more or less a global problem. The difference, if any, is only of degree not of kind. It is directly linked with socio-economic and cultural factors. Karl Marx proclaimed that the result of purchasing children at an immature age by the capitalist is not only a physical deterioration but a social degeneration as well. It is a matter of satisfaction that worldwide awareness regarding upliftment of child labour is increasing now. In this regard, the UNO and its agencies especially ILO have gone through many resolutions, programmes and regulations. Being enlightened by the activities of the World organigations and government of different nations all over the world irrespective of their political ideologies adopted so many measures protected its constitution and laws either to eliminate child labour or at least to regulate their wages and working conditions. No doubt, much has been done and a lot has to be done. India has also taken so many legislative measures for welfare of the children but slur of child labour still remains on its head. The problem of child labour is very intense in India though there is difference in estimates of magnitude of child labour.

Concept of Child Labour

The term 'child labour' is generally used to refer "any work by children that interferes with them in their full physical development, the opportunities for a desirable minimum of education and of their needed recreation". Children aged between 4 to 14 doing work on family farms or in occupations without wage or in factories, farms outside home for wages constitute child labour. Now-a-days child labour is a widespread phenomena. It is not only confined to work on family farms or in traditional family jobs and occupations, but it has also extended to other fields. They work in agriculture and allied activities, unorganised small scale sector and even in organised industries.

The phenomenon of child labour, which is a consequence of the exploitative system operating at the national and international levels, not only closes the future of millions of children in the third world countries, but it also restricts the development prospects of these countries drastically. The existence of child labour is a threat to overall world development, to the solidarity and peace in the world.

The problem of child labour is symptom of the disease, which is widespread due to exploitative structure, lopsided development, iniquitous resource ownership with its correlation of large-scale unemployment and abject poverty among the countries. The existing international economic order perpetuates this harsh reality because powerful multi-national corporations operate and use child labour directly or indirectly, to maximise profits and minimise costs. The poor third world countries faced with acute foreign exchange crisis, permit and encourage export of goods using cheap and vulnerable child labour in the hope of improving their foreign exchange reserves and balance of payments crisis. India carpet industry, lock industry, gem and precious metals, etc. are examples. It is true that extreme poverty and unemployment force the poors to send their children to work as a part of their survival strategy; greed for profit and desperate competition for markets in the developed world encourage employers to use child labour for economic advantage. Lack of firm commitment to the goal of eradication of child labour results in a haphazard and ineffective intervention from the government, which is quite conducive to the interest of MNCs and other vested interests.

Causes of Child Labour

Although there is no single factor responsible for the participation of the children below 15 years of age in the highly competitive job market, poverty seems to be one of the most dominant reasons. In spite of high claims by the government, the study by Institution of Public Opinion reveals that 41.2 per cent of the population is still below the poverty line. Therefore, child labour is no longer a medium of exploitation but it is necessitated by the economic necessities of the parents and in many cases that of the child himself. Inadequate income of the parents does not fulfil the minimum requirements of the children, which in most of the cases, inspires the children to inter into the job market.

Poverty is most often supplemented by other socio-economic factors to expose the child to manual jobs. Due to high degree of illiteracy and ignorance of the parents, the children are deprived of getting proper counseling for building up their future career and at the time of economic necessity, the children move into the job market to eke out their subsistence. Most of the times, a bigger family size adds to the misery of the parents to maintain the children properly, which motivates some of them to search for a job even in their teens to supplement the family income. Since education has become expensive these days, those who cannot afford to educate their children, indirectly encourage them to go for a job instead of sitting idle. As unemployment creates havoc in our country and there is no adequate provision for maintenance allowance to the unemployed, the children of unemployed parents immediately jump to the job market. Besides these handicaps of the children, the employer finds child labour as the cheapest labour, malleable and can be easily controlled. Hence, the encouragement also comes

IV. METHODOLOGY

The present study is based on primary data made available through a questionnaire of envisaging different aspects as well as to test the impact of socio-economic conditions of child labour. As the study has been applied to examine the different variables of the problems of child labour and correlation among them, sampling is based on random samples. It has been collected from the area concerned on interview basis. Utmost care has been taken and respondents from all castes, categories and religions have been included in our sample. Hence, the source of information is based on primary data.

Sample Size

The present study is confined to the tea-stalls, sweet-shops and *dhabas* located at Musallahpur area in Patna, Bihar. We have selected a few pockets of these establishments to analyse the working conditions of the child workers. The reason for making selection of 55 establishments is that it is not possible to conduct a comprehensive survey of the entire tea-stalls, sweet-shops and *dhabas* located in Patna. Thus, 55 samples establishments have been chosen for the study. Among them; there are 12 tea-stalls, 16 sweet-shops and 27 *dhabas*. These are mainly located at Musallahpur area in Patna.

Obstacles during Fieldwork of Research Study

During the fieldwork of research study, we have faced a variety of obstacles from child labour and their employers, which has taken additional time in completing the fieldwork. The major obstacle we faced was that majority of the respondents were either illiterate or less educated and incapable to understand the questions asked by the investigator while few of them were not giving much importance because there was no any advantage from such surveys. We also found lack of awareness among child labours and this was mainly due to poor economic condition, illiteracy and also threat from employers. Some respondents also tried to furnish wrong information, which was detected through supplementary and counter questions during filling up of questionnaire.

V. FINDING OF THE STUDY

Child labour, which constitutes a large section of the workforce in India, is probably the most deprived and disadvantaged group in the country. The Government has initiated several measures since independence to ameliorate their conditions. Although their levels of living have somewhat improved particularly during the previous decade, the child labourers have been largely bypassed by the general socio-economic development witnessed after independence. Various public works programmes and social security measures sponsored by the state have played an important role in India towards mitigating the plight of child labour.

Workers' Allocation

The study of 55 establishments revealed that 212 workers were working in these establishments, carrying out all sorts of jobs which include cooking, cleaning, sweeping, serving, preparation of the tea and sweets, etc. It is revealed from the study that 80 child workers were engaged in various services by their owners of the tea-stalls, sweet-shops and *dhabas*. It is evident from the Table 1.

Table 1 shows that out of 212 total workers, the number of children were 80. It constitutes 37.74 per cent of the total employment given to the workers in the 55 establishments. The number of adults was 132, which comes to 62.26 per cent when compared with the child workers in the establishments surveyed.

Mode of Employment

Further Table 2 reveals that the mode of employment followed by the owners of the establishments are of three kinds viz., employment through self, employment through relationship and other sources. Out of 80 child workers; 20 have got employment through self-persuasion, 36 through their relationship and remaining 24 have been introduced to the owners through other sources.

TABLE 1

Workers' Allocation

Nature of Establish-ments	*Number of Establish-ments*	*Total Employees*	*Adults*	*Children*	*Percentage*
Tea-stalls	12	34	19	15	44.11
Sweet-shops	16	67	44	23	34.32
Dhabas	27	111	69	42	37.87
Total		55	212	132	80

Source: As per survey.

TABLE 2

Mode of Employment

Mode of Employment	*Number of Children*	*Percentage*
Self	20	25
Through Relations	36	45
Other Sources	24	30
Total	80	100

Source: As per survey.

Age Composition of Child Workers

Table 3 throws light on the age composition of the child workers in the 55 establishments surveyed by the researcher. During the survey, it was found that 14 children were less than 9 years of age, which constitute 17.5 per cent of the total child workers interviewed. There were 38 children between the age group of 9-12 years and 28 children between the age group of 12-14 years, which constitute 47.5 per cent and 35 per cent respectively of the total child workers.

Wages Earned by Child Workers

Similarly, the study of Table 4 discloses that the wage-range of child workers varies from Rs. 0-350 and above. Out

TABLE 3

Age Composition of Child Workers

Age-Range in Years	*Number of Child Workers*	*Percentage*
Less than 9	14	17.5
9-12	38	47.5
12-14	28	35.0
Total	80	100.0

Source: Same as Table 1.

TABLE 4

Wages Earned by Child Workers

Wage-Range in Rs.	*Number of Child Workers*	*Percentage*
Below 150	15	18.75
150-250	44	55.00
250-350	19	23.75
350 and Above	2	2.50
Total	80	100.0

Source: Same as Table 1.

of 80 child workers; 15 get their wages below Rs. 150, 44 child workers are given wages between Rs. 150-250 and 19 get their wages between Rs. 250-350. There are only 2 child workers who have stated their wages above Rs. 350. Thus, it is quite evident that only 2.5 per cent working children get their salary above Rs. 350 and remaining 97.5 per cent child workers draw their wages below Rs. 350. There are 23.75 per cent child workers who have their wage between Rs. 250-350 and 18.75 per cent get a poor wage of Rs. 0-150 from their employers.

Working Hours of Child Workers

It is also evident from the statements of the child workers that they have to work without rest pauses from morning till late night. It is revealed from the study of Table

5 that all the child workers are to work from 8-15 hours without any rest. 15 per cent of the total child workers have stated that they work for 8-12 hours a day, 72.5 per cent child workers have stated that their working hours vary between 12-15 hours and 12.5 per cent have mentioned that they have to work tirelessly for 15 hours or above every day. It is generally found from the statement made by child workers that their employers do not follow any child labour welfare legislation. As the child workers are whole-time servants and live in the premises provided by their employers, they usually work from early hours of the morning to late hours in the night without taking any rest.

TABLE 5

Working Hours of Child Workers

Working Hours	*Number of Child Workers*	*Percentage*
0-8	0	0.0
8-12	12	15.0
12-15	58	72.5
Above 15	10	12.5
Total	80	100.0

Source: Same as Table 1.

Leave Availed by Child Workers

Table 6 deals with the nature of leave allowed by owners of these establishments to the child workers. The study reveals that 70 per cent of child workers have been allowed no leave in any shape. However, 1.25 per cent of them have mentioned that their employers have allowed them 10 days as the leave with full pay, 13.75 per cent have reported that they have been given 12 days as a leave period with full benefits annually, 5 per cent have stated that they avail annually 15 days as a leave period with full wages while 2 workers (2.5%) out of 80 child workers have committed in their response that they avail 24 days as leave period and their owners make full payment for the above said days and 3 child workers (3.75%) of the sample units have mentioned 36 days as the leave period with full wages

TABLE 6

Leave Availed by Child Workers

Leave Availed (Annually) No.	*Number of Child Workers*	*Percentage*
Leave	56	70.0
10 days	01	1.25
12 days	11	13.75
15 days	04	5.0
24 days	02	2.5
36 days	03	3.75
52 days	03	3.75
Total	80	100.0

Source: Same as Table 1.

as agreed to by their owners. It is also clear from the Table 6 that 3 child workers (3.75%) get 52 days leave annually.

Entertainment Facilities for Child Workers

Similarly, the data collected and tabulated under Table 7 represents the mode of entertainment provided to the child workers in these establishments. According to the study, 58.75 per cent of the child workers have mentioned that there is no entertainment facility provided to them. However, 25 per cent of child workers have stated that they entertain themselves through radio and tape recorders and 15 per cent have mentioned that their employers have given them television. The child workers have made it clear in their statements that they can avail the entertainment facilities only in the late hours in the evening and night when there is no rush of work for want of customers.

So far as nature of their duties is concerned, they are engaged in washing utensils, cleaning of tables and chairs, sweeping of rooms, preparation of tea and sweets, etc. Despite large number of such establishments, they are not covered by any law or regulation and are supposed to carry out jobs of mixed nature.

TABLE 7

Entertainment Facilities for Child Workers

Mode of Entertainment	*Number of Child Workers*	*Percentage*
No Provision	47	58.75
Radio	11	13.75
Tape Recorder	10	12.50
Television	12	15.00
Total	80	100.00

Source: Same as Table 1.

Educational Profile of Child Workers

Table 8 shows the educational profile of child workers in these establishments. It reveals that 36 child workers (45%) of the total child workers are illiterate, 35 child workers (43.75%) are those who had joined the study but could not complete even fifth standard. The study further reveals that 9 child workers are those who have passed primary education but could not go beyond the middle standard. The percentage of these child workers is recorded as 11.25 per cent when compared with the total strength of the child workers of 55 establishments. It is also important to note that none of the 80 child workers was matriculate or above as evidenced from the educational profile of child workers given in Table 8.

TABLE 8

Educational Profile of Child Workers

Education Level	*Number of Child Workers*	*Percentage*
Not Educated	36	45.00
0-5th	35	43.75
5th-8th	9	11.25
Above 8th	0	0.00
Total	80	100.00

Source: Same as Table 1.

VI. CONCLUSION OF THE STUDY

The data collected in the present survey depicts a clear picture of the working conditions of the child workers in tea-stalls, sweet-shops and *dhabas* located at Musallahpur area in Patna Town.

The child workers have stated that they have got the occupation through three different modes viz., self, through relationship and other sources. It is clear from the survey that 25 per cent child workers got their occupations by their individual initiative, 454 per cent through media of their relationship and 30 per cent could get their employment through other sources. The main reason of joining the occupation by these child workers is stated as "poverty". It is the poverty, which seems to have been responsible to generate the evils of child labour in each and every establishment of our society.

The survey also reveals that the working conditions of the child workers are far from satisfactory. The owners of these establishments do not adhere to laws made to regulate the hours of work as prescribed under the Child Labour (Prohibition and Regulation) Act, 1986. It has been observed that the daily working hours of child workers vary between 8 to 15 hours as against 6 hours prescribed under Section 7, Clause (3) of the Child Labour (Prohibition and Regulation) Act, 1986. To the surprise of the investigator, 10 child workers have stated that they are forced to work even for more than 15 hours a day without any rest. The data collected reveals that the child workers are not allowed for any rest during the entire course of their work in a day. Almost all the child workers interviewed have mentioned that there is no specific period given to them for the purpose of rest. This practice is highly in contravention to Section 7(3) of the Child Labour (P & R) Act, 1986 wherein every employer is under statutory obligation to arrange the period of work on each day in such a manner that no period should exceed three hours and no child should work for more than three hours before he had an interval of rest for at least one hour. It is also observed during the interview of child workers that they have to work even in the late hours of the evening and there is no bar on the employers to restrain them as the employment of the children between 7.00 P.M. and 8.00 P.M. is totally prohibited under Clause 4 of Section 7 of the Act.

It is also quite evident that the child workers do not get any weekly holiday. 70 per cent of the child workers interviewed have stated that they are not entitled to any kind of leave. Only 30 per cent of the respondents have mentioned that they get annual leave ranging between 10 to 52 days. The survey results, therefore, show that the mandate of Section 8 of the Child Labour (P & R) Act, 1986 is not at all obeyed by the owners of tea-stalls, sweet-shops and *dhabas.*

So far as the wage is concerned, it has been generally observed from the study that they are poorly paid and even get their wages between a poor range of Rs. 0-350 which claims 97.5 per cent of the total child workers. There are only two children who have mentioned their wages above Rs. 350 per month. The survey, therefore, discloses that the poor child workers are not paid even the minimum wages by their employers which is sheer in contravention to the decision of the Supreme Court given in *M.C. Mehta* Vs. *State of Tamil Nadu* (AIR) 1991 (SC 417). The Hon'ble Court in this case has held that the child workers must get at least minimum wages which comes to 60 per cent of prescribed minimum wage for adult employees doing same job to be given to child in view of special adaptability of child's tender age to such work.

It is also observed from the survey that the educational profile of the child workers is very poor. None has stated his education above 8th standard. 45 per cent of the child workers have been found totally illiterate and only 55 per cent of the child workers upto 8th standard. It is observed that the majority of child workers have joined these occupations because they were basically poor and need wages as a source of their livelihood. There is hardly any night school for those who want to continue their studies. It is also revealed from the study that there is lack of appreciation on the part of their employers to give them education while serving in their establishments. The findings of the study, therefore go against the spirit of the decision of the Supreme Court in *M.C. Mehta* Vs. *State of Tamil Nadu.*

VII. SUGGESTIONS OF THE STUDY

On the basis of previous discussion, the following points may be considered useful for reappraising the strategy for preventing child labour as well as ameliorating their conditions:

1. A constitutional obligation of providing free and compulsory education to all children upto the age of fourteen years of age must be fulfilled without any further delay. Education should be made compulsory and free.
2. There is a need to bring consciousness among the children so that they may be aware of their constitutional rights and get relief accordingly. This is again possible with the help of radio, television, spread of education and literacy campaigns.
3. The problem of child labour is directly connected with the poverty and illiteracy of Indian people. There should be every possible effort on the part of Government and NGOs.
4. Further, supportive measures for child labour such as removal of poverty and unemployment ensuring minimum wages, meaningful education policy, medical and health support, proper nutrition, recreation and cultural activities, family planning, apprenticeship and vocational training facilities, etc. must be given much importance besides legislative measures.
5. The raising of public awareness and supporting community action should be given top priority in any scheme concerning child labour.
6. Government should implement such action plans in the areas where child labour concentration is much higher. These areas should get priority.
7. Unemployment allowance, old-age pension and red-card schemes for supplying the grains at half price among the poor all should be properly and

fairly implemented. Benefits should reach genuine and needy people.

8. Poverty alleviation programmes should be formulated and implemented in a decentralized manner with the participation of people at the grass-root level through village panchayats, panchayat samitis, zila parishads, etc.
9. In urban areas; slum-dwellers, casual workers, small artisans, vendors, minority community people, SC/ST and Backward Classes of the population should be the main beneficiaries of anti-poverty programmes.
10. Productivity may be augmented through land-based activities like minor-irrigation, dry farming, horticulture and even farm forest tree.
11. Land reform programmes should be strictly implemented. Land to the landless must be provided as most of the families of child labour and landless.
12. Since more than 80 per cent people of the state still depend on agriculture, this sector should be developed in a proper way. It provides employment to a sizeable population.
13. Child labour should not be under the jurisdiction of the Ministry of Labour. The rehabilitation programmes come under Education Department, Health Department, Rural Development Department, etc. Co-ordination with these departments is often a major hurdle. Therefore, the issue of child labour should be placed under the Ministry of Welfare because it would be better suited to deal with the problem in its various dimensions.
14. Minimum Wages Act should be strictly followed and the Act concerning it must be ammended and reformulated to avoid loopholes in them.
15. Apart from general education, vocational training should be imparted to the children to make them economically independent in their adulthood.

To sum up, a strong political will power and dedicated welfare activities are necessary to check this evil practice. There is the need for change in social attitude and in this context; mass media should be assigned a constructive role. This will certainly help in reducing child labour and eliminate it through improving enforcing legislations, promoting school enrolment, raising public awareness, supporting community action and targeting hazardous environment. Last but not the least, the prevailing corruptions in the government machinery must be checked very effectively and properly otherwise our all efforts in elimination of child labour will be like filling a vessel which has a whole in it.

References

GoI, Economic Survey, 2002-03.

Government of Bihar (2001), Census of India, Provisional Population Totals, Director of Census Operations, Bihar.

Hirway, Indira, Cottyn, J. *et. al.* (1991) (Eds.), Towards Eradication of Child Labour, Oxford and IBH Publishing Company, New Delhi.

Marx, Karl, *Das Capital*, Translated from German Edition by S. Moore and E. Aveling and Edited by F. Engels, George Allen and Unwin, London.

Rodgers, G. and Standing, G. (1981), "The Economic Roles of Children: Issues for Analysis" in *Child Work, Poverty and Unemployment* (Eds.), ILO, Geneva.

Shandilya, T.K. and Khan, S.A. (2003), Child Labour, A Global Change, Deep & Deep Publications (P) Ltd, New Delhi.

Sharma, Alakh N. (1979), "Child Labour in Patna", A.N. Sinha Institute of Social Studies, Patna (Memio).

Singh, B.P.and Mohanty, Shukla (1993), "Children At Work", Problems and Policy Options (Eds.), B.R. Publishing Corporation, Delhi.

Stein, E. and Davis, J., (1940) (Eds.), "Labour Problems in America", F. Farraer and Richer, New York.

10

Infrastructure and Inter-regional Disparities in India

G.C. Tripathi, Poonam Jaiswal and Abhishek Kumar Pandey

The overall objective of the country is 'growth with social justice', where social justice means—removal of poverty, unemployment and removal of regional disparities. Through proper regional development people can have decent levels of living. All the Five Year Plans stressed the importance of balanced regional development and policies were designed to direct more investments to the relatively backward areas. India is shining but existence of regional disparity as a spot can be seen everywhere in India. There exist severe regional disparities in economic performance across the States/UTs and such disparities are even more pronounced within the states/UTs.

Ahluwalia (2000) argues that 'while inter-state inequality as measured by the Gini coefficient has clearly increased, the common perception that the rich states got richer and the poor states got poorer is not entirely accurate'. It is true that rich states like Punjab and Haryana recorded lower growth in the 1990s than 1980s. The growth rates of poorer states (U.P., Bihar, Orissa) declined in the 1990s. In the case of Rajasthan and Madhya Pradesh there was no increase in the growth rate in the 1990s compared to 1980s. Therefore, in five major states there was no acceleration in the growth rate in the post-reform period. In contrast, acceleration occurred in Western and Southern States and West Bengal. Intra-rural inequalities have not risen while intra-urban inequalities have increased. Present paper attempt to understand the different issue and challenges related to disparities in infrastructure. Regional development is important not only for raising economic growth but also human development.

SECTION I

INCOME POVERTY AND DISPARITIES

According to Adwait K. Mohanty (1989), Poverty in India is widespread and deep-rooted. At the beginning of the planning era, it was expected that overall economic growth would automatically trickle down the benefits of development to the poorest of the poor. But it did not happen. So, since the seventies the government took measures for a direct assault on poverty. It was realised that the poor are asset less. Therefore, steps were taken to increase their asset-base and employ them gainfully. The asset distribution measures did not work well due to inadequacy of assets and administrative inefficiency. Self-employment programmes failed because of the unpreparedness of the poor. Government sponsored wage employment programmes did not give employment of enduring type. Employment elasticity is declining in the over-crowded agricultural sector, which employs 70 per cent of the country's work force.

Poverty is concentrated in a few states. The share of six states (Bihar, U.P., M.P., West Bengal, Orissa and Assam) in all India rural poor increased from 68.8 per cent in 1993-94 to 74.4 per cent in 1999-00. According to official estimates, poverty declined from 37.3 per cent in 1993-94 to 27.1 per cent in 1999-00. It declined 10.2 percentage points over the six year period indicating a 1.7 percentage point decline per annum. Deaton and Dreze show that the growth rate of average per capita consumption expenditure (APCE) during 1993-94 and 1999-00 is

TABLE 3

Indicators of Medical and Health Infrastructure

Indicators of Medical and Health Infrastructure
No. of primary health centres/lakh population
No. of health/sub-centres/lakh population
No. of hospital beds per lakh population
No. of doctors/lakh population
No. of nursing personnel/lakh population
No. of primary health centres/100 sq.km.
No. of sub-centres/100 sq.km.

Index of Social and Economic Infrastructure

The index of social and economic infrastructure was much higher than all India in seven states viz., West Bengal, Maharashtra, Gujarat, Haryana, Tamil Nadu, Kerala and Punjab in both 1995 and 2000. The Table 4 shows that in general, there is a positive relationship between infrastructure and growth. However, there are some outliers. Punjab did not record high growth in spite of high level of infrastructure while Rajasthan registered high growth despite low infrastructure; because Infrastructure is necessary condition for growth and human development but its not sufficient condition. Similarly, Karnataka and Andhra Pradesh have similar levels of infrastructure but the former recorded much higher growth than the latter. Data also shows that the key infrastructure sectors of power, roads, tele-communications, posts and banking are better developed in richer and middle income states as compared to poorer states.

SECTION III

INVESTMENT AND CAPITAL FLOWS

Investment generally flows to the states where infrastructure facilities are high. Ahluwalia (2000) examines the relationship between state plan expenditure as a percentage of GSDP and growth rates in GSDP. His study finds that plan expenditure as per cent of SDP declined in

TABLE 4

Index of Social and Economic Infrastructure

States	*Index*		*Rank*	
	1995	*2000*	*1995*	*2000*
Andhra Pradesh	99.19	103.3	10	9
Assam	81.94	77.72	12	13
Bihar	92.04	81.33	11	11
Gujarat	123.01	124.31	6	5
Haryana	158.89	137.54	3	4
Karnataka	101.20	104.88	9	8
Kerala	205.41	178.68	2	2
Madhya Pradesh	65.92	76.79	14	14
Maharashtra	121.70	112.80	7	6
Orissa	74.46	81.00	13	12
Punjab	219.19	187.57	1	1
Rajasthan	70.46	75.86	15	15
Tamil Nadu	149.86	149.10	4	3
Uttar Pradesh	111.80	101.23	8	10
West Bengal	131.67	111.25	5	7
All India	100.00	100.00	–	–

both the better performing states as well as the poor performing ones. The lack of correlation between state plan ratio and growth rate of GSDP indicates that total investment, which includes private investment, is more important than state plan expenditure. The per capita public and private investment in Gujarat (Rs. 33,875) was 10 times more than that of Bihar (Rs. 2,852) and U.P. (Rs. 3304). The per capita total credit utilisation in Maharashtra was more than 20 times that of Bihar and nine times of UP. Shetty's study (2003a) shows that the credit-deposit (C-D) ratios have fallen in all regions of the country in the 1990s—the decline being much steeper in backward states and regions. For example, in the eastern region, the C-D ratios declined from 54 per cent in 1981 to 50 per cent in 1991 and to 37 per cent in 2001.

The states ranking higher in respect of social and economic infrastructure could attract greater foreign direct investment (FDI). Between 1991 and 2003, the top five states in terms of attracting FDI, viz., Maharashtra, Delhi, Tamil

Nadu, Karnataka and Gujarat, accounted for 52 per cent of total FDI approvals in the country. Despite its reforms, Andhra Pradesh managed to attract only about 4.6 per cent of total FDI in the country. There seems to be a positive relationship between FDI inflows and physical and human infrastructure. Generally speaking, there is a positive relationship between higher levels of infrastructure/income and capital flows, particularly the per capita total investment. There are some exceptions like Orissa.

Study shows that both public and private insurance companies has playing a significant role in infrastructure development in India but the requirement of Infrastructure sector is consistently going towards upstream. According to India Infrastructure Report the level of investment in infrastructure needed to be increased from 5.5 per cent of GDP to about 7 per cent by 2000-01 and 8 per cent by 2005-06, to attain a GDP growth of 7 per cent by 2000-01 and 8 per cent by 2005-06. The funding requirements of various sectors in the infrastructure area aggregate to about Rs. 1,020,000 crore by the year 2005-06. The estimated availability of financing from Indian Financial Institutions and banks for infrastructure is expected to be about Rs. 1,20,000 crore. The total Investment required during the Tenth Plan Period (2002-07) is projected at about rupees 50,000 crore and a massive project of "Bharat Nirman" needs rupees 1,74,000 crore in the next four years for rural Infrastructure development. Organisation both national and international have always pointed about the possibility that funding of such large infrastuctural projects like roads, power, water, sanitation, ports, housing, irrigation and telecommunication could usefully be done by insurance companies through their life and pension funds. However, this would still leave a large funding gap which would have to be met through other sources that is bilateral/multilateral/government funding. For the insurance sector it is possible to provide funds for infrastructure because of IRDA's investment guidelines which gives provision for life insurance companies are bound to invest at least 15 per cent in infrastructure and social sector while the non-life insurers shall invest not less than 10 per cent in the same. The life insurance sector invested a total of

Rs. 31335.89 crore in the infrastructure sector in the year 2002-03 out of which the contribution of Life Insurance Corporation was Rs. 30998.16 crore which was 98.92 per cent of the total investment in infrastructure.

Section IV

SUGGESTIONS AND CONCLUSIONS

A multi-pronged strategy is needed to narrow down regional disparities, there is need of modified development strategy so that low performing region can have proper development. The major thrust of strategy has to be fast human capital development (i.e. education, health and nutrition).

- In the post-reform period, due to deregulation, the degree of control of the central government declined in many sectors. Now State governments can take more initiatives for economic development. Also, the role of private sector is becoming more important as compared to the public sector.
- Public investment is crucial for raising physical (irrigation, power, roads, etc.) and human (health and education) infrastructure. There is a potential for public-private partnerships (PPPs) to contribute more and help bridge the infrastructure gap in India. The role of private investment has become more important in the post-reform period.
- Investment should be increased in less developed states for higher growth and reduction in poverty. Resources have to be used for infrastructure from central assistance, including externally aided projects and the state's own resources. The central government's role is important in allocating more resources to the less developed states.
- Fiscal management of states must improve in order to allocate more expenditure for physical infrastructure and health and education. Many

state governments are facing severe fiscal problems although there are signs of improvement in recent years.

- The less developed states are facing both low economic growth and high population growth. These states have to focus on policies for reducing population.
- Agriculture sector problems have to be solved in backward states. Public investment has declined as have credit-deposit ratios for rural areas. There seems to be an increase in farmer's suicides. There is also a challenge of involving small and marginal farmers in diversification. Investment in irrigation and watershed development is important, particularly for dry land areas.
- Productive employment should be generated in order to reduce poverty in low income states. Employment can be increased if economic growth is labour-intensive. Development of agriculture and rural non-farm sector will improve employment and wages in rural areas. Direct employment programmes such as wage and self-employment schemes have to be effectively implemented in less developed areas.
- Social sector performance should be improved in backward regions. It is necessary to ensure the expansion of public services for the poor at a low cost, effective public regulation of private services like health care, and accountability of these systems, public as well as private, to the local communities. Improvement in health and education in backward regions would improve economic growth and human development.
- Decentralisation would increase accountability. For improving accountability and development, there is a need to involve more finances, functions and powers for panchayats in order to make these institutions self-sustaining. Governance has to be improved in less developed regions. There is a need to garner support for the reform process

from wider sections of the population by encouraging participatory models of development.

- Infrastructure projects are characterised by large capital costs and long gestation period. In order to collecting funds Insurance sector can play a crucial role. A well developed insurance sector is needed for economic development as it provides long-term funds for infrastructure development.
- Agro-based industries operate as a catalytic agent for the development of infrastructure, which would bridge the gap between the rural and urban economies. It integrates rural and urban economics by eliminating regional imbalances. Therefore, employment programmes for the illiterate and unskilled poor are to be planned in the agro-industries, which require less capital but provide large productive employment of an enduring type. There is a need to plan for agro-industries at the regional level, with keeping in mind the regional constraints and potential.

CONCLUSION

Economic performance of states reveals that inter-regional, inter-class and rural-urban regional disparities have increased in the post-reform period. The disparity between the group of eastern and northern states and the group of western and southern states has increased. India cannot 'shine' unless we reduce these disparities through better public policies. Physical and social infrastructure is important for economic growth as well as higher human development. In order to improve levels of living of human body; there is need to invest in infrastructure development of the human capital, the collective efforts are needed for proper regional development. The pattern of investment must be so devised as to lead to balanced regional development. A well developed insurance sector is needed for economic development as it provides long-term funds for infrastructure development. Region specific and product specific policy should be considered. During the off-seasons there is need to provide better employment opportunities to labour. Agro-industry can be vibrant segments. Through proper policy we can achieve regional development and can have better levels of living, it will be just like growth with human face.

References

Mohanty, Adwait K. (1989), Poverty Alleviation and Agro-Based Industries, published in *Indian Journal of Agricultural Economics,* Volume 44, No. 3, July-September.

Bhattacharya, B.B. and S. Sakthivel (2004), 'Regional Growth and Disparity in India: Comparison of Pre and Post-Reform Decades', *Economic and Political Weekly,* 29(10), 6 March.

Bhullar, D.S., "Regional Economic Disparities and Area Planning", Published by ABD Publishers, Jaipur.

Deaton and Jean Dreze (2002), 'Poverty and Inequality in India: A Re-examination', *Economic and Political Weekly,* 7 September.

Economic Survey, 2005-06, Published by Government of India, Ministry of Finance.

GOI (2003), 'Tenth Five Year Plan, 2002-07', Planning Commission, Government of India, New Delhi.

Infrastructure Development Report, 2006.

Joshi, B.M., "Infrastructure and Economic Development in India", Published by Ashish Publishing House, New Delhi.

K. Sundaram and S.D. Tendulkar (2003), 'Poverty in India in the 1990s: Revised Estimates', *Economic and Political Weekly,* 38(46), 15 November.

K.V. Sundaram (1982), "Measurement and Analysis of Development at the Regional and Local Levels: Some Issues and Problems".

M. Govinda Rao, R.T. Shand and K.P. Kalirajan (1999), "Convergence of Incomes Across Indian States—A Divergent View", *Economic and Political Weekly,* 27 March.

Montek S. Ahluwalia (2000), "Economic Performance of States in Post-Reform Period", *Economic and Political Weekly,* 6 May.

National Human Development Report, 2001.

Dholakia, R.H. (2003), "Regional Disparity in Economic and Human Development in India", *Economic and Political Weekly,* 27 September.

Rastogi, A. (2006), "Infrastructure Sector in India, 2005", *Infrastructure Development Report,* 2006.

Shetty, S.L. (2003), 'Growth of SDP and Structural Changes in State Economies: Inter-state Comparisons', *Economic and Political Weekly,* 6 December.

Murty, S., "Infrastructure and Social Sector Development for Economic Growth", Published by RBSA Publishers, Jaipur.

11

Glaring Regional Disparities in Economic Development in India

Niraj Kumar

Economic welfare of a nation or region depends upon its level of economic development. In material terms economic development means availability of more and better goods and services. But in reality, this definition may not be appropriate because the efforts and sacrifice, that go into obtaining such goods and services, must also be taken into account. Economic development means more leisure, better health, more time to read, even more time to contemplate the good life.

The ultimate goal of development is the improvement in the quality of life, which depends upon not only material production or per capita real income, but also on social and welfare services, satisfaction, self-reliance, self-esteem and economic freedom.

Balanced regional growth is necessary for the harmonious development of a federal state such as India. India however, presents a picture of extreme regional variations, in terms of such indicators as economic growth as per capita income, the proportion of population living below the poverty line, working population in agriculture, the percentage of urban population to total population and the percentage of workers in manufacturing industries, etc.

Economic welfare does not merely depend upon the level of development but also on its distributive aspect. As development takes place, side by side, the forces—growth promoting and thus distributing the benefits of growth—come in conflict. Consequently the gap between the development level of resourceful and less resourceful regions goes on widening. Economic history proves that the process of development starts first in regions which are rich in resources and these regions attract investment and the process of development becomes cumulative, but the problem in India can not be explained with reference to endowments of natural resources alone. There are some 'rich' regions having good base of natural resources but are still economically 'backward'.

To repeat, economic welfare does not merely depend upon the level of development but also on its distributive aspect. Unfortunately the fruit of economic development is not equally distributed among different groups of people and parts of the country, causing disparities and imbalances in economic development.

In India regional disparities in economic development are glaring as much as to cause anxieties. Relatively speaking, some states are economically advanced while others are relatively backward. Even within each state, some regions are more developed while others are almost primitive. The co-existence of relatively developed and economically depressed states and even regions within each State is know as regional imbalance. Regional imbalances may be natural due to unequal natural endowments or manmade in the sense of neglect of some regions and preference to others for investment and development efforts. Regional imbalances may be inter-state or intra-state; they may be total or sectoral. Economic backwardness of a region is indicated by symptoms like high pressure of population on land, excessive dependence on agriculture leading to high incidence of rural employment, absence of large-scale urbanisation, low productivity in agriculture and cottage industries, etc.

An important indicator of regional disparity is the growth rate of net state domestic product (NSDP) observed during the last two decades. For own purpose, we have classified the major states of India into forward and backward states

(Punjab tops on list as it has the highest per capita income and Bihar is at the bottom in the list of backward states as it has the lowest per capita income).

Table 1 clearly pointed out:

TABLE I

State-wise Net State Domestic Product at Factor Cost

(At 1980-81 prices)

State	*(Rs. Crores)*			*Annual Average Growth Rate*	
	1980-81	*1990-91*	*1997-98**	*1980-81 to 1990-91*	*1990-91 to 1997-98*
Forward States					
Punjab	4,449	7,505	10,142	5.3	4.4
Maharashtra	15,163	27,244	42,932	6.0	6.7
Haryana	3,032	5,719	7,545	6.5	4.0
Gujarat	6,547	10,839	18,433	5.2	7.9
West Bengal	9,594	14,458	22,767	4.2	6.7
Karnataka	5,587	9,112	13,683	5.0	6.0
Kerala	3,823	5,262	7,782	3.2	5.8
Tamil Nadu	7,218	12,423	18,193	5.6	5.6
Andhra Pradesh	7,324	11,723	17,936	4.8	6.3
Sub-total	62,737	1,04,265 (55.0)	1,59,413 (54.8)	5.2 (57.8)	6.3
Backward States					
Madhya Pradesh	7,012	11,107	14,748	4.7	4.1
Assam	2,298	3,426	4,302	4.1	3.3
Uttar Pradesh	14,012	22,780	27,365	5.0	2.6
Rajasthan	4,126	8,473	11,138	7.4	4.0
Orissa	3,443	4,345	6,013	2.3	4.7
Bihar	6,349	10,253	10,653	4.9	0.6
Sub-total	37,240	60,384 (38.8)	72,219 (31.7)	4.9 (26.9)	3.0
All-India	1,10,340	1,90,218 (100.0)	2,75,895 (100.0)	5.6 (100.0)	5.5

Source: RBI, Hand Book of Statistics on Indian Economy (1999).

(a) In 1980-81, out of a total net domestic income of Rs. 1,10,340 crores for the whole country, the 9 forward states accounted for 55 per cent while the 6 backward states accounted for nearly 39 per cent. But in 1997-98 the same forward States raised their share to 58 per cent, while the share of the 6 backward states in net national product declined to 27 per cent. In other words, the forward states were becoming more forward or richer, while the backward states were becoming still more backward and poorer.

(b) The above fact is made clear by the difference in the growth rates of NSDP of the forward and backward states.

NSDP in forward states indicated an annual growth rate of 5.2 per cent during 1980-81 to 1990-91—the pre-reform period, however, the synthesis showed a marked improvement in these states and they showed a higher annual average growth rate 6.3 per cent during 1990-91 to 1997-98.

As against them, the backward states indicated a growth rate 4.9 per cent during the pre-reform period but this growth rate decelerated in the post-reform period.

It may also be noted that as compared to average All-India growth rate of 5.5 per cent in the post-reform period, two major states of India, viz. Uttar Pradesh and Bihar; showed an average growth rate of 2.6 per cent and 0.6 per cent respectively—a miserable performance indeed. In fact none of the six states included in the backward group showed a growth rate higher than the national average.

Table 2 provides per capita NSDP at 1993-94 access for both forward and backward states. Punjab has greatest per capita income both in 1990-91 and in 2000-01. Orissa had the lowest per capita income in 1990-91, both in 2000-01, Bihar has recorded the lowest per capita income. During the decade, Karnataka has recorded the highest annual average growth rate while Bihar has extended minus 2.8 per cent rate of growth. Further, while accepted states have recorded smart annual rates of growth (2.6% in Haryana and 6% in

TABLE 2

Per capita Net State Domestic Product at Factor Cost

(At 1993-94 prices)

State	*1990-91*	*2000-01**	*Annual Average Growth Rate 1990-91 to 2000-01*
Forward States			
Punjab	11,779	15,390	2.7
Maharashtra	10,248	15,172	4.0
Haryana	11,125	14,331	2.6
Gujarat	8,788	12,975	3.9
West Bengal	6,013	9,778	5.0
Karnataka	6,629	11,910	6.0
Kerala	6,851	10,712	4.6
Tamil Nadu	7,872	12,79	4.9
Andhra Pradesh	6,873	9,982	3.8
Backward States			
Madhya Pradesh	6,321	7,003	1.0
Assam	5,574	6,157	1.0
Uttar Pradesh	5,342	5,770	0.8
Rajasthan	6,771	7,937	1.6
Orissa	4,300	5,187	1.9
Bihar	4,476	3,345	-2.8
All-India	7,321	10,254	3.4
Ratio Between Maximum and Minimum Per Capita NSDP	2.74	4.60	

Source: Ministry of Finance, Indian Public Finance, Statistics (2001-02)

Karnataka). Backward states have registered extremely poor rates of growth between 1 and 1.9 per cent, with Bihar registering negative rate of growth.

This is a clear indication of the forward rates providing a higher per cent capita income to their profile while the backward states failing to catch up with the forward states. The gravity of the problem has increased to the extent that it has been threatening the political and economic stability in

India. Lack of basic amenities, difference in level of living and employment opportunities, misconception of economic exploitation, cultural and linguistic differences, etc. have encouraged social tensions, violence and separatist tendencies in Punjab, Jammu and Kashmir, Assam and Nagaland, etc. The forces of regionalism have become so strong in India that the economic cost of buying political conformism to shore up politically unstable and economically deprived regions has assumed huge proportion in the form of current expenditure on unproductive items (Mitra, 1987)

Existence of regional disparities in economic development, in vast developing countries like India, is a common phenomenon. The degree and extent of inequality may vary from period to period. Many studies in India highlighted the facts that regional disparities in India have increased over the plan period. The studies by Sampath (1977), Nair (1983), Singh (1985) and Tiwari (1985) shows that regional disparities in India are diverging despite the measures adopted by the Government of India to reduce the divergence among the states in respect of development.

The importance of balanced regional development in a federal political structure needs no emphasis. It is, of course, true that perfect regional balancing is neither feasible nor economically desirable. Balanced Regional Development does not mean equalisation of all regions in every aspect of development. It means the maximum utilisation of all the potentialities of an area and thereby giving its inhabitants the full benefit of possible progress in relation to overall economic growth. Therefore, the solution of the problem of regional disparities and imbalances lies not in perfect balanced regional development but in regional development. (Kantewala and Rao, 1992)

Liberalisation and globalisation of the economies do not reduce the importance of regional policies and strategies. Only the emphasis may shift from direct participation to market-friendly policies for formulation of development plans and programmes. Concerted efforts are needed for consistent and coherent programmes for balanced regional development. Thus regional policies are not only going to stay, but need to be improved, strengthened and made more effective.

Therefore, there is urgent need for re-examination of pattern of development, particularly of industrialisation in the context of balanced regional development in the country. Governments in states and at the centre, with greater co-ordination, should envisage a major programme in human resource development through education, technical training, family welfare, etc. especially in rural areas. Substantial improvement in the human resources in backward areas would help in the reduction of inter-state disparities in India. Moreover, expansion of service sector in backward areas would promote the small scale industries as well as agro-based industries in these areas, thereby leading to enlargement of the share of secondary sector employment so as to absorb the labour released by the primary sector. This would not only help in removing poverty and unemployment but also reducing the regional disparities.

References

Gulati, Rajinder Kumar (1999), Regional Disparities in Economic Development, Deep & Deep Publications Pvt. Ltd.

Dutt, Ruddar and KPM Sundharam (2006), Indian Economy, S. Chand, New Delhi.

Villard, H. Henry (1963), Economic Development, Holt, Rinehart and Winston Inc. New York.

12

Regional Disparity in Economic Development: Comparative Analysis

S.K.L. Das and Manindra Kumar Singh

INTRODUCTION

It is rather shameful that even after more than 59 years of independence, we are talking about regional disparity in growth process. We all are aware that there are many intricate economic models and statistical techniques, which have been used to measure poverty line. However, it is the stark reality before us that for decades we have not been able to solve the crucial problems facing many millions of our people living in different regions of the country.

Regional disparity in India is a serious concern today. It is well known that in a large economy different regions have uneven growth path over time. One of the reasons why centralized planning was advocated earlier was that it could restrain the regional disparity in economic development. In spite of planning the regional disparity remained a serious problem here in our country.

A new controversy in this respect is whether growth rates and levels of living in different regions of the country would eventually converge or not. The convergence theorem of Barro postulates that when the growth rate of the economy accelerates, initially some regions having affluent resources would grow faster than others. But after some time, when the law of diminishing marginal returns set in, first growth rates would converge, due to differential marginal productivity of capital and it ultimately would bridge the gaps in the levels of income of different regions.

The empirical evidence on this is however very controversial. It has also been observed that when an economy is liberated especially after controls on investment are lifted, then regions with better infrastructure would abstract more investment through market mechanism. It would lead to regional disparity during early hours of reforms.

In India growth rate of Gross Domestic Product (GDP) accelerated since 1980. The average annual growth rate in the first three decades (1950-80) was only 3.6 per cent. During 1980-89 the GDP growth rate accelerated to 5.6 per cent and after economic reforms in 1991, it has further improved to 6 per cent. The economic reforms led to a lot of structural changes in the Indian economy, such as liberalisation of trade, exchange rate, interest rate, capital flows and prices as well as delegation of domestic and foreign investment. With this policy public investment has declined from 45 per cent in 1980 to one-third in 2002-03. The RBI data on capital flow shows that few states have received the major chunk of foreign direct investments, while poor states with inadequate infrastructure are not able to attract foreign investment. Hence regional disparity has gradually widened. In respect of poverty estimation there is regional disparity. The poverty ratios for total population in major states show that it declined significantly since 1983. (Table 1)

In spite of reduction in poverty, some of the states are having very high poverty ratios for the total population. In 2004-05 it was more than 40 per cent in Orissa and Bihar and between 30 to 40 per cent in Madhya Pradesh and UP and between 25 to 30 per cent in Maharashtra and Tamil Nadu, Karnataka and West Bengal. A group of four states comprising Bihar, MP, Orissa and UP had a share of about 50

TABLE 1

SDP at Constatant Prices

(% per annum)

States	*1980-90*	*1990-2000*	*1980-2000*
AP	4.81	5.12	5.02
Assam	3.91	2.47	3.99
Bihar+Jharkhand	5.20	3.47	3.85
Goa	5.71	8.23	7.47
Gujarat	5.71	8.28	6.80
Haryana	6.68	6.71	7.80
HP	6.10	6.91	6.20
Karnataka	6.10	7.07	6.53
Kerala	4.50	6.00	5.97
MP	5.18	5.45	5.89
Maharashtra	5.98	6.80	6.30
Orissa	5.85	3.60	3.90
Punjab	5.14	4.63	4.70
Rajasthan	7.17	6.46	6.95
Tamil Nadu	6.35	6.65	6.51
UP	5.88	4.33	5.15
W.B.	5.20	7.24	6.11
All India	5.60	6.03	5.66

Source: NSSO.

per cent in rural poor of the country in 1983. This share increased to 55 per cent in 1993-94 and further to 61 per cent in 2004-05. Similarly, the share of seven states (Bihar, Karnataka, MP, Maharashtra, Rajasthan, Tamil Nadu and UP) in urban poor rose from 61.6 per cent in 1983 to 70 per cent in 1993-94 and to 76 per cent in 2004-05.

Large number of studies in this regard throw light that regional disparity in rural and urban areas has widened. State domestic product growth rates have indicated that there is a fair degree of variation. While some states have witnessed rapid and phenomenal growth, the rest lagged behind the all India growth rate.

The comparative average growth rates of State Domestic Product for some states as indicated in the above table show that AP, Assam and Kerala have less than 5 per cent growth during 1980s against All India growth rate of 5.6 per cent per annum. However, there was a comparatively balanced regional growth during 1980s, even though the disparity widened across the states. In 1990s while Gujarat and Maharashtra grew at over 8 per cent, A.P., Punjab and other poor states registered much lower growth than India average.

Poor states like Bihar, UP, Orissa, Assam have witnessed less foreign capital and performed badly with SDP growth rate less than 4 per cent per annum. Apart from lack of investment, poor infrastructure combined with poor governance might have also restrained growth in these states. The coefficient of variation of average growth rates among states has jumped from 0.14 in the 1980s to 0.29 in the 1990s. This reflects an uneven regional development in the post-reform years. Ahluwalia's study made in 2000 shows that there is a significant degree of dispersion in growth across states.

The growth of per capita SDP for some states indicates that the regional disparity in standard of living has increased in 1990s. While Assam recorded the lowest per capita SDP growth at 1.7 per cent per annum, Tamil Nadu the highest at 4.8 per cent during 1980s. In 1990s the disparity rate has again widened from 0.7 per cent for Assam to as high as 6.7 per cent for Goa and 6.4 per cent for Gujarat. While standard of living improved faster in 1990s in comparison to 1980s as most states, the opposite happened in Assam, Bihar, Orissa, Punjab, Rajasthan and UP. Due to higher growth of population in these states disparity in standard of living has gone up. Generally southern states performed better than eastern and central states.

The regional disparity becomes even more serious if we consider its relationship with population growth. Table 2 indicates the growth rates of population in terms of per cent per annum.

Some of the states like Bihar, UP, Rajsthan and Orissa have upward growth of population, which has a great impact on the economic growth. If we correlate the population growth and economic growth we find that the correlation coefficient reverses the sign and becomes –0.57, which is a significant at one per cent level. It appears that economic growth and population growth have become inversely related in India in recent period. Those states have higher population growth registered low economic growth.

TABLE 2

States	*1980-90*	*1990-2000*	*1980-2000*
A.P.	2.19	1.72	2.03
Assam	2.14	2.13	2.20
Bihar	2.16	2.14	2.15
Goa	1.82	1.30	1.38
Gujarat	2.02	1.76	1.86
Haryana	2.46	2.19	2.36
H.P.	1.82	1.71	1.76
Karnataka	2.03	1.49	1.75
Kerala	1.42	1.35	1.34
M.P.	2.38	1.98	2.28
Maharashtra	2.29	1.97	2.21
Orissa	1.82	1.81	1.84
Punjab	1.88	1.91	1.92
Rajasthan	2.64	2.06	2.35
T.N.	1.48	.98	1.25
U.P.	2.33	1.75	2.10
W.B.	2.20	1.72	2.09
All India	2.16	1.88	2.04

Source: NSSO.

Regional disparity can also be viewed on the basis of poverty trend in different areas of the country. There are differences between rural and urban areas regarding trends in poverty at all India level. Some of the states are having very high poverty ratios for the total population. In 2004-05, it was more than 40 per cent in Orissa and Bihar and between 30 and 40 per cent in MP and UP and between 25 per cent and 30 per cent in Maharashtra, TN, Karnataka and WB. It may be noted that Orissa and Bihar's poverty level was almost six times that of Punjab in 2004-05. Even urban poverty was 30 per cent or more in Bihar, MP, Orissa and UP in 2004-05. The number of rural poor increased in three states, viz. MP, Orissa and UP in 2004-05 as compared to 1993-94. A group of four states comprising Bihar, MP, Orissa and UP had a share of 49.8 per cent in the rural poor of the country in 1983. This share increased to 55 per cent in 1993-94 and further to 61 per cent in 2004-05. Similarly the share of seven states (Bihar, Karnataka, Maharashtra, Rajasthan, Tamil Nadu and UP) in urban poor rose from 61.6 per cent in 1983 to 70 per cent in 1993-94 and to 76 per cent in 2004-05. Poverty for total population (rural+urban) is getting concentrated in five states, Bihar, UP, Orissa, MP and Maharashtra, their share being 65 per cent of the total poor in 2004-05.

TABLE 3

Absolute Number of Poor in Millions

States	*1983*	*1993-94*	*2004-05*
A.P.	16.82	15.47	11.85
Assam	7.65	9.59	5.87
Bihar	46.39	50.89	50.49
Gujarat	11.12	10.99	9.25
Haryana	3.11	4.32	3.27
H.P.	0.79	1.49	0.76
Jammu & Kashmir	1.51	1.41	0.54
Karnataka	15.24	15.74	15.34
Kerala	10.43	7.86	4.79
M.P.	27.30	29.91	32.96
Maharashtra	28.65	30.76	31.65
Orissa	18.07	16.22	18.41
Punjab	2.97	2.82	2.14
Rajasthan	13.88	13.34	13.49
T.N.	26.85	20.26	18.62
U.P.	55.22	61.51	63.92
W.B.	30.98	24.02	22.08
All India	324.34	324.55	315.48

TABLE 4

Growth Rates and Urban-Rural Differences in MPCE

	Rural		*Urban*	
States	*1983-94*	*1994-2005*	*1983-1994*	*1994-2005*
A.P.	1.02	1.09	0.02	2.49
Assam	-0.26	2.00	2.84	2.29
Bihar	0.62	1.23	1.62	1.57
Gujarat	0.39	1.02	1.32	3.17
Haryana	0.01	2.18	0.12	2.03
H.P.	-1.02	2.51	1.96	-0.07
Jammu & Kasmir	0.91	2.36	2.92	0.47
Karnataka	0.21	0.43	0.10	1.90
Kerala	0.86	3.80	1.71	2.45
M.P.	0.72	0.26	0.86	3.17
Maharashtra	1.09	1.00	0.90	1.17
Orissa	2.02	0.72	1.15	0.40
Punjab	-0.31	1.07	.88	3.26
Rajasthan	-0.54	0.49	0.43	1.51
T.N.	2.34	1.21	1.04	1.03
U.P.	0.36	1.03	1.81	1.60
W.B.	2.70	1.09	1.68	1.95
All India	0.83	1.16	1.43	1.94

Source: NSSO Report 508, December 2006.

The percentage of very poor is higher than all India level in these states. The table indicates that concentration of the poor in populated states, like UP, Bihar, AP, Orissa, Maharashtra and West Bengal is more.

The growth rate in monthly per capita expenditure (MPCE) was higher in 10 states in rural areas in post-reform period. The table indicates all such things clearly.

One of the concerns in the post-reform period relates to the widening disparities between rural and urban areas. Even inflation has made a significant impact on increasing the disparity of growth in different regions. The poorer regionswhich depend on primary sector has witnessed that the share of this sector has declined significantly over the last two decades. In Bihar the share of the primary sector, which was about 60 per cent in SDP in 1980s has now come down to 30 per cent in 2005-06.

No doubt the Economic Survey 2006-07 casts its eye, India is shining. Economy is growing at 9.2 per cent but up and down pattern in agriculture has made the regional disparity more vulnerable. States, which depend on agriculture, its growth pattern has been related with the agricultural growth. From 2001-02 to 2006-07 the sectoral real growth rates in GDP at factor cost shows that there is a wide variation in it. While in 2001-02 it was 6.3 per cent and in 2006-07 it registers only 2.7 per cent. This indicates that variation in agricultural growth had widened the regional disparity in economic development.

CONCLUSION

The regional disparity in growth rates becomes sharper in terms of per capita income. The poorer states have not only performed poorly but their failure in controlling the population has left them in worse condition. The growing regional disparity has become a matter of serious concern. Levels of living in backward regions tell a different story. A large number of people are living in abject poverty. It means economic growth is not evenly distributed all over the country.

With deregulation of private investment, faster growth in turn would induce more investment, and this in turn would further accentuate regional disparity. The problem is compounded by the negative relationship between population growth and income growth. Backward regions with higher population are not able to attract both public and private investments due to poor infrastructures as well as poor governance. Bihar is the burning example in this regard. Due to positive governance situation is fast changing here in Bihar in comparison to previous government.

Hence a pro-active public policy is significant to induce investments in backward regions either through public investment or through fiscal incentives. Efforts should be made to restrict or contain population and quality of governance should be given more positive attention at state level. The inverse relationship between population growth and income growth at the state level in the recent years can become an explosive issue not only economically but also politically. States with higher population growth and lower income growth would tend to have higher unemployment rate. Migration from poor region to well-off region can only partially mitigate this problem of unemployment and regional backwardness, rather large scale migration in a country with wide diversities in religion, language, caste and education levels can create socio-political problems. It is quite evident in regions and states.

If the inverse relationship between population growth and income growth persists it would have a serious impact between regions in terms of distribution of resources. In our country allocation of resources through Finance Commission is a pointer in this regard. The per capita transfer of resource from the Finance Commission as well as the Planning Commission was lower for many of the less developed states. However in 11th Finance Commission situation has improved in favour of less developed states, but in a federal democratic country there are limits to such statutory transfers, particularly because many of our developed states too are poor in absolute terms.

The simmering unrest in several less developed regions of the country indicates that without major initiatives at national level, the regional disparities in development, may accentuate further to crisis proportions threatening social harmony and national integrity, apart from depriving the country for sustainable development. Even the Mid-term appraisal of the 10th Plan indicates that regional disparity is a cause for concern. To bring regional balance is the need of the time. The Mid-Term Appraisal projects several proposals to strengthen the resource position of backward states, such as raising the royalty for the poorer states which are rich in forests and minerals, helping them through better project preparation. By refocusing Bharat Nirman project for rural infrastructure development as well as central sector expenditure from different ministries for development of the less developed regions of the country. Apart from this the solution of such difficult situation would be to accelerate reforms in backward regions for attaining a balanced regional growth.

References

Ahluwalia, Montek S. (2002), *State Level Performance Under Ecnomic Reforms in India*. Oxford University Press, New Delhi.

Ahluwalia, Montek S. (2000), "Economic Performance of States in Post-reform Period", *Economic and Political Weekly*, May 6.

Barro, Robert J. (1991), Economic Growth in a Cross Section of Countries-*Quarterly Journal of Economics*, 106, May.

Bhattacharya, B.B. and Arup Mitra (1990), Excess Growth of Tertiary Sector in Indian Economy, *Economic and Political Weekly*, Nov. 3.

Drez, Jean and Sen, Amartya (2002), *India: Development and Participation*, Oxford University Press, New Delhi.

Rao, C.H. Hanumanth and S. Mahendra Dev (2003), Economic Reforms and Challenges Ahead: An Overview.

Reddy, G.R. (2005), Twelfth Finance Commission and Backward States-Centre of Economic and Social Studies.

Sen, Abhijit and Himanshu (2004), Poverty and Inequality in India, *Economic and Political Weekly*, Vol. 39, No. 38.

Sundaram, K. and S.D. Tendulkar (2003), Poverty in India-*Economic and Political Weekly*, Nov. 15.

Economic Survey, 2006-07, Ministry of Finance, Government of India.

13

Health Situation in India: Regional and Gender Disparities

Arun Kumar Thakur and Rabindra Nath Ojha

Health, defined as a state of complete physical, mental and social well-being by the World Health Organisation, is of crucial instrumental value in the development process apart from being of intrinsic importance to the individual. Good health has implication not only for quality of life but also for production of economic goods and services contributing to the national wealth. It is not only a meahs to achieve economic development, but an end in itself. Poor health limits the productive capacity of the affected person including his ability to enjoy good health. According to World Development Report 1993; improved health contributes to economic growth in four ways :

(i) It reduces production losses caused by worker illness.
(ii) It permits the use of natural resources that had been totally or nearly inaccessible because of disease.

(iii) It inceases the enrolment of children in schools and makes them better able to learn.

(iv) It frees for alternative uses of resources that would otherwise have to be spent on treating illness.

The report further adds that the economic gains are relatively greater for poor people, who are typically most handicapped by ill health and who stand to gain the most from the development of underutilised natural resources.

Health can be measured in different ways. One of the easiest to understand and most commonly used indications is the difference between life and death. Infant Mortality Rate, Under 5 Mortality Rate, Death Rate, Life Expectancy, etc. can be easily quantified and understood. Hence we will use these indicators to understand the problem, however, these indicators are not commonly accepted as the best as they present certain weakness.

HEALTH SITUATION IN COUNTRY

Since independence, there has been an improvement in the health status of the Indian population; though India is still for away from its objectives of ensuring good health to its citizens as one third of its population is poor, illiterate, malnourished and without proper health facility. Lack of proper health institutions as also easy accessibility to the available services, lower mother and child's nutrutional status and other socio-economic and demographic hindrances are responsible for poor health of mass of the population in country. A substantial failure of Indian public health policy has been in controlling the relatively high incidence of infectious or communicable diseases, which are normally associated with low levels of sanitation and public hygiene, poor quality of drinking water and undernutrition. Amongst the countries with low human development, India has the highest percentage of pregnant women having anemia. Thils in combination with low age at first pregnancy for a large number of women puts the infant at considerable risk of loss of life apart from hampering the growth and development of the child.

It is clear from above discussion that the health status of our country is far from satisfactory. The health status in rural areas is much worse compared to urban areas. There are considerable inter-state variations in health indicators. Following table shows some selected indicators of health development in India-statewise :

TABLE I

Differentials in Health Status

State	% of Population below the Poverty Line		Death Rate	Infant Mortality Rate	Rural Infant Mortality Rate	Maternal Mortality/ Lakh
	1987-88	1999-00	2000	2000	1998	2000
Punjab	13.2	6.2	7.4	52	58	–
Maharashtra	40.4	25.0	7.5	48	58	135
Haryana	16.6	8.7	7.5	67	72	-
Kerala	31.8	12.7	6.4	14	15	87
Tamil Nadu	43.4	21.1	7.9	51	58	79
Madhya Pradesh	43.1	37.4	10.3	87	103	498
Uttar Pradesh	41.5	31.2	10.3	83	89	707
Orissa	55.6	47.1	10.5	96	101	498
Rajasthan	35.2	15.3	8.5	79	87	607
Bihar	52.1	42.5	8.8	62	68	707
India	38.9	26.1	8.5	68	77	408
Rural	–	27.09	9**	75*	–	–
Urban	–	23.62	6.3*	44*	–	–

Source : Census of India, 2001.

Ministry of Health and Family Welfare, Government of India, New Delhi.

It is clear from above table that :

1. The health status in rural areas is much worse compared to urban areas. According to latest report the rural Infant Mortality Rate in 2001 was 72 whereas in urban areas it was 42. Low birth weight has been identified as a major cause of

infant mortality in India; and almost a third of the children born belong to the category of low birth weight babies.

2. There are considerable inter-state variations in health indicators. Kerala emerges as the example of a state which indicates higher rate of health development whereas Madhya Pradesh, Uttar Pradesh, Orissa and Bihar are lagging far behind.
3. There exist not only rural urban and inter-state variations in health indicators but is much worse for rural women. Gender equality and empowerment of women is recognised globally as a key element to achieve progress in all areas. In India maternal morbidity and mortality is highest if we compare it with developed countries and even with most of the developing countries. Maternal morbidity and mortality affect not just the mother but the entire family. A majority of young women belonging to the lower socio-economic group in India is undernourished.
4. Development of children represent nation's greatest resource for the future but the health status of children is also poor in our country. Infant and early childhood mortality data reflect the extent of awareness and knowledge of mothers about different aspects related to health and nutrition needs of children. They also reflect the extent of immunisation of children, the availability of health services, the food availability and distribution patterns in the families, accessibility to safe drinking water and sanitary living conditions and the extent to which major causes of child morbidity and mortality have been tackled. while malnutrition is high among children, it is even higher among female children because of tradition and social practices leading to discrimination against girls.

HEALTH FOR ALL AND GOVERNMENT INITIATIVE

The Government's initiative for health for all is a move in the right direction. The Government of India has launched a National Rural Health Mission (NRHM) on 12th April 2005; with objectives to provide integrated, comprehensive and effective primary healthcare to the unprivileged and vulnerable sections of the society especially women and children by improving access, availability and quality of public health services.

Now the Government has taken timely note of India's abysmally poor health indicators. The NRHM objectives indicates the motivation in part of Government to correct the rural-urban, inter-state and gender inequalities in health as a priority. No country, whose 40% population lives in abject poverty with minimal health, hygiene, safe drinking water, educational facilities and without much law, order or justice can ever shine and develop. United Nations Human Development Report (UNHDR) 2005 states that India does well on economic growth but poorly on human development. High infant and maternal mortality rates, skewed sex ratio, rising rural unemployment and stagnating agricultural wages are some areas of grave concern. Some recent studies have shown that contrary to earlier perceptions as high growth cannot be sustained when income gaps are huge. Economic growth is meaningless without proportional social development. Most of the Government operated rural health sub-centres, primary health centres and Anganwadi centres are on the verge of collapse.

UPA-led Government consecutive budget shows that attempts have been made to develop social sector and initiatives have been made in this direction. There are eight flagship schemes for social sectors which would be large extert benefit rural development. The total allocation for these schemes were Rs. 34,927 crore in 2005-06 and this stepped up to Rs. 50,015 crore, representing an increase of Rs. 15,088 crore, i.e. 43.2 per cent in 2006-07. The provision for the National Rural Health Mission has been increased to Rs. 8,207 crore from Rs. 6,553 crore in above mentioned period. The total allocation for the above mentioned eight development programmes has been raised from Rs. 50,015 crore to Rs. 56,494 crore in 2007-08. Out of which 15,291 crore will be spent on health and family welfare, i.e. 22 per cent higher than previous year. According to Dr. Siddhartha Roy, Economic Advisor, Tata Group, "One of the major positive features of the Budget has been its prime focus on education and healthcare. The Budget aims at improving access to social services and provides a social safetynet". All districts in the country will complete preparation of District Health Action Plans by March 2007 and the allocation for the NRHM has been increased from Rs. 8,207 crore in 2006-07 to Rs. 9,947 crore in 2007-08. The allocation for Integrated Child Development Services scheme has been increased from Rs. 4,087 crore in 2006-07 to Rs. 4,761 crore in 2007-08.

SUGGESTIONS FOR IMPROVEMENT IN HEALTH STATUS

But a close look at them, however, gives the impression that most of rural development schemes are repackaged versions of ongoing schemes. Its achievement will mostly depend on qualitative difference in the delivery system at operational level. More funds for education, health, nutrition, safe drinking water may not necessary mean more education, more health, more nutrition and better safe drinking water. What matters is how the money is spent.

The importance of community participation forms the cornerstone of the concept of primary health care to achieve the goal of 'Health for All'. For the success of the program it is essential to encourage and ensure full community participation through the effective propagation of relevant information through which individuals, families and community can assume responsibility for their health and well-being. Regular interactive sessions with mothers, parents group, old age persons added by audio-visual demonstration along with household contact and monitoring, development of local resource groups, etc. should be incorporated.

Scrutiny of various health programmes show that partnership and network initiatives can alone ensure lasting impacts with focus on communities especially the deprived sections of society. So the Government should take initiatives in this regard for success of the programme.

accounts for one-fourth of India's National Income and one-third of India's workforce directly engaged for its livelihood.

Agriculture is the foundation of our economy which occupies a place of pride in the country's progress. It is the main stay of any developing country of the World and performances of other sectors are largely dependent on the progress of agriculture. Agriculture is the backbone of our economy in terms of Gross National Produce and largest means of livelihood of mass population. Since Independence, agriculture contributes to the largest share of GDP, though the share is declining from 48.6 per cent (1950-51) to 21 per cent of GDP at present.

Agriculture provides livelihood, employment, social justice, prosperity, peace and harmony in the society and it is a major source of raw material for many industries. Agriculture provides employment to 64 per cent and earns 13 per cent of India's foreign exchange. Agriculture sector is considered as dynamic leading sector of our all economic development of the country. It is a powerful tool for poverty alleviation, employment and anti-migration force from rural to urban area.

Nobel Laureate W. Arther Lewis focused on two sector models of economic development that emphasised on the structural transformation of primary subsistence economy. According to this model industrial expansion with an *"Agricultural Surplus"* stimulating industrial growth by means of cheap food and surplus labour.

Agriculture sector and rural economy are the dynamic path of development of rural areas without which rural development cannot sustain. Performance of economy is crucially dependent on agriculture for food, and fiber requirement of 70 per cent of mass resides in rural area.

SCENARIO OF AGRICULTURAL DEVELOPMENT

Indian agriculture has only performed well but has also shown improvement in its performance. India inherited a stagnant agriculture at the time of Independence in 1947.

TABLE 1

Key Figure of Indian Agriculture

1.	Total geographical area	328.7 Million Hect.
2.	Gross cropped area (2000-01)	187 Million Hect.
3.	Net cropped area (2000-01)	141.4 Million Hect.
4.	Gross irrigated area (2000-01)	74.14 Million Hect.
5.	Net irrigated area	54.68 Million Hect.
6.	Drought prone area	260.00 Million Hect.
7.	Flood prone area	40.00 Million Hect.
8.	Area under high yielding varieties	116.00 Million Hect.
9.	Fertiliser consumption (2005-06)	NPK—20.67 Million tonnes 108 Kg./Hect. $N:P_2O_5; K_2O$ Ratio—5.2:2.1:1
10.	Operational holdings (million Nos.)	1.4%
11.	Contribution in GDP (2005)	21%

Source: FAI Statistics.

Green Revolution

The changes in agricultural growth in the country can be observed in the three distinctive phases:

(a) Pre-green revolution phase
(b) Green revolution phase
(c) Diversification and commercialisation phase

Agricultural production in the country has shown a remarkable growth in food grain production since green revolution.

TABLE 2

Year	*Food grain production (MT)*
1950-51	50.80
1955-56	60.90
1960-61	80.20 (GR)
1970-71	108
1990-91	176
1999-00	209
2001-02	211
2003-04	213
2004-05	204
2005-06	208 (Provisional)

Source: FAI Statistics.

TABLE 3

Compound Growth (Agriculture)

Year	*Compound growth rate %age*
1951-61	2.62
1964-65	2.72
1971-81	1.70
1981-91	3.90
1992-93	2.20
1995-96	1.65
2003-04	3.13
2004-05	2.30
2005-06	1.80

Source: Economic Survey, GOI.

TABLE 4

Total Cropped Area and Population (Million Hect.)

Year	*Total Cropped Area (Million Hect.)*	*Population (In Million)*
1951-52	133.20	363
1960-61	152.77	432
1970-71	173.00	684
1990-91	185.00	846
2001-02	193.00	1027

Source: Economic Survey, GOI.

Green Revolution

The Spectacular Progress made in agriculture sector since inception of new technologies in the mid-sixties, has changed the agricultural scenario of the country from a stable of "begging bowl" to the stage of self-reliance in food production.

The grow of food production during four decades has been shown in the Table 2 which has been associated with well known "Green Revolution".

Agriculture in fact needs to be termed as the largest industries in India. Green revolution has three main factors which accelerated food grain production and made the country from sip to mouth to self-sufficient in food grain production. Three key factors were: (a) seéds (HYV), (b) fertilizers, and (c) irrigation.

Fertiliser

Dr. Norman, E. Borlogue has rightly said on green revolution "if high yielding wheat and rice varieties were catalysts than that ignited the green revolution is the 'chemical fertilisers' was the fuel that powered its forceful thrust."

Fertiliser has played and would continue to play a vital role in increasing agricultural production in the country. Fertiliser being the key input in food grain production contributes more than 50 per cent increase alone as a single input.

India is bountiful and blessed by mature through diverse agro-climatic conditions and having vast resources, green revolution was the boon to Indian agriculture. Fertiliser use in India started in 1920s and was very limited during late 40s synthetic Ammonia plants developed at Sindri (Jharkhand) during 60s sow a rapid growth in indigenous fertiliser production of Nitrogenous and Phosphatic and complexes. Potassic fertilisers are not manufactured in India and being imported only.

There is an increase in population @ 2 per cent annually whereas agricultural production growth rate is 1.83 per cent only. It is expected that our population will be 1.29 crore by 2012. To feed this population 337.3 million tonnes of foodgrains will be required for which 28 million tonnes of N, P_2O_5 and K_2O to be added to overcome with this challenges. Fertiliser, therefore has to be stepped up in the coming years particularly in the low consuming areas to ensure sustainable food security besides increase in other agricultural crops. To achieve the 9 per cent GDP growth 4 per cent growth in Agriculture annually is required only then this challenges can be meet out to feed up the vast growing population in future.

COMPARATIVE STUDY OF LEVELS OF AGRICULTURAL DEVELOPMENTS IN NORTHERN REGION AND EASTERN REGION

Though there are a vast difference in agro-climatic, credit facilities, irrigation and other regional disparities which affect the fertiliser consumption among the northern and eastern states. For Agricultural Development point of view the northern regional states comprises of: (a) Haryana, (2) Punjab, (3) Uttar Pradesh, (4) Uttaranchal, (5) J&K, (6) Delhi, and (7) Himanchal Pradesh. In the eastern regional states comprise of: (a) Assam, (2) Bihar, (3) Jharkhand, (4) Orissa, (5) West Bengal, and (6) North-Eastern States (Arunachal, Manipur, Meghalya, Mizoram, Nagaland, Sikkim and Tripura).

For comparative study three major states from Northern Region comprising of: (1) Uttar Pradesh, (2) Punjab, (3) Haryana and from Eastern states: (1) Bihar, (2) West Bengal, (3) Orissa will be taken for the study.

Uttar Pradesh (U.P.)—U.P. is the largest state of India, covers 2,94,000 KM^2 having different type of land—alluvial, clay, sandy, rocks, mixed, red and black soils. U.P. is also known as most populous state having abouot 13.91 crores population (1991 Census) which has crossed 16.60 in 2001 and projected to increase 24.29 crores by 2016 when India's population will be 126.35 crores during that period. About 20 per cent of the population will be in U.P. U.P. is having 14 per cent share of Gross cropped area of the country and 21per cent share in N, P, K consumption of all India's total fertiliser consumption.

Scenario of Food Supply in U.P.

Fertiliser consumption in U.P. (2004-05) 128.20 Kg./ Hect. N, P, K ratio of U.P. is 16.2 : 5 : 1

Northern regional states nutrients consumption has increased by 9.6 per cent over the previous year.

U.P. continued to be the highest fertiliser consuming state in the country. Total consumption of fertiliser nutrients has increased 3.310 million tonnes (2004-05) to 3.660 million tonnes (2005-06) which is 10.80 per cent increase. N, P, K use

TABLE 5

Consumption of Fertilisers (N, P, K) Vs. Food Grain Production (1951 to 2005-06)

Year		N	P_2O_5 ('000 tonnes)	K_2O	Production of foodgrains (MT)
1950-51		55.0	8.8	6	50.8
1951-52		58.7	6.9	—	52.0
1952-53		57.8	4.6	3.3	59.2
1953-54	I Plan	89.3	8.3	7.5	69.8
1954-55		94.8	15.0	11.1	68.0
1955-56		107.5	13.0	10.3	66.9
1956-57		123.1	15.9	14.8	69.9
1957-58		149.0	21.9	12.8	64.3
1958-59	II Plan	172.0	29.5	22.4	77.1
1959-60		229.3	53.9	21.3	76.7
1960-61		211.7	53.1	29.0	82.0
1961-62		249.8	60.5	28.0	82.7
1962-63	III Plan	333.0	82.8	36.4	80.2
1963-64		376.1	116.5	50.6	80.6
1964-65		555.2	148.7	69.3	89.4
1965-66		574.8	132.5	77.3	72.4
1966-67		737.8	248.6	114.2	74.2
1967-68		1034.6	334.8	169.6	95.1
1968-69		1208.6	382.1	170.0	94.0
1969-70		1356.0	416.0	210.0	99.5
1970-71		1479.3	541.0	236.3	108.4
1971-72	IV Plan	1798.0	558.2	300.6	105.2
1972-73		1839.0	581.3	347.6	97.0
1973-74		1829.0	649.7	359.8	104.7
1974-75		1765.7	471.5	336.1	99.8
1975-76		2148.6	466.8	278.3	121.0
1976-77	V Plan	2456.9	634.7	319.2	111.2
1977-78		2913.0	866.6	506.2	126.4
1978-79		3419.5	1106.0	591.5	131.9
1979-80		3498.1	1150.9	606.4	109.7
1980-81		3678.1	1213.6	623.9	129.6
1981-82	(Feb./January)	4068.7	1322.3	676.2	133.3
1982-83	(April/March) VI Plan	4242.5	1432.7	726.3	129.5
1983-84		5204.4	1730.3	775.4	152.4
1984-85		5486.1	1886.4	838.5	145.5
1985-86		5660.8	2005.2	808.1	150.4
1986-87		5716.0	2078.9	850.0	143.4
1987-88	VII Plan	5716.8	2187.1	880.5	140.4
1988-89		7251.0	2720.7	1068.4	169.9

1989-90		7385.9	3014.2	1168.0	171.0
1990-91		7997.2	3221.0	1328.0	176.4
1991-92		8046.3	3321.2	1360.6	168.4
1992-93		8426.8	2843.8	8839	179.5
1993-94		8788.3	2669.3	908.7	184.3
1994-95	VIII Plan	9507.1	2931.7	1124.8	191.5
1995-96		9822.8	2897.5	1155.8	180.4
1996-97		10301.8	2976.8	1029.6	199.4
1997-98		10901.8	3913.6	1372.5	192.3
1998-99		11353.8	4112.2	1331.5	203.6
1999-00		11592.5	4797.9	1678.4	209.8
2000-01	IX Plan	10920.2	4214.6	1567.5	196.8
2001-02		11310.2	4382.4	1667.1	212.0
2002-03		10474.1	4018.8	1601.2	182.6
2003-04		11076.3	4123.8	1597.6	212.1
2004-05		11640.4	4479.1	1995.7	204.6
2005-06		11330	4.190		206-210

Source: FAI Statistics.

TABLE 6

N, P, K Use Ratio (India)

Year	*NPK Use Ratio*
1951-52	79 : 0.9 : 1
1961-62	8.9 : 2.2 : 1
1971-72	6.0 : 1.9 : 1
1991-92	5.9 : 2.4 : 1
2001-02	6.8 : 2.6 : 1
2002-03	6.5 : 2.5 : 1
2003-04	6.9 : 2.6 : 1
2004-05	5.7 : 2.2 : 1
2005-06	5.2 : 2.1 : 1

Source: FAI Statistics.

ratio changed from 13.2 : 4.1 : 1 during 2004-05 to 11.9: 4: 1 during 2005-06. Fertiliser consumption per hect. of nutrient use has increased from 141 Kg. in 2005-06 from 128 Kg. 2004-05. Agricultural credit has also increased 14.7 billion (2005-06) from 13.60 billion in 2004-05. Total sales point increased from 65,124 (2004-05) to 67,339 (2005-06).

Punjab

Punjab occupies 1.5 per cent of total geographical area and contributes 23.40 million tonnes of food grains and

TABLE 7

State-wise Consumption of Primary Nutrient and their Ratio (2003-04)

Rank	*State*	*N, P_2O_5, K_2O (Kg./Hect)*	*N, P_2O_5, K_2O*
1.	Punjab	184	31 : 9 : 1
2.	Haryana	167	48 : 15 : 1
3.	Andhra Pradesh	136	5 : 2 : 1
4.	UP	126	15 : 5 : 1
5.	WB	122	2.5 : 1.3 : 1
6.	Tamil Nadu	112	2 : 1 : 1
7.	Gujarat	95	9.3 : 5 : 1
8.	Bihar and Jharkhand	80	2.3 : 3 : 1
9.	Karnataka	74	2.6 : 1 : 1
10.	J&K	71	16 : 6 : 1
11.	Maharashtra	65	5 : 2.4 : 1
12.	Kerala	63	1.3 : 0.6 : 1
13.	M.P.	55	12 : 7 : 1
14.	Assam	46	7 : 1 : 1
15.	Chhattisgarh	46	8 : 3 :1
16.	Orissa	41	4.1 : 4 : 1
17.	Rajasthan	40	49 : 17 : 1

Source: Indian Journal of Fertiliser, Dec. 2005.

contributes 59 per cent of wheat and 52 per cent of rice in the Central pool of the country. Punjab has recorded 8 per cent growth in total nutrient consumption from 1.563 million tonnes (2004-05) to 1.688 million tonnes during 2005-06. N, P, K use ratio changed from 27.8 : 7.3 : 1 (2004-05) to 19.8: 5.8 : 1 (2005-06). Fertiliser nutrient consumption per hectare has also increased 192.5 kg. (2004-05) to 208 kg. per hectare (2005-06). Agriculture credit has increased from 337.9 million (2004-05) to 412.8 million (2005-06), total number of fertiliser sales point increased from 10,469 (2004-05) to 10,690 during 2005-06.

Haryana

Fertiliser consumption has increased by 7 per cent over the previous year from 1.05 MT (2004-05) to 1.129 MT. N, P, K use ratio narrowed from 40.3 : 12.3 : 1 during 2004-05 to 29.6 : 8.8 : 1 (2005-06). Fertiliser nutrients increased from 166.2 kg./hect. (2004-05) to 178.6 kg. (2005-06).

TABLE 8

All India State-wise Consumption of Fertiliser (NPK Kg/ Hect.)

Zone/State	2003-04				2004-05			
	N	P_2O_5	K_2O	Total	N	P_2O_5	K_2O	Total
East	*46.8*	*15.1*	*10.5*	*72.5*	*48.3*	*17.2*	*12.6*	*78.1*
Arunachal Pradesh	1.6	0.7	0.4	2.7	1.7	0.7	0.4	2.8
Assam	22.8	13.0	12.0	47.8	19.7	12.9	9.4	41.9
Bihar	79.0	5.8	3.3	88.1	78.4	9.0	5.3	92.7
Jharkhand	32.1	20.1	2.3	54.5	36.5	20.6	2.1	59.1
Manipur	105.1	14.7	6.5	126.3	78.9	11.1	4.4	94.4
Meghalaya	9.9	6.6	0.6	17.1	10.3	6.9	0.6	17.8
Mizoram	5.2	4.2	3.1	12.5	5.2	4.3	2.5	12.0
Nagaland	0.9	0.7	0.3	1.9	0.8	0.6	0.2	1.6
Orissa	23.9	7.6	5.6	37.1	25.4	8.9	6.1	40.4
Sikkim	2.2	1.1	–	3.3	3.3	1.4	–	4.7
Tripura	17.7	6.4	5.6	29.7	22.1	6.1	3.6	31.8
West Bengal	59.5	31.1	23.5	114.1	64.5	34.7	29.7	129.0
North	*103.4*	*32.2*	*5.3*	*140.9*	*104.6*	*31.0*	*6.0*	*141.6*
Haryana	121.6	37.6	2.5	161.7	124.9	38.1	3.1	
Himachal Pradesh	32.3	9.1	7.5	48.9	32.1	8.9	7.4	48.4
Jammu and Kashmir	50.5	18.3	3.2	72.0	45.6	19.5	2.9	68.0
Punjab	146.5	41.9	4.8	193.2	150.6	39.7	5.4	195.7
Uttar Pradesh	92.0	29.7	5.9	127.6	92.6	28.6	7.0	128.2
Uttaranchal	76.4	23.0	9.3	108.7	69.5	17.4	6.2	93.1
Chandigarh	3.3	–	–	3.3	3.3	–	–	3.3
Delhi	20.8	9.4	0.2	30.4	10.4	0.4	–	10.8
South	*62.8*	*27.3*	*20.1*	*110.2*	*71.4*	*34.6*	*26.8*	*132.8*
Andhra Pradesh	89.3	37.2	18.8	145.3	90.7	42.3	22.9	155.9
Karnataka	42.3	20.6	16.0	78.9	56.2	31.2	23.4	110.8

Kerala	28.5	13.0	22.6	64.1	29.5	14.0	23.9	67.4
Tamil Nadu	60.8	25.5	28.3	114.6	77.5	33.9	41.4	152.8
Pondicherry	565.4	253.1	193.8	1012.3	586.7	258.7	232.6	1078
A & N Islands	7.3	7.0	1.4	15.7	6.1	3.9	1.6	11.6
West	*36.3*	*16.3*	*4.2*	*56.8*	*39.4*	*19.3*	*5.9*	*64.6*
Gujarat	64.1	23.8	6.8	94.7	70.2	27.6	9.0	106.8
Madhya Pradesh	30.8	18.3	2.6	51.7	32.4	20.6	2.9	55.9
Chhattisgarh	29.2	11.3	3.7	44.2	41.2	17.3	6.3	64.8
Maharashtra	38.1	18.4	7.7	64.2	42.6	23.5	11.5	77.6
Rajasthan	27.1	9.8	0.5	37.4	26.1	9.8	0.8	36.7
Goa	16.6	9.2	10.5	36.3	15.2	8.8	10.3	34.3
Daman and Diu	–	–	–	–	2.0	–	–	2.0
D & N Haveli	21.7	12.3	1.7	35.7	22.3	11.7	1.3	35.3
All India	*58.2*	*21.7*	*8.4*	*88.3*	*61.6*	*24.3*	*10.8*	*96.7*

Source: FAI Statistics.

Eastern Regional States: The total nutrient consumption increased by 16.3 per cent in the eastern region.

Bihar

The population of Bihar is 8.3 crores (1991) and 89 per cent population resides in rural area. Total geographical area 579 lakh hectare. Bihar having 2.8 per cent of India's total irrigated area 33.5 lakh hectare and share and most populous state of India. Total net area sown 56 lac hectare and gross cropped area is 79 lakh hectare.

Fertiliser Consumption: The consumption of total fertiliser nutrients in the state recorded sharp increase of 29.9 per cent from 0.732 million tonnes during 2004-05 to 0.951 millioon tonnes during 2005-06. The consumption of all the three nutrients (N, P, K) has increased in 2005-06. N, P, K use ratio has reduced from 14.7 : 1.7 : 1 during 2004-05 to 6.1 : 1.3 : 1 during 2005-06.

Kharif : Rabi share in total consumption marginally changed from 42.58 during (2004-05) to 41.59 during (2005-

TABLE 9

Season-wise Share of Consumption of N, P_2O_5 and K_2O by States - Kharif

Zone/State	*2002-03*				*2003-04*				*2004-05 (P)*			
	N	*P_2O_5*	*K_2O*	*Total*	*N*	*P_2O_5*	*K_2O*	*Total*	*N*	*P_2O_5*	*K_2O*	*Total*
East	*48*	*43*	*40*	*45*	*49*	*40*	*38*	*46*	*48*	*37*	*35*	*43*
Arunachal Pradesh	44	21	20	33	55	25	36	44	58	25	36	46
Assam	51	51	49	50	49	51	48	50	47	44	50	47
Bihar	45	48	56	46	49	27	13	46	47	23	8	42
Jharkhand	69	62	52	66	70	67	52	68	68	58	50	64
Manipur	76	70	57	74	74	72	71	73	65	69	43	65
Meghalaya	57	56	50	57	61	60	56	60	54	61	28	56
Mizoram	54	58	56	56	56	54	50	54	56	55	60	56
Nagaland	48	48	40	47	70	68	60	68	55	55	43	53
Orissa	75	70	64	73	74	68	68	72	73	64	64	70
Sikkim	69	48	–	54	48	47	–	48	70	61	–	68
Tripura	45	33	43	42	49	28	21	39	44	36	41	42
West Bengal	37	33	33	35	37	30	32	34	36	29	32	33
North	*43*	*29*	*29*	*39*	*44*	*32*	*33*	*41*	*44*	*25*	*39*	*40*
Haryana	32	25	41	31	38	25	51	35	40	25	59	37
Himachal Pradesh	53	17	12	39	52	17	11	39	51	19	13	39
Jammu and Kashmir	50	47	12	49	46	41	52	45	49	40	12	45
Punjab	47	34	61	45	48	39	58	46	45	28	59	42
Uttar Pradesh	43	28	21	39	44	31	24	40	44	24	34	39
Uttaranchal	54	28	38	48	52	36	46	48	51	30	28	46

Chandigarh	50	–	–	50	–	–	–	–	100	–	–	100
Delhi	21	20	–	21	24	10	100	20	17	100	–	20
South	*48*	*48*	*48*	*48*	*45*	*45*	*47*	*45*	*49*	*51*	*49*	*50*
Andhra Pradesh	46	48	45	47	47	44	44	46	49	48	46	48
Karnataka	59	53	58	57	52	51	53	52	61	59	57	60
Kerala	50	47	49	49	48	50	51	50	62	62	59	61
Tamil Nadu	35	40	42	37	31	36	44	35	34	44	41	38
Pondicherry	39	35	34	37	34	37	35	35	43	41	40	42 A
A&N Islands	46	36	31	40	41	45	50	43	67	94	71	76
West	*52*	*53*	*52*	*53*	*50*	*49*	*51*	*49*	*49*	*50*	*49*	*50*
Gujarat	45	48	36	45	49	50	39	48	48	53	41	49
Madhya Pradesh	37	40	46	39	30	32	36	31	38	41	44	39
Chhattisgarh	89	87	86	88	86	81	79	84	81	74	75	79
Maharashtra	62	59	54	60	63	56	58	60	60	56	50	57
Rajasthan	39	48	41	42	41	52	35	44	32	39	32	34
Goa	59	61	63	61	60	61	63	61	61	60	64	61
Daman and Diu	100	–	–	100	–	–	–	–	100	–	–	100 D
N Haveli	76	78	40	75	77	78	40	76	78	77	25	75
All India	*47*	*43*	*45*	*46*	*46*	*41*	*44*	*45*	*47*	*42*	*45*	*45*

Source: FAI Statistics.

TABLE 10

Target Growth Rate of GDP and Population and Agricultural Crops during 9th, 10th and 11th Plan Periods

Items	*Per Annum Growth (%)*		
	9th Plan 1996-97 to 2001-02	*10th Plan 2002-03 to 2006-07*	*2007-08 to 2011-12*
GDP	6.5	7.70	8.1
Population	1.57	1.57	1.45
Agricultural Crop	3.82	4.54	4.27
Rice	2.75	3.08	2.73
Course Cereals	2.20	2.40	2.43
Pulses	3.50	4.93	5.66
Oil Seeds	5.25	8.85	5.16
Sugarcane	4.00	6.16	6.07
Fruits and Vegetables	7.00	8.01	7.89
Tea	5.00	6.16	6.07
Coffee	5.00	6.16	6.07
Other Agril. Products	2.63	3.08	3.04
Total Agriculture	4.50	5.30	5.10

Source: Indian Journal of Fertilisers News, Dec. 2005.

TABLE 11

Projected Population, Foodgrains Production and Consumption, Input Use by the End of the 11th Plan

Item	*2011-12*
Population (Million)	1,196.4
Per capita foodgrains consumption (Kg.)	223.4
Foodgrains requirement (MT)	337.3
(a) Rice	128.2
(b) Wheat	130.4
(c) Course cereals	48.9
(d) Pulses	29.8
(e) Oil seeds	58.6
(f) Sugarcane	679.6
Gross area sown (Million hect)	219.2
Net area sown (Million hect.)	142.0
Gross Irrigated area (Million hect.)	105.5

Source: Indian Journal of Fertilisers News, Dec. 2005.

TABLE 12

Production of Foodgrains (Million Tonnes)

Year	*U.P.*	*India*
1951	11.7	50.8
1980-81	24.9	129.6
1995-96	3.4	180.4
1997-98	41.6	192.3
1998-99	40.4	203.5
1999-00	45.2	208.9
2001-02	43.1	211

Source: Statistical Outline of India, 2002-03 and Economic Survey, 2000-01.

06). The per hectare consumption of fertiliser nutrients increased significantly from 92.70 Kg./hect. during 2004-05 to 120.4 Kg. during 2005-06. Fertiliser sales point 1059 in co-operative and 45,000 in private during 2005-06.

West Bengal

Total fertiliser consumption nutrient-wise grew 7.9 per cent from 1.261 million tonnes (2004-05) to 1.36 million tonnes during (2005-06). The consumption of N, P_2O_5, K_2O has increased 2.5 per cent over the previous year. N, P, K use ratio has changed from 2.2:1.2:1 during 2004-05 to 2.0:1.3:1 during 2005-06.

Kharif : Rabi share in total fertilizers consumption changed marginally from 33:67 during 2004-05 to 34 : 66 during 2005-06.

Fertiliser nutrient consumption per hectare increased 129 Kg. per hect. (2004-05) to 139.2 Kg. per hect in 2005-06. Total number of fertiliser sales point increased from 37,771 duirng 2004-05 to 37,970 during 2005-06.

Orissa

Fertiliser consumption in Orissa has increased by 16.3 per cent from 0.355 million tonnes during 2004-05 to 0.413 million tonnes during 2005-06. The consumption of all three nutrients also increased. N, P, K use ratio changed from 4:2: 1.5:1 during 2004-05 to 3.8:1.3:1 during 2005-06.

West Bengal	Area	6069.1	434	6557.9
	Production	15256.7	961	16326.1
	Yield	2514	2215	2490
Orissa	Area	4500.0	7.0	4695.7
	Production	7148.4	10.6	7280.1
	Yield	1589	1514	1550

Source: FAI Statistics, 2002-03.

Kharif : Rabi share in total fertiliser consumption changed from 70:30 to 65:35 during 2005-06. Fertiliser nutrient consumption per hectare increased from 40.4 Kg. (2004-05) to 47 Kg. per hect. (2005-06). Fertiliser sales point remains unchanged 25,320 during 2005-06.

CONCLUSION AND RECOMMENDATIONS

Fertiliser has played and would continue to play a major role in enhancing crop production. Fertiliser is the key input for achieving higher target of growth in agriculture. Though, there are temporary disturbances in the growth of agricultural production such as weather, flood, drought and others but in spite of all that agricultural growth has been establised by the use of fertilizers.

The current fertiliser consumption of Northern States are higher than that of Eastern States. U.P. is having fertiliser consumption per hectare 141 Kg. whereas Bihar is having only 120 Kg. per hectare (2005-06). Fertiliser (N, P, K) nutrient consumption (2005-06) of U.P. is 3628 thousand tonnes whereas in Bihar only 949 thousand tonnes. U.P. continued to be the highest fertiliser consuming state about 21 per cent of total consumption of India.

N, P, K use ratio in U.P. is 11.9 : 4 : 1 (N:P:K) whereas in Bihar 6.1 : 1.3 : 1 only. Total foodgrains production of U.P. is 40,814 tonnes and average yield 2,356 Kg./hect. whereas in Bihar is 11,284 tonnes and average yield is 1779 Kg./hect.

This regional disparities and difference in Agricultural production and productivity in Northern States (e.g. U.P) and Eastern States (Bihar) is such more. Though the agro-climatic factors, availability of credit, use of new technology, marketing infrastructure affect the development.

The stimulation of agricultural growth of the State occupies a prime place in the overall development. To achieve the desired rate of growth in agriculture we have to increase the fertiliser consumption at par with the other fast growing States like, U.P., Haryana and Punjab. Availability credit, infrastructure of marketing and technical know-how to be provided to the farmers in co-ordination with agricultural university and extension department of government of Bihar.

Bihar being the flood prone area hence interlinking of rivers check dams and other irrigation schemes to be launched and fastened the pending projects. Pisciculture and Makhana raising can increase the revenue of the villages. Bihar is very potential in Rice cultivation but instead of traditioanal rice, Basmati, other scented rice should be produced to get revenue. Maize crop in Bihar has revolutioned the crop production. Several products like Popcorn, Cornflake and Maize floor can be manufactured. The need of the crop dominated agriculture has been the need of the past because high requirement of foodgrains, crop diversification is to bring desirable change in the existing cropping system towards more balanced system.

Floriculture is much attractive and has ample future scope of getting revenue by adopting practices like rose water, scent and essential fragrances.

Fruits like Mango, Lichhi, Banana and Chikku can be cultivated in small areas also which is an ultimate source of livelihood/revenue. A very bright future for HERBAL FARMING is knocking the doors which can be used as several Aurvedic medicines and extraction of oil for medicinal use. These crops require small holding and less cost in comparison with wheat and rice crops.

Diversification of Agriculture in the state must be supplemented with small scale cottage rural base industries like Basket-making, Madhubani painting and fancy items from Bamboo and making of rope with Hexian (Jute). Crop production diversifications with dairying, piggeries and poultry farming can be beneficial and generate employment also.

Vegetable cultivation and mushroom cultivation can be adopted in small areas also which increased the revenue of the villagers.

Application of new bio-technology in agriculture has shown a great promise particularly in evolving genetically modified crops. Use of tissue culture for Banana cultivation is the boon for Hazipur, Sonepur and other areas. Development of transgenic to improve nutritional quality of rice, potato with balanced protein and tomato with Oxalate free are the few examples of Bio-technology.

Bihar is having ample potential for agricultural growth in future. Revival of closed sugarcane mills, tobacco-based industries, fishries, mackana cultivation, canning of mango, Lichi and other pulpy fruits are the major source of earning foreign currency. Bihar is hub of tourists. Tourism industries has a great potential for its succession. Places like Mithila, Rajgir, Lauriya, Arc Raj, Patna, Sasaram, Vaisali, Buxar, Parasnath, Sitamarhi and other places attract the ancient glory of the past. Tourism constitutes the largest industry in the terms of turnover and employment which Bihar can exploit by making awareness among the people and can earn foreign exchange also.

At last but not the least the development of Bihar underlies on its agricultural growth and development. Agricultural Research and Extension, fund allocation for flood control, irrigation project and credit facilities should be extended to small and marginal farmers at minimum interest rate. The development of State should be kept on priority and make sincere efforts by each individual in positive manner by "lighting a candle rather cursing the dark". Pt. Jawahar Lal Nehru always used to say, "we have to run twice as fast as to stay where we are" which is very true in the development of Bihar to acquire the past glory. "The best administrated states of India".

References

Bihar Economic Journal, (2003) Conference Volume.

Economic Survey, (2001-04), Government of India.

Fertiliser Statistics (2001-05).

Indian Journal of Fertiliser (various issues), FAI, Publication, New Delhi.

India Economic Journal, (2004) Conference Volume.

The Economic Times, Business Daily, New Delhi.

15

Regional Development and Level of Living in India

Ravi Ranjan and Satendra Prajapati

I. INTRODUCTION

While exploring a comparative study of various regions in their economic growth and standard of living, the first and foremost there come the necessity of some tools basing upon which the difference can have been located and objective inferences drawn. Here, among such tools to be applied to measure the level of growth of the regions undertaken, important are per capita income, and domestic product, credit extension to the regions by financial institutions, growth and developmental networking of infrastructure, consumptions of power, human resource development, capital investment and proposal for future investment, and so on. This paper, *ab-initia* relies itself on such ingredients to measure the level of development and level of living in various regions of India.

Relying upon the government's data for per capita income the position of Punjab was first among the list of India's states and Orissa was placed at the bottom of the list.

In 1990-91 Punjab topped the list with Rs. 23,693 crores as its net domestic products at the price level of 1993-94, and the same figure for Orissa was of Rs. 4300. In regard to per capita income the order was the same, e.g. Punjab being at the top and Orissa at the bottom of the list of States.

II. REGIONAL IMBALANCES IN PRE-REFORM AND POST-REFORM PERIOD

In the Pre-reform period the differential rate of domestic production between the forward states like Punjab, Maharashtra, and the backward states was wide enough to create on wide differences in the living standard of these two categories of states. In the forward states the growth rate of domestic product in the said period was 5.6 per cent and the corresponding figure for the backward states was 1.7 per cent per annum. These widespread disparity between the forward and backward states aggravated regional imbalances in the post-reform periods. Some of the backward states like West Bengal, Karnataka, Gujarat managed their economic to receive high growth rate, that was realised in their growth acceleration more than 6 per cent per annum; while the backward states like Madhya Pradesh, Orissa, Assam, Bihar, etc. witnessed very low growth rate during the 12 years period, between 1990-91 and 2002-03. The most distressing fact was about Bihar which indicated a negative trend in its growth rate—0.7 per cent per annum on average for the aforesaid 12 years. The case of Uttar Pradesh, whose total population represented 16.2 per cent of India's total population acquired only a very nominal growth rate of 2.1 per cent and Madhya Pradesh also showed a dismal performance with 0 growth rate of 0.4 per cent. The general perusal of facts is an indicative that states with larger population like Bihar, U.P. and M.P. have been acting as a drag on the growth process of the Indian economy. States like Orissa and Rajasthan have picked up the line and have succeeded to give a formal boost to their growth with 4.1 and 3.5 per cent respectively. On the other side, there are forward states like Punjab and Haryana, whose growth rates have assumed a decelerating trend. But still they are the star performers in the Indian economy.

Secondly, if per capita Net State Domestic Products (NSDP) is regarded as an indicator to measure the regional balance in economy the positions of these two types of states, forward and backward present the picture as given below :

In 1990-91 Punjab emerged with the highest per capita income but in 2002-03 Maharashtra superseded it. In 1990-91 Orissa was the lowest per capita income state but in 2002-03 came to the bottom of the list with negative growth rate. Among the backward states West Bengal recorded the highest per capita growth rate that surmounted to 6 per cent approximately. It is a clear indication of the forward states providing greater rates of growth while the backwards states failing miserably to catch up the forward states.

III. INFRASTRUCTURAL DISPARITY

Above given facts denotes the common trend of growth rates in regard to NSDP, owing to which regional economic disparity, among states has been widened to the extent of valconic eruption.

Such an uncomfortable phenomenal development of the economy, the regional imbalances that have given birth to various unpleasant political and economic consequences, require that a probe be made into this development process to inquire into reasons responsible for this unpleasant trend of growth. The answer to this question, first and foremost has to be explored in the trend in investment and financial assistances, the manner of financial assistances and the amount allocation to various states.

N.J. Kurian has made an intensive investigation into this aspect of problem and inferred that nearly two-third of investment proposals, to be exact 69.2 per cent, in the post-reform period have been concentrated in the forward state, and the same policy has been endorsed in the matters of financial assistances extended by the various financial institutions including the scheduled commercial banks. Nearly all financial institutions, no matter whether they are all India or State financial institutions had extended 67.3 per cent of their credit to forward states till 31 March, 1997 of all 9 forward states the four of them viz. Maharashtra, Gujarat, Tamil Nadu and Andhra Pradesh, maneuvered to grab more than 51 per cent of the total institutional financial assistances. Even in the case of State Financial Corporations, 70 per cent of total assistances were received by forward states. In general analysis the secret of regional disparity has unearthed the fact the reform process has opted forward states for financial assistances an allocation of investment proposals.

The prevailing infrastructural disparity is one of the potent factors that explains the extent of regional imbalances in the economy. Dr. N.J. Kurian's findings on infrastructural disparity among various states of India is very wide. Nearly all the forward state's per capita power consumption is more than the average for all India, as in 1996-97 the average figure for them was 338 kwh but the backward states particularly U.P. and Bihar are far behind the per capita average all India power consumption, as this figures for them are 145 kwh and 194 kwh respectively. In general inference it appears to be imperative that unless industrialisation picks up speed in these states their backwardnesses would be continuing.

According to the infrastructure index developed by CMIE with weightage Punjab has the highest value of Infrastructure Development Index (IDI) as 191.4 followed by Tamil Nadu and Haryana as 144.0 and 141.3 respectively. The lowest value of IDI was for Madhya Pradesh, 75.3 followed by Assam 79.9 and Bihar 81 per cent. Although U.P. has the value of IDI 103.3 higher than that of all India level yet in terms of foodgrain production and poverty removal it was far behind Karnataka, West Bengal and Tamil Nadu; which had relatively lower IDI values.

Regarding irrigation infrastructure Punjab had 95 per cent of irrigated areas as a proportion of gross cropped areas, it had the highest productivities per hectare. In U.P. this proportion even though being high, that is 63 per cent yet its per hectare productivity was relatively low. This clearly evidenced that Punjab and Haryana successfully harnessed the irrigational facilities to give an upward boost to their economy but U.P. miserably failed to gear up its productivities of foodgrains.

Human resource development is one of the important indicators to show the economic health of a region. Kerala and Tamil Nadu are the two states which have proved the human resource development, can be explore without much economic growth. On the other hand, there are states like Bihar, Orissa, Madhya Pradesh which have shown their utter failures to make adequate allocation of fund for acceleration of education and health. Particularly in case of female education their literacy rate is too meager to give any sort of upward boost to human resource development. Consequently their child mortality rate is higher, birth rate is higher and life expectancy is lower than many states. Under the schemes and reforms introduce under the aegis of the concept of globalisation some educational institutions in the field of higher education and some private hospitals and clinics have been appearing mushroomly. But their expensive charges are beyond the financial capabilities of the underdog masses and these educational and health clinics have kept themselves fully aloof from welfarism. How the economy in India with providing greater opportunities to private sector and minimising the economic role of public sector has geared up the process of regional imbalances has been commented by N.J. Kurian. He writes; "The better-off states are able to attract considerable amount of private capital investment, both domestic and foreign to improve their development potential because of the existing favourable investment climate including better socio-economic infrastructures. The backward states are unable to attract private investment because of unfavourable investment climate including poor infrastructure. They are unable to improve the existing poor infrastructure facilities due to lack of resources. Their lack of resources is linked to their poor development. Thus, they are truly in a vicious circle.

The above illustrated are the disparities among various regions, which have been caused due to certain objective as well as subjective reasons as geographical conditions and isolation, inadequacy of economic overheads like transport, labour technology, etc.

The genesis of regional backwardnesses or regional disparity in development can be traced in the policy of the colonial rulers who preferred to develop only these regions which possessed greater facilities for development of manufacturing and trade. The Indian port cities like Calcutta, Bombay and Madras were found to be much amicable for the British colonial rulers for their economic activities. Consequently, their growth as prosperous cities remained a factor and the rest of the areas in the country remained backward.

Secondly, the land system of British India was so harsh and exploitative as it placed rural areas under the condition of a complete pauperisation. Peasantry in general was the most oppressed class and the classes which grabbed the income from the land, were *Zamindars,* money lenders and greedy British bureaucracy which drained out from the agrarian sector whatever incomes they could. In absence of effective land reforms the structure in rural areas remained by and large inimical to economic growth and caused disparity between urban and towns.

IV. CONCLUDING REMARKS

In developing countries like India developed regions are generally confined to urban centres. This is because physical geography controls economic growth to a great degree. Some regions which are developed to day, have been located for economic ventures due to their physical locations and material availabilities for growth.

However under liberalisation and globalisation which have completely removed restrictive provisions for economic activities and private sector has been opted to play pivotal role in economy regional embalances home got themselves enshrined in the very concept of growth. The growth of forward states and regions are ensured on the cost of exploitation of one region by the another. This is the natural characteristics of a private economic system and what India has been experiencing since several decades has been caused not by the indifferences on the part of the people by the policy that government has been following since several decades back.

References

Ministry of Finance, *Indian Public Finance Statistics*, 2004-05.

Kurian, N.J., (2000), "Widening Regional Disparity in India", *Economic and Political Weekly*, February 12-18.

16

The Level of Living of Agricultural Labour in Bihar during 1985-2001: An Analysis

RAMESH KUMAR SINGH

The purpose of the study is to assess the levels of living of agricultural labour in Bihar during 1985-2001, the period which is marked by 'Economic Reforms.' It is also a period when agriculture was being treated as industry and was expected to bring more income to the agriculturists. Strangely the level of living of agricultural workers do not show any significant rise during the period. This may throw light on the fall of real incomes of the workers in spite of the Reforms.

We have selected some indicators to measure levels of living of agricultural workers during the said period:

1. Percentage of agricultural labour,
2. Level of wages of agricultural workers,
3. Average percentage of outstanding of agricultural household according to different asset groups,
4. Average annual consumption expenditure, and
5. Level of nutritional value of diet.

I. PERCENTAGE OF AGRICULTURAL LABOUR

Following table shows the proportion of agricultural households to total rural labour households which remained more or less the same at about 30 per cent between 1986-87 to 1994-95. The proportion of agricultural labour to total working force however went up from 22.97 per cent in 1991 to 38.92 per cent in 2001 which meant an increase of dependence on the same holdings by greater number of family workers. Thus the per head share of agricultural labour went down.

The Table 1 shows that the agricultural labour to households was the same whereas the agricultural labour in relation to total labour has increased. The percentage distribution of scheduled caste agricultural labour was 39.86 per cent in Bihar according to the census 1991-92. The Third Rural Labour Enquiry however recorded the figure at 45.70 per cent in 1994-95. This meant an increase of 5.84 per cent within a span of three years. It is possible that this sudden increase in percentage was due to difference either in procedures adopted by these two surveys or due to an actual increase in the population of schedule caste agricultural

TABLE I

Size of Operational Holdings in Bihar, 2001

Classification/ years	*(%)age of Agricultural household*	*(%)age of Agricultural to labour rural tolal working force*	*(%)age of SCs Agri-cultural labour*	*(%)age of STs Agri-cultural labour*	*(%)age of OBCs Agri-cultural labour*
1986-87	29.60	–	–	–	–
1991-92	–	22.97	39.86	5.35	54.79
1994-95	28.00	–	45.70	5.30	48.80
2000-01	–	38.92	–	–	–

Source: (A) 1986-87: Agricultural Labour in India Report.
(B) 1991-92: 1991 Census.
(C) 1994-95: Rural Labour Enquiry Final Report.
(D) 2000-01: 2001 Census.

labours. Quite differently, the percentage of schedule tribe population of agricultural labour was constant at 5.35 per cent in the 1991 Census. This shows that the per head share of SCs went down but that of the STs remained constant.

The percentage distribution of 'other backward classes of agricultural labour' belonging to the different backward castes (OBCs) like—*yadavas, kurmis, koyaris* and *kunjra,* etc. stood at 54.79 per cent according to the 1991 Census. It went down at 48.8 per cent in 1994-95. This means a fall of 5.99 per cent of agricultural household labour within four years. However since the estimation procedures are different for the two surveys, we cannot compare these figures the subsequent census in 2001 as well as the N.S.S surveys do not provide any information on 'other backward classes of agricultural labour.' As such, we cannnot say anything about the percentage increase or fall in this class of agricultural labour. It is however clear that they formed a considerable population of rural Bihar. This explains the falling percentage of OBCs depending on agriculture, so that those remaining increased their per head income.

2. LEVEL OF WAGES OF AGRICULTURAL WORKERS

Different types of agricultural workers work different types of activity in agriculture. There also differ in the wages and duration of work in different places in Bihar. The wages of agricultural workers show increase due to more labour days and prices. During 1985-2001, enforcement of minimum wage of act has also some role. The wages of agricultural workers have increased and their standard of living has some impact due to this. The tables show their economic conditions as in Table 2.

The average annual earning per agricultural worker household show a subsequent increase over the years from Rs. 420 in 1986-87, to Rs. 608 in 1994-95 and by 2000-01, to Rs. 1001 at current prices. But at a constant price base of 1991, we see that the average annual earning per agricultural labour household actually fell down from Rs. 424.24 in 1986-87 to Rs. 405.33 in 1994-95. There was, however an increase in 2000-01 when the average annual earning went up to

TABLE 2

Classification/ Year	*Avg. no. of agri. employment per year*	*Avg. annual earning per agri. households (Rs.)*	*Annual per capita income (Rs.)*
1986-87	190 Days	420 (424.24)	88.03(89.19)
1994-95	198 Days	608 (405.33)	129.04 (86.27)
2000-01	–	1001 (485.92)	241.00 (117.37)

Note: Figures In Brackets are all In Terms of 1990-91 Prices.
Source: 1986-87 to 2000-01 N.S.S. Reports on Current Prices.

Rs. 485.92. It means that the condition of the real wages of agricultural workers in general had a marginal increase.

The annual per capita income of an agricultural worker household was Rs. 88.03 in 1986-87, Rs. 129.04 in 1994-95 and Rs. 241.00 in 2000-01 at current prices. If, however we deflate these figures at 1990-91 prices, we see that the annual per capita income actually fell down from Rs. 89.19 in 1986-87 to Rs. 86.27 in 1994-95, whereas the average annual per capita income went upto Rs. 117.37 in 2000-01.

Thus this indicator indicates little improvement in real wages and level of living of agricultural workers during the period.

3. THE AVERAGE PERCENTAGE OF OUTSTANDING LOANS OF AGRICULTURAL HOUSEHOLD ACCORDING TO DIFFERENT ASSET GROUPS

According to the sources of N.S.S. from 1986-87 to 2000-01, the average debt per indebted household was 143.33 in 1986-87 which came down to Rs. 141.38 in 1994-95. This further fell down in 2000-01 when it declined to 78.99. It proves that level of debts of agricultural labour in Bihar during this period has increased with increase in asset position.

The following table shows that the biggest amount of loan outstanding of Rs. 875.54 belonged to the asset group of Rs. 3000 to Rs. 4999. It may also be observed that the loans granted increased as the asset position (the credibility) of the agricultural labour increased. This means that low asset groups were not getting sufficient loans and so the low position of loans explain that low asset groups have little benefits from loans.

4. AVERAGE ANNUAL CONSUMPTION EXPENDITURE

Following table explain the average annual consumption expenditure of an agricultural labour household at Rs. 623.23 in 1986-87. It went up to Rs. 681.33 in 1994-95 but then it fell down to Rs. 442.31 in 2000-01. Quite similarly, the annual per capita consumption expenditure was Rs. 131.13 in 1986-87. It went up to Rs. 142 in 1994-95. But then it also fell down to Rs. 134.80 in 2000-01. If we compute this the monthly per capita consumption becomes very low figures of Rs. 10.94 in 1986-87, Rs. 11.83 in 1994-95 and Rs. 11.23 in 2000-01.

It shows that average annual consumption expenditure and annual per capita consumption of agriculture labour has not improved during this period in Bihar.

TABLE 3

Per Household Value of Assets and Loan Outstanding on Date of Survey by Asset Group Wage Earner Households in Bihar

Asset Group	*Amount in Rs. ('000)*	
	Total asset	*Loan Outstanding*
Less than 100	47.06	53.62
100-299	181.79	115.52
300-499	389.04	141.48
700-999	569.11	198.83
1000-2999	1515.33	230.53
3000-4999	3250.80	875.54
5000-9999	6780.54	287.17
10000 and Above	11,363.64	509.09
All Classes (Total)	753.56	167.72

Source: N.S.S. July 2000 to June 2001.

TABLE 4

Classification/ Year	*Average annual consumption expenditure of agriculture labour household*	*Annual per capita consumption expenditure*
1986-87	623.23	131.30
1994-95	681.33	142.00
2000-01	442.31	134.80

Source: N.S.S, 1986-87 to 2000-01.

5. LEVEL OF NUTRITIONAL VALUE OF DIET

It is worth mentioning here that in the famous debate about agriculture labour in Bihar during this period various specific considerations for india in terms of availability as well as consumption habits, took into account the different requirements of persons of different age, sex, groups. Sukhatme's minimum rule of diet are presented in the following table in comparison to some other estimates:

TABLE 5

Minimum Per Capita Monthly Consumption Expenditure for Rural Consumers, July 2000 to June 2001

Sl. No.		*Sukhatme*	*F.A.O.*	*Patwardhan*	*N.S.S. estimate for non-cultivating wage earner*
A.	Value of minimum diet	15.71	18.26	11.60	—
B.	Total expenditure of food corresponding to minimum diet	16.59	19.59	12.64	9.14
C.	Total consumption expenditure corresponding to minimum diet	22.73	25.60	15.63	11.23

Source: N.S.S. Twenty-fifth round (No. 232).

As it would be easily seen, the total expenditure on all food intems as incurred by the household member lies below the prescribed minimum advocated by all the three standards. Quite analogously, the actual total consumption expenditure also falls short of the minimum diet prescribed by each of these standards.

Policy Implications

Though some indicators give hints of some improvement in wage and consumption factors and also in indebtedness and nutritional factors the basic reason for the poor living standards has been little growth in agricultural production and paucity of employment opportunities to the agricultural labour. This has increased dependance on agriculture and more labour has fallen on small holdings and so they have not been able to improve their standard of living. It is therefore necessary that more employment opportunity is created in villages so that the agricultural labour is diverted to other jobs in the village itself. It also gives further scope of land reforms for small farmers and landless labour. Here village panchayats have to play a positive role.

17

Regional Development and Living on the Edge of SGSY in Jharkhand

A Case Study of Chas Block (Jharkhand)

D.B. GOSWAMI AND KUNAL VIKRAM

The paper examines four aspects of Swarnajyanti Gram Swarozgar Yojana in terms of its contribution in resolving "Prisoner's Dilemma" problem, these are :

(i) The various projects undertaken by SGSY in Chas Block to foster communication among the villagers about what they are doing in fact with their poverty alleviation programs.

(ii) The many requirements that SGSY imposes on target groups in defining co-operative behaviour.

(iii) A number of exceptions to the objectives of SGSY but do not require villagers to deviate from bare necessities of their livelihood.

(iv) The new dispute settlement mechanism that SGSY provides the incentive for the target group to conform to all the paradigms.

In the end SGSY is viewed as a remarkably well-conceived solution to the complex problems of the Panchayat Samities with assistance of Gram Sabha and DRDA in a cluster manner.

While the macro-economic indices of growth have shown tremendous increase in the country's Gross National Product (GNP) in the recent past which has also increased the average per capita income in the past 50 years of planning efforts in India at the same time the gap between rich and poor, educated and illiterate as well as between those who are clearly a part of the mainstream of the country's economic progress and those who remain unseen, unheard and disregarded continues to be widened. Even after 57 years of independence, implementation of Nine Successive Five Year Plans, resort to green revolution drive, nationalisation of major Commercial Banks for providing credit facilities to weaker sections, propagation of *Garibi Hatao* slogan and forceful; implementation of hundred days employment guarantee programs, generation of economic development has done little to improve the living conditions of a large portion of the teeming millions, inflicting a grim comment upon economic development strategies which had as one of their main designs, the elimination of poverty and unemployment.

For development to be in consonance with the people's wishes and aspirations the emphasis has been shifted towards participation of people in development process through Self Help Groups and Panchayati Raj Institutions. *Gram Sabhas* have been assigned important responsibilities and aim is to make it a vibrant form of governance. Top priority has also been accorded to rural development in terms of progressively increasing the allocation of resources for the implementation of the poverty alleviation programs.

The budgetary allocation for the Annual Plan 2004-05 is to the tune of Rs. 16,000 crores. It is also expected that within a year another 2300 crores will be provided additionally from the payment of foodgrains. Ministry of Rural Development stands committed to efface poverty and hunger from the face of Rural India. Two Main Schemes—one for providing Wage Employment—*'Sampoorna Grameen Rozgar Yojana'* ***(SGRY)*** and the other for providing Self Employment *'Swarnajayanti Gram Swarozgar Yojana'* ***(SGSY)*** to the rural people are under implementation to face the biggest challenge of unemployment specially in the rural areas of our country. The major schemes that have been under taken by the Rural Development Department for enhancement of income and employment opportunities to the rural poor fall into two categories.

(a) Centrally Sponsored Schemes: The Swarnajayanti Gram Swarozgar Yojana, Indira Awas Yojana, Employment Assurance Scheme and The Drought Prone Area Programme.

(b) State Plan Schemes: The Community Development Programme, Basic Minimum Services, Panchayats and the Minimum Needs Programme.

To begin with, IRDP was the only Self Employment Programme by the Ministry of Rural Developments, Govt. of India. A number of allied programmes have been added in course of years, such as Training of Rural Youth for Self Employment (TRYSEM), Development of Women and Children in Rural Areas (DWCRA), Supply of Improved Toolkits to Rural Artisans (SITRA), and Ganga Kalyan Yojana (GKY). With the coming into force TRYSEM, DWCRA, SITPA, GKY and MWS are no longer in operation. The unspent balances, as on 01.04.1999 under these head SGSY and utilized as per the new guidelines. Quality will be the hallmark of SGSY, which has to be imaginatively used to bring people above the poverty line. The State Government earmarked Rs. 3635.43 lakhs towards state share during 2000-01. During 2001-02 Rs. 3549.67 lakhs has been earmarked to meet the state share. Besides, the state government will provide the establishment cost of Block Strengthening and Direction and Administration at the headquarters and contribution towards state share of the DRDA Administration. DRDA Administration is a new scheme started from the financial year 1999-2000. This is meant to meet administrative expenditure of DRDA establishment.

It is holistic programme covering all aspects of self-employment such as organisation of the poor into SHG, Training Credit Facilities, Technical Infrastructure and Marketing. Families below poverty line in rural areas constitute the target group of SGSY. Within the target group special safeguards have been made provided to vulnerable sections by way of reserving 50 per cent benefits for SCs and STs, 40 per cent for women and 35 per cent for disabled persons. "This programme SGSY aims at improving the socio-economic conditions of the rural poor at the block level, it was also found correct in funding for this scheme through the government of India and Government of Jharkhand on 75:25 sharing basis.

This has proved to be a comprehensive scheme of self-employment of rural poor of Jharkhand with the chunk of beneficiaries called Swarozgaries. The basic objectives have been found here :

(i) To enable the rural poor to improve the socio-economic conditions for increased earnings.
(ii) To organize the rural poor into Self Help Group to build their self-confidence
(iii) Capacity building through vocational training.
(iv) Providing economic assistance through banks for taking up the vocational/trade (pottery trade) thereby creating income-generating assets.

Here SGSY has been conceived as a holistic program indeed for creating Swarozgaries. Such as selection of key activities organising the poor into SHG, planning of activities clusters and their capacity building with requisite faculties. SGSY in Chas Block has undertaken following projects during the period under reference :

(i) The approved project for disabled cost Rs. 1.90 crores and plan period is 2 years.
(ii) District Central Cooperative Bank has accepted to finance the disabled group by availing refinance from NHFDC with a service charge of 2 per cent.

(iii) The Central Government has released 39 lakhs towards first instalment of the plan 2003-04 to assist the target group.

(iv) The maximum amount of loan to each beneficiary has been provided upto Rs. 15001 and the repayment period has been fixed upto 24 months.

(v) The locally prevalent trade i.e., pottery 25 such major activities have been grouped so far and being imparted vocational training to them.

18

Regional Development and Level of Living in India

GAGAN KUMAR AND ANAND KISHORE

One can see five stages in the evolution of thought on economic growth. The chronological sequence is not without some overlap. In the first stage, the major concern was simply to accelerate economic growth. Growth was identified with the increase in the availability of material goods and services and was to be achieved through capital formation. Better life was identified with enhanced production of goods and services. The need for accelerating growth in this was felt even more strongly in developing economies, which started out with very low living standards. Eradication of poverty was to be achieved through faster economic growth. In the second stage, a distinction was made between growth and development. A greater concern with the distribution of income emerged. Development was seen as going beyond mere economic growth and bringing about changes in the structure of the economy. Equitable distribution of the benefits of economic growth became an independent goal. Balanced regional development also became a concern in large economies. In the third stage, the concept of equity was interpreted to mean the provision to everyone of what came to be described as basic needs which included the basic requirements of life such as food, education, safe drinking water and health services. In essence this approach stressed the need to provide to all human beings the opportunities for a richer and more varied life as one of out plan documents put it. The next stage in the evolution of economic thinking on growth was the emergence of the concept of sustainable growth which acquired importance in the context of the environmental degradation caused in the process of economic growth. Sustainable development focuses attention on balancing today's concerns with tomorrow's requirements. In the current stage of thinking on growth, the concept of basic needs has been widened and the objective of growth is set as "human development" which means an improvement in the quality of life of the people. Enhancement of human development should lead on the one hand to the creation of human capabilities through improved health, knowledge and skills and on the other the opportunities for the people to make use of these capabilities in a broader sense, human development implies human rights and participation and freedom of choice. In addition, the assent has shifted from the mere processes and the dynamics of growth to include also the institutions which should deliver the benefits of growth to the poor and disadvantaged. Under this approach, economic growth becomes an aspect of human development.

REGIONAL DISPARITIES

Various studies in recent years have revealed the fact that there has been wide variations in economic development of various regions of the country in post-liberalisation era. In the post-liberalisation era those states benefited which had better infrastrure and other resources but the backward states like Bihar, U.P., M.P., Rajasthan and Orissa lagged far behind. S.K. Mishra (2006) in his study opined that market-led growth benefits those who are economically competent and socially when placed to take advantage of the opportunities of capital-intensive and labour displacing global technologies and that growth rates of national and per capita incomes and also rate of reduction in poverty ratio can not ensure social justice at the state level. This paper looks at regional disparities in important economic indicators in the post-reform period.

We first examine trends of overall economic growth by sectors and the trends of GDP growth rates since independence and then a comparative study of regional variations in growth rates of both net state domestic products as well as per capita net domestic products in respect of major states of the country. The following Table 1 provides

TABLE 1

Trends in Growth Rates of Real GDP: 1950-51 to 2000-01

Period	*Agriculture* %	*Industry* %	*Services* %	*Non-Agri* %	*GDP* %
1950-51 to 1960-61	3.03	6.18	4.14	4.85	3.85
1960-61 to 1970-71	2.31	5.44	4.62	4.93	3.83
1970-71 to 1980-81	1.50	4.02	4.34	4.22	3.04
1950-51 to 1980-81	2.28	5.21	4.36	4.66	3.50
1980-81 to 1990-91	3.48	7.22	6.50	6.79	5.58
1990-91 to 2000-01	2.79	6.03	7.70	7.06	5.83
1980-81 to 2000-01	3.13	6.62	7.10	6.92	5.71

Source: Dholakia (2001).

sector-wise trend of growth rates during 1951-2001. Table 2 provides compound annual growth rates in net state domestic product and per capita net state domestic products for two time periods. A comparative analysis of the regional pattern of growth rates both net domestic products and per capita incomes reveals the fact that during the first period some of the poorer states like Bihar, U.P., M.P. and Rajasthan did better in the pre-reform period. At the same time some of the richer states like Haryana, Punjab and Tamil Nadu also did better in the pre-reform years than in the post-reform years. The shortfall in case of Punjab and Haryana is partly due to near stagnation in the agricultural sector. Services and rural non-farm sector performed better in the post-reform period.

TABLE 2

A Comparative View of Growth Rates of Net State Domestic Products and Per Capita Net State Domestic Products in Two Time Periods in Case of Selected States of the Country

Sl. No.	*States*	*CARG NSDP 1981-82 to 1990-91*	*CARG NSDP 1993-94 to 2003-04*	*CARG Per Capita NSDP 1981-82 to 1993-94 to 1990-91*	*CARG Per Capita NSDP 2003-04*
1.	Andhra Pradesh	6.63	5.406	4.56	4.313
2.	Bihar	5.76	2.96	3.764	0.72
3.	Guiarat	4.8	6.03	2.992	4.16
4.	Haryana	6.7	6.217	4.43	3.988
5.	Karnataka	5.2	5.59	3.4	4.21
6.	M.P.	7.9	3.7	5.6	1.75
7.	Maharashtra	6.5	4.6	4.32	2.85
8.	Orissa	3.7	4.66	2.012	3.36
9.	Punjab	5.6	3.54	3.8	2.017
10.	Rajasthan	7.6	5.55	5.26	3.266
11.	Tamil Nadu	5.7	4.6	5.033	3.65
12.	U.P.	6.05	3.87	3.89	1.78
13.	W.B.	5.84	6.7	3.96	5.26
14.	All India CARG of GDP	5.578	6.2		

Source: Compiled from Economic Survey, 2005-06.

Note: 1. CARG stands for compound annual growth rate.

2. Data for NSDP and NSDP Per Capita has been deflated with Wholesale Price Index taken as average of weeks for the respective years.

A statistical analysis of data on per capita NSDP for all the states and UTs as shown in the Appendix, reveals the fact that the coefficient of variation has increased over the years in the post-reform period. The ratio of minimum to maximum per capita incomes after a declining trend till 1995-96 again went up in 1996-97 and after that it started marginally declining again till 2001-02 but after that it started going up indicating that disparities are widening.

EXTENT OF POVERTY

The extent of poverty is the most important parameter of under-development. There are diversities among various states in terms of extent and magnitude of poverty and there are wide gaps in rural and urban poverty. States like Bihar and, Orissa are far behind the national averages. The percentage of poor in rural areas for India as a whole is 38.27 per cent according to the table whereas in Bihar and Orissa 51.52 and 54.97 per cent of the population are poor respectively.

Food Security

Among the parameters determining level of living, one of the important ones is extent of food security. It is often said that India is self-sufficient in foodgrains production. But the erratic trends of the past still continues. India's food output in recent years has been around 202 million tonnes per year. In the year 2003-04 it was 213.5 million tonnes. The annual compound growth rate in foodgrains production during the last 13 years preceding 2003-04 at around 1.48 per cent had generally outstripped the growth in population, which stood at around 2 per cent per annum. The total production of foodgrains during 2003-04 was 213.5 million tonnes whereas in the next year i.e., 2004-05 the production actually fell down to 205 million tonnes and the growth rate was negative and during 2005-06 the production increased by 6 per cent over the previous year.

TABLE 3

Poverty Ratios Using the Nutrition Poverty Line in India

States	*1993-94*		*1999-00*	
	Rural	*Urban*	*Rural*	*Urban*
Bihar	60.51	35.08	51.52	34.59
Orissa	55.19	41.25	54.97	40.48
Kerala	27.89	27.50	16.58	22.62
Puniab	13.32	12.78	12.95	08.25
All India	45.28	33.83	38.27	27.54

Source: Extracted from 2001(2005).

For long the government believed that the food produced in the country did not reach certain sections of the population. The Government of India, therefore made two interventions. One, it set-up the public distribution system (PDS) and two, it eastablished the system of price incentives to the farmers, to grow more food and sell them to the government for feeding into the PDS. Started in early 1960s, PDS entails supplying to the vulnerable sections of the society essential commodities at subsidised rates, to shield the poor from the volatility of prices and fluctuations in the supply of essential commodities. In the macro-micro terminology, the PDS in India is intended to translate the macro-level self-sufficiency in foodgrain production to micro-level food security by ensuring access to food and other essential commodities to poor families. The PDS in India has a network of over 4,00,000 fair price shops (FPS) and serves about 160 million families and is probably the largest such distribution system in the World. Many noted commentators, including Sen (1998), maintain that India could avoid large-scale families and saved millions of lives because of PDS, something that other countries which did not have such a system, such as China, failed to prevent.

There has been a serious neglect of agriculture in post-reform years. Higher growth in agriculture sector can be achieved only through a significant increase in the productivity levels through modernisation of the Indian agriculture. Both public and private investment must be stepped up in agriculture. There should be a significant growth in total cropped area which can be achieved by increasing area under irrigation. Effective application of high yielding variety of seeds in dry land farming should also be part of the strategy to improve the productivity.

Inflationary Trend in Prices of Essential Commodities

The index numbers of food and non-food articles during the post-reform period of 1994-95 to 2004-05 reveal the fact that there has been a persistent rise in the prices of non-food articles over the years along with a sharp rise in the prices of fuel, power, light and lubricants, but foodgrains prices increased more than the non-foodgrains during the concerning period.

The cost of living is indicated by consumer price indices released by Government of India. The Government of India releases index numbers for consumer prices in case of industrial labourers, urban non-manual employees and agricultural labourers. But, the base years taken are different for these categories. Though, there are difficulties in comparison, these indices do reveal the increasing cost of living of these people. The dearness allowances of industrial labourers and other white collar employees in the organised sector are linked to the rise in their respective indices, though there are time lags. However, in case of agricultural labourers who are the single largest category of labourers under unorganised sector do not have the wage increases simultaneously. So, the price rise causes greater hardships to them. There has been 250.12 per cent rise in price level in 2004-05 over that of 1986-87 level.

Availability of Safe Drinking Water

Another important determinant of quality of life is access to safe drinking water. The following table which is based on secondary data shows the relative condition in major states in terms of provision of safe drinking water in households in percentage terms at three points of time namely 1981, 1991 and 2001. We see that in rural M.P., Orissa, and Rajasthan the condition has improved in 2001 as compared to 1991 but the percentages are much below the national average. The condition has improved in Bihar and U.P. and these backward states have surpassed the national average in this respect.

Human Development

Explaining the conundrum of why accelerated income growth has not propelled India into a faster poverty reduction track, the HDR 2005 says that extreme poverty is concentrated in the rural areas of the northern poverty-belt States including Bihar, Madhya Pradesh, Uttar Pradesh and West Bengal, while income growth has been most dynamic in other States, urban areas and service sectors. At a national level, rural unemployment is rising, agricultural output is increasing at less than two per cent a year, farm incomes are stagnating and growth is virtually jobless.

TABLE 4

Access to Safe Drinking Water in Households

Sl.. No.	*States/UTs*	*Tap/Handpump/Tubewell*								
		1981			*1991*			*2001*		
		Total	*Rural*	*Urban*	*Total*	*Rural*	*Urban*	*Total*	*Rural*	*Urban*
1.	Bihar	37.6	33.8	65.4	58.8	56.5	73.4	86.6	86.1	91.2
2.	U.P.	33.8	25.3	73.2	62.2	56.6	85.8	87.8	85.5	97.2
3.	M.P.	20.2	8.1	66.7	53.4	45.6	79.4	68.4	61.5	88.5
4.	Orissa	14.6	9.5	51.3	39.1	35.3	62.8	64.2	62.9	72.3
5.	Rajasthan	27.1	13.0	78.7	59.0	50.6	86.5	68.2	60.4	93.5
	All India	38.2	26.5	75.1	62.3	55.5	81.4	77.9	73.2	90.0

Source: Economic Survey, 2005-06.

The Human Development Report 2006 (UNDP) refers to India's disappointing performance in improving its Human Development Index (HDI). India ranked 126th out of 177 countries. The HDR 2006 says the country's record in human development continues to remain less than impressive. The report notes that the incidence of poverty in India has fallen from 36 per cent in 1990 to 25-30 per cent and appears to be on track to achieve the Millennium Development Goal (MDG) of reducing by half the proportion of people living on less than a dollar a day by 2015. However, on most other indicators, especially health (reducing child and maternal mortality), achieving universal primary education and gender equality, it may reach the MDG goals only some time between 2015 and 2040. Painting a grim picture, the HDR points out that one in every 11 children dies in the first five years of life and that India alone accounts for 2.5 million child deaths annually, one-fifth of the world total.

Human development is now being recognised as an important dimension of socio-economic development. There have been wide variations in repect of various indicators of human development among the states of the country. Selected indicators of human development like life expectancy, infant mortality rates, birth and death rates reveal the fact that backward states like Bihar, U.P., Rajasthan and Orissa are lagging behind in all these respects. Birth and death rates are still higher than the national averages in these states. Infant mortality rates also present the similar trend per 1000 live births.

Access to Education

Access to education increases the self-esteem and social dignity of an individual and reduces deprivation. Data on extent of education in some major states of the country shows that backward states like Bihar, U.P., M.P., Orissa are far behind the developed states like Karnataka, West Bengal, Maharashtra, and also far behind the national average.

CONCLUSIONS

During the post-reform period the overall economic growth of the country has increased. Growth rates of services and the non-agricultural sectors in particular has increased, but agriculture has stagnated. All the sectors of the economy, thus, did not benefit equally in the post-liberalisation period. Further, there are imbalances in regional development. Those states benefitted which had got economic infrastructure. Poor states like Bihar, U.P., M.P., and Rajasthan lagged behind and at the same time some of the rich states like Punjab, Haryana and Tamil Nadu also could not do better. Gujarat, Karnataka, West Bengal and also Orissa benefitted. The coefficient of variation reveals the fact that regional disparities have increased over the years in the post-reform period. The ratio of minimum to maximum per capita incomes after a declining trend till 1995-96 again went up in 1996-97 and after that it started marginally declining again till 2001-02 but after that it started going up indicating that disparities are widening. Among the parameters determining level of living poverty ratios reveal the fact that poorer states like Bihar and Orissa have largest percentage of people below the poverty line. Agricultural production had an erratic trend and the net availability of foodgrains has been affected over the years casting a deep concern for the level of food security in the country. Another important factor affecting the standard of living is the price trend of the food and non-food articles and the cost of living. The foodgrain prices increased more than the prices of non-foodgrains, and there was a sharp rise in the price of fuel, power, light and lubricants as a group. Access to safe drinking water has improved in rural M.P., Orissa, and Rajasthan in 2001 as compared to 1991 but the percentages are much below the national average. The condition has improved in Bihar and U.P. and these backward states have surpassed the national average in this respect. Wide variations have been noticed in respect of various indicators of human development among the states of the country. Backward states like Bihar, U.P., Rajasthan and Orissa are lagging behind in terms of selected indicators of human development like life expectancy, infant mortality rates, birth and death rates. These backward states also lag behind the national average in terms of access to education.

References

Rangarajan, C. (2007), Strategy for Bihar's Economic Growth, Valedictory Address at the Global Meet for a Resurgent Bihar at Patna, January 21.

Mishra, S.K. (2005), "Economic Reforms and Regional Disparity in Economic Development in India", *Varta*, Vol. XXVI, April and October, Nos. 1 and 2, p. 39.

Dholakia, Bakul H. (2001-02), Sources of India's Economic Growth and the Vision of Indian Economy in 2020, *The Indian Economic Journal*, April-June, Vol. 49, No. 4, p. 30.

Dholakia, Bakul H. (2001-02), Sources of India's Economic Growth and the Vision of Indian Economy in 2020, *The Indian Economic Journal*, April-June, Vol. 49, No. 4, p. 40.

Economic Survey, 2005-06 and *Economic Political Weekly*, Feb. 3-9, 2007, Current Statistics 5.

Mukherjee, Amitava, 2001-02, Micro-level Hunger in Contemporary India: Perspectives of the Hungry, *The Indian Economic Journal*, April-June, Vol. 49, No. 4, p. 23.

Sen, Amartya (1998), Hunger in the Contemporary World, STICERD London School of Economic, London.

Naik, S.D. (2005), Human Development Index—Conundrum of Rising Income, Growing Poverty, *Financial Daily*, Tuesday, Sept. 27, *The Hindu* Group of Publications.

HDR, 2005 and 2006.

APPENDIX

	1993-94	1994-95	1995-96	1996-97	1997-98	1998-99	1999-00	2000-01	2001-02	2002-03	2003-04
σ	3946.503	4711.167	5259.584	6305.345	7490.494	8574.977	9351.654	10560.26	10991.33	12468.34	12210.1
Average	8789.28	10005.84	11242.88	12818.9	14422.59	16153.09	17437.34	18896.5	20184.72	22256.59	22847.72
C.V.	44.9	47.08	46.78	49.187	51.5358	53.0856	53.63	55.8847	54.4537	56.02	53.44
Min	3037	3372	3041	4001	4014	44495	4794	5157	5007	5683	5780
Mix	19761	22824	26734	31158	34583	40248	44349	49693	51076	53092	57621
Ratio of Min. to Max.	0.1536	0.147	0.1137	0.1284	0.116	0.11158	0.108	0.10377	0.098	0.107	0.1003
Medium Value	7694	8762	10108	1009	11666	133185	14784	16683	18064	19865	20896

19

Regional Development and Levels of Living in India

A Case Study of North-East Region

N.C. JHA

'INDIA' being a welfare state has a rule to provide maximum economic as well as social advantages to the citizens especially to the backward regions so that it could be developed into a strong economic unit possessing a paramounting political image at the international standards. Since independence and inception of planning era, the proces of regional development is going on but due to the operation of certain economic and non-economic obstacles, the desired result could not be attained. The concept of balanced regional development has become increasing popular only recently with the social awakening in the field of economic development. This certainly advocates to attain social economic development of the whole region. But in underdeveloped countries like India undoubtedly suffer from the regional inequality because every state differs with each other with quality of development such as Punjab is comparatively more advanced in agriculture. Kerela has the highest educational achievement, Gujarat and Maharashtra have achieve record development in textile industry, Garments and cotton ginning industries, Karnataka, A.P. have attained the record in technological field especially in Engineering, Bio-Technology, Information technology, etc. but the states of Bihar, M.P., U.P., Jharkhand, Uttaranchal, Chhattisgarh, H.P. Manipur, Nagaland, etc. fail to attain any recognition in any field rather they are well-known as the most 'Backward Region' of the Indian Union because the concept of 'Regional Development' has fully failed in these states.

Infact the 'Balanced Regional Development' necessary clarifies the term Region which means in Indian context as a state within the union of India which is formed on linguistic basis. A Region is thus explained as an economic entity within a state it may be a district or a town or a village. Regional Development does not mean equal development of the whole region such as Eastern Region, Southern Region, Western Region or Northern Region. It simply implies the fullest development of the potentialities of an area according to the capacity so that inhabitants of the region may have shared the fruit of development in most equitable manner and society seems to be structured as equally balanced with economic, social and other factors. But the ultimate aim of regional development is to raise the living standard of the people of the region because there is a direct positive correlation between regional development and the level of living because the former affects all the determining factors—'Economic' as well as 'Non-economic' factors of the level of living. Thus the regional development means the economic development of all the regions raising their per capita income and living standard and fully exploiting their natural and human resources.

But in Indian context, there exists serious regional imbalances in respect of economic development and levels of living among the people of different regions and areas, which has arisen due to haphazard over concentration of Industries in certain areas leaving the other untouched due to certain constraints. But it is not only an Indian problem rather a global problem. But this concept of regional development is not only a political flavour but an economic necessity of the backward regions because it contains the power to break through the various circle of poverty which keeps the poor to be poor with both demand and supply side as well as other side too. Due to poverty, which is certainly a curse to the certain regions of the Indian economy, keeps the level of living at the lowest. The poverty ratio in India in 1993-94 was 36 per cent as a whole but the highest concentration is in Bihar, Orissa, M.P., U.P. which is 55 per cent, 48.6 per cent, 42.5 per cent and 40.9 per cent which has gone down to 42.6 per cent, 47.2 per cent, 37.4 per cent and 31.2 per cent in 1999-2000. In 2005-06 the recent study reveals that India still has some poverty—34.71 of India's poorest population, the population that lives on 3/4th of the poverty line or less, still have less than US $ 2 per day. The N.S.S.O. estimated that 26.1 per cent of the population was, monthly consumption goods below Rs. 211.30 for rural areas, and Rs. 454.11 per 'Urban Areas' 75 per cent of the poor are in rural areas (27.1% of total rural population) with most of them comprising daily wages, self-employment households and landness labours. The major causes for poverty are unemployment or under-employment, low ownership of assets and literacy. The Poverty has direct impact on the level of living and if such population suffer from this disease, how may you imagine even the average level of living standards for such people in India.

The level of living is directly controlled by the process of economic development, which is influenced by two factors—Economic and non-economic.

The economic development of an economy/Region/State is dependent upon its natural resources, human resources, Capital Enterprises and technology, etc. but the former is not possible so long as the social institutional environment and political awareness are not prevailing at the optimal level. The factors which affect the 'Regional Development' and thus the level of living may be discussed as follows.

Natural Resources

In India, the principal factor affecting the regional development and thus the level of living is the natural resources which are consisted of land (area, situation, location and technology, etc.) Minerals (Climate, Water resources, etc.) which are developed at different degree in different regions make the region as developed and underdeveloped—to make the people rich and poor and thus determines the level of living which differentiate them as civilized illiterate for the later. In India in different regions the availability of land especially the irrigated areas and net sown areas differ, makes the production yield different and thus differentiates them by way of level of living. The states of Punjab, Haryana, and Net sown areas, thus higher sources of income and thus higher level of living but the states such as Bihar, Jharkhand, M.P. Orissa, Chhattisgrah, etc. have less irrigated and Net sown areas, thus lower productivity, yield of the inhabitants shows lower sources of income and thus reflects comparatively low of living.

Per Capita Income

The next most important factor determining the level of living of region/state is the per capita Income of the related state/region because both income and level of living are directly related, higher per capita income leads higher level of living and *vice-versa*. The following table can be used as showing the per capita Net Domestic Product and its reflection of determining the level of living.

Note. Bihar includes Jharkhand, Madhya Pradesh includes Chhattisgrah and Uttar Pradesh includes Uttarnchal upto 1990-91 in 2001-02, Bihar excludes Jharkhand, M.P. excludes Chhattisgrah and U.P. excludes Uttaranchal.

The above Table 1 explicitly shows the changing trend of per capita net domestic product between 1960-61 to 2001-02 which clearly explain that the state of Punjab, Maharashtra and Haryana have continuously maintained a considerable lead over other states. In 1960-61 Maharashtra was the first state having the highest per capita income but was pushed to the second place by Punjab in 1964-65 and since then the place has been comfortably occupied and the per capita income has far ahead other states. It clearly shows that the level of living in Punjab is undoubtedly and comparatively higher than other states.

TABLE I

Per Capita State Net Domestic Product in 15 Major State of India

(At current Prices)

Sl. No.	*State*	*1960-61*	*1971-72*	*1980-81*	*1990-91*	*2001-02*
1.	A.P.	314	627	1467	4816	17916
2.	Assam	349	548	1329	4432	11034
3.	Bihar	216	415	1022	2966	5445
4.	Gujarat	380	827	2089	6343	20195
5.	Haryana	359	960	2437	7721	24820
6.	Karnataka	292	698	1644	4975	17518
7.	Kerala	278	592	1835	5110	19603
8.	M.P.	274	534	1609	4798	12027
9.	Maharashtra	419	808	2492	7612	24246
10	Orissa	226	437	1352	3166	10027
11.	Punjab	383	1121	2629	8177	25246
12.	Rajasthan	271	560	1424	4883	13738
13.	Tamil Nadu	344	648	1666	5541	20315
14.	U.P.	244	497	1402	3937	9753
15.	W.B.	386	779	1925	5072	17875
	Average	305	660	1741	5365	17823

Sources: Directors of Economic and Statistics of respective state.
Per Capita NNP at Current Prices.

Differential Growth Rates

Dipankar Das Gupta *et al.* have estimated annual percentage growth rate of per capita SDP for various states at 1980-81 prices. For simplicity the table is reduced to 14 Major states which are as follows. *Economic and Political Weekly,* July 1, 2000.

The Table 2 clearly shows that during 1970-71 to 1995-96, the poorest states have certainly not performed better-off because the annual rates growth in these states varies between 1.4 to 1.9 per cent. This is certainly an index of level of living of these poorest states because of the annual per capita growth. Yate certainly determines the level of these

TABLE 2

Estimated Annual Percentage Growth Rate of Per Capita SDP for 14 Major States at 1980-81 Prices

Sl. No.	*State*	*Annual Percentage Growth (1970-71 to 1995-96)*
1.	A.P.	1.9
2.	Assam	1.7
3.	Bihar	1.8
4.	Gujarat	2.7
5.	Haryana	3.1
6.	Karnataka	2.2
7.	Kerla	1.7
8.	M.P.	NA
9.	Maharashtra	3.0
10.	Orissa	1.4
11.	Punjab	3.0
12.	Rajasthan	1.9
13.	Tamil Nadu	2.4
14.	U.P.	1.8
15.	W.B.	2.3
	All India	2.1

Note 1. D. Dasgupta *et al.* have not provided estimates of Growth rate for M.P.
2. All India Growth rates to per capita net National product.

Source: Dipankar Dasgupta at Growth and Inter-state Disparities in India, Table 2.

poorest states because of the annual per capita growth rate certainly determines the level of consumption which depends on income which is low, thus, a low level of living of the people of these poorest states is the reality on the other hand the richer states Haryana, Punjab, Maharashtra and Gujarat shows the growth rate of per capita income between 2.7 per cent and 3.1 per cent which certainly reflects high income high consumption and thus a high level of living is being maintained moreover the gap between the rich over the two and a half decades certainly dignifies a different and wide range of level of living among these states regions in the Union of India.

CONSUMPTION EXPENDITURE

In India the level of living is directly influenced by the consumption expenditure which is directly influenced by the level of income of the states region. N.S. Iyengar and P.R. Brahmanand have presented a calculation known as 'Gini-Lorenz Ratios' of the size distribution of nominal per capita household private consumption expenditure. They have used the N.S.S. data on consumption expenditure for this purpose which we may explain with the help of following Table 3.

From the results given in Table 3 one would be tempted to draw the following concludes: (1) since during the 1950s the average Gini-Lorenz. Ratios for both rural and urban areas were higher than the Gini-Lorenz Ratios for the subsequent decades inequalities in the distribution of consumption expenditure have declined over time. (2) From the 1960 onwards up to the end of the sixth plan the Gini-Lorenz Ratio of the rural areas was stable at around 0.30 whereas for the urban areas was stable at 0.33 thus clearly shows more consumption expenditure in urban areas than the rural one which certainly distinguishes the level of living. (3) The Gini-Lorenz Ratios for the urban areas are about 10 to

TABLE 3

Plan-wise Avetagegini–Lorenze Fatoo

Plan	*Number of Observations*	*Rural*	*Urban*
First (1951-56)	6	0.34	0.38
Second (1956-60)	6	0.33	0.37
Third (1961-65)	4	0.33	0.35
1966-68*	3	0.30	0.33
Fourth (1969-73)	4	0.29	0.33
Fifth (1974-79)	1	0.31	0.33
1979-80*	N.A.	N.A.	N.A.
Sixth (1980-84)	1	0.30	0.33

*Annual Plan Years.

Source: N.S. Iyengar and P.R. Brahmananda Estimated Distribution Parameters and their Behaviour in P.R. Brahamananda and V.R. Panchamukhi, etc. The Development Process of the Indian Economy, Bombay, 1987, p. 87.

12 per cent higher than the Gini-Lorenz Ratios for the rural areas. This clearly suggests that inequalities are higher in the urban areas than in the rural areas.

According to Iyengar and Brahmananda's study if the income distribution has not improved through overtime distribution of private consumption expenditure in money term has undergone a change for the better thus might lead a better level of living both in rural and urban India.

The world Bank estimates for 1983, 1989-90, 1994 and 1997 the percentage share of household Expenditure by percentile groups of household which is as follows.

From the Table 4 according to the World Bank's estimates of household expenditure distribution, it is clear that between 1883 and 1989-90 there was very little change in the expenditure distribution, thus, the Table 4 shows that during 1983-97 the percentile household expenditure remains more or less constant and thus the level of living too constant if we take household expenditure as an index.

TABLE 4

Percentage Share of Household Expenditure by Percentile Groups of Household

Households	*1983*	*1989-90*	*1994*	*1997*
Lowest 20 Per cent	8.1	8.8	9.2	8.1
Second quintile	12.3	12.5	13.0	11.0
Third quintile	16.2	16.2	16.8	15.0
Fourth quintile	22.0	21.3	21.7	19.3
Highest 20 per cent	41.4	41.3	39.3	46.1
Highest 10 per cent	26.7	27.1	25.0	33.5

Source: The World Bank, World Development Report, 1992, Table 30, pp. 276-77, World Development Report, 1993, Table 30, pp. 296-97 and World Development Report, 1999-2000, Table 5, pp. 238-39.

SAVING

The level of living can be explained with the help of the saving which is a direct function of the level of income and if the level of income is so low, it remains negative and if it is greater than zero, it certainly explains that the income is certainly as high as to maintain the necessity and thus have certain surplus income. Since the five decades of planned economic development, there has been considerable rise in the rate of saving which we may explain with the help of following table.

The Table 5 shows the trend of gross domestic savings between 1950-51 and 2003-04 which explains the trend of household doctor, private corporate sector and public sector respectively, the table certainly reveals the rising trend of household sector which has gone up from 6.2 per cent in 1950-51 to 24.3 per cent to 4.1 per cent but the public sector's

TABLE 5

Gross Domestic Savings (as Per cent of GDP at Current Market Prices)

Year	*Gross Domestic Savings* Household Sector	*Private Corporate* Sector	*Public Sector*	*Total (1+2+3)*
1950-51	6.2	0.9	1.8	8.9
1955-56	9.6	1.2	1.7	12.6
1960-61	7.3	1.6	2.6	11.0
1965-66	9.4	1.5	3.1	14.0
1968-69	8.6	1.1	2.4	12.2
1978-79	15.4	1.5	4.5	21.5
1980-81	13.8	1.6	3.4	20.1
1985-86	14.3	2.0	3.2	19.5
1990-91	19.3	2.7	1.1	23.1
1994-95	19.7	3.5	1.7	24.8
1999-00	20.8	4.4	-1.0	24.1
2000-01	21.6	4.1	-2.3	23.5
2001-02	22.6	3.6	-2.7	23.4
2002-03	22.6	3.6	-1.1	26.1
2003-04	24.3	4.1	-0.3	28.1

Note: Ratios of savings of individual sector may not add to totals because of rounding off.

Source: Govt. of India, Economic Survey, 2004-05 (Delhi, 2005), Table 1.5, pp. 5-8 and 5-9).

trend shows changing nature because between 1950-51 to 1978-79 it has risen from 1.5 per cent to 4.5 per cent but since 1980-81, it has declined from 3.4 to -0.3 in 2003-04. But the G.D.S. has a moderate rising trend which has increased from 8.9 per cent in 1950-51 to 28.1 per cent. We certainly conclude that over the year's the level of living in India and in different regions have risen because G.D.S. has shown a rising trend, thus reflecting a rising surplus income and better level of living.

PER CAPITA CEREAL CONSUMPTION

Level of living is also associated with cereal consumption and since the inception of 'Green Revolution' in India. Food production shows a rising trend because according to S. Radhakrishna (2002) (in India Development Report, p. 48). It has almost attained 3.77 per cent aggregate and 1.62 per cent per capita food production growth rate between 1981-83 to 1991-93 but during 1991-93 to 1997-99 there is a marginal fall and it has been 2.72 per cent and 0.90 per cent respectively. If we go into the detail of per capita cereal consumption according to the N.S.S.O. quinquennial survey between 1970-71 to 1999-2000, it has marginally decreased from 15.35 kg per month to 12.70 kg per month for the urban sector. The declining trend is discernible in most of the states, especially in Punjab where the decline is as much as 6 kg per capita per month. What is most conspicuous state like Punjab (10.58 kg in rural and 9.21 kg in urban areas in 1999-2000) and higher intake in a backward state like Orissa (15.09 in rural and 14.51 kg in urban areas). The sharp decline in cereal consumption can be attributed to changes in consumer tastes, from food to non-food items and within the food group from 'Coarse' to 'fine' cereals (Radhakrishna and Ravi, 1992). More recently, Rao (2001) has shown that decline in cereal consumption has been greater in the rural areas where the improvement in rural infrastructure has made other food and non-food items available to rural households. It has been argued that a reduction in hard manual work in agriculture due to farm mechanisation might have reduce nutritional requirements. Rao further observes that a reduction in the intake of cereals on this account should not be taken as deterioration in human welfare, (Food and Nutrition Security in India, M.K. Sinha, *Bihar Economic Journal*, 2005, 1996-97). This shows that the level of living has changed both in rural areas and urban areas because there is shift in cereal or coarse cereal to fine cereal or non-cereal consumption which certainly reflects a better level of living in the States/Region of India.

CHANGING PATTERN OF MONTHLY PER CAPITA EXPENDITURE

The NSS estimates of changing pattern of monthly per capita expenditure for rural India reveal that the total food expenditure has been declining in rural areas (from 8.73% in 1997 to 54.99% in 2002). The data also highlights that the monthly per capita expenditure has been falling in the same period (from 21.89% in 1997 to 18.20% in 2002) due to the increase in non-food items expenditure and that of pulse products and milk products has been decreasing in the same period (from 3.75% to 3.27% in 2002 and 9.95% to 8.53% in 2002) the data also focus that the monthly per capita vegetables and beverages expenditure has upward trend (from 5.34 in 1997 to 6.62 in 2002 and 3.69 in 1997 to 4.61 in 2002). The percentage of monthly per capita cereal expenditure has been falling in all the states, that of pulses and products expenditure has declined from 1997 to 2002 in all the states except Haryana and Orissa, that of milk and milk products expenditure has decreased in all the states except M.P, U.P. and T.N., Orissa has the lowest monthly per capita milk and milk products expenditure (2.26 in 2002 and that of vegetables expenditure has been increasing except M.P in the same period. The above description certainly explains the changing level of living in India and the regional development of its role which is explicitly visible in the changing variables of different states of India.

NORTH-EASTERN REGION

In India the North-Eastern Region comprises the

'Special Economic Zone' (SEZ) because the boundary of these states is related with the international line of control—China, Bangladesh, Myanmar, Bhutan, the total geographical area of this region is 7.76 per cent of India whereas the proportion of population to India is concerned it is 3.74 per cent. But this region is rich with respect to the proportion of total forest area which is 64.31 per cent to the total forest area of India, these states are—Arunachal Pradesh, Assam, Manipur, Meghalaya, Mizoram, Nagaland, Tripura. For the development of these states of Eastern Region, many steps have been taken by the central.

As well as the state government which shown by the increase in per capita income and other facilities which we may explain with the help of the following Table.

From the Table 6 the per capita Net Domestic Product (at Current price in 1980-81) for the states of North-Eastern

TABLE 6

Per Capita Net Domestic Product, Percentage of Electrified Villages, Infant Mortality Rate, Poverty Ratio, and Availability of Safe Pure Drinking Water in Eastern Region States and India

Name of the states	*Per Capita NDP at Current Prices (in Rs.) 1980-81*	*Per Capita NDP at Current Prices (in Rs.) 2000-01*	*Percentage of Electrified Villages (1991)*	*Availability of Safe Pure Drinking Water*	*Infant Mortality Rate (2001)*	*Poverty Ratio in Percentage 1973-74*	*Poverty Ratio In Percentage 1999-2000*
Arunachal P.	1522	14587	59.00	70.02	49	51.93	33.47
Assam	1329	10198	77.00	45.86	78	51.21	36.09
Manipur	1396	12823	81.00	38.72	25	49.96	28.54
Meghalaya	1538	13114	46.00	36.16	52	50.20	33.87
Mizorum	1399	14909	98.00	16.21	23	50.32	19.47
Nagaland	1607	12594	96.00	53.37	N.A	50.81	32.67
Tripura	1645	14348	94.00	37.18	49	51.00	34.44
India	16707	86.00	62.30	71	54.88	26.10	

Sources: 1. Statistical Pocket Book India, 2000, pp. 240-41.
2. Economic Survey, 2002-03, pp. S-11-12 and S-113-14.
3. Economic Survey, 2001-02, p. 239.

region varies between Rs. 1329 and Rs. 1645 whereas in 2000-01 it varies (at current price) Rs. 10198 and 14909 but undoubtly it is less than the per capita net Domestic Product at Rs. 16707. The rise in per capita income in all these North-Eastern states certainly reveals that the level of living has gone up in all these States because income and the level of living are directly and functionally related but not as fast as the other developed states of India, Punjab, Haryana, Maharashtra, etc.

Level of living in all these North-Eastern states has certainly improved because the percentage of electrified villages (in 1991) varies between 46 per cent and 96 per cent since this index is improving. Except Meghalaya and Arunachal Pradesh which is 46 per cent and 59 per cent the all states, Assam 77 per cent, Manipur 81 per cent, Tripura 94 per cent, Nagaland 96 per cent and Mizoram 98 per cent whereas 86 per cent, all India, all these percentage are truly reflecting the rising level of living.

The another index for explaining the level in these states in the availability of safe pure drinking water which is certainly less than the all India average (62.30) except Arunachal Pradesh 70.02 per cent because Assam has 45.86 per cent, Mizoram 38.72 per cent, Meghalaya 36.16 per cent, Mizoram 16.21 per cent, Nagaland 53.37 per cent and Tripura 37.18 per cent. If we analyse this index as the level of living it certainly refers as low level because most states except Arunachal Pradesh has not found the ways for availability of safe drinking water for all people, the worst is in Mizoram only 16.21 per cent of population avails this facility which is indeed a worrying factor for the rise in level of living.

Next, we may also use Infant Mortality rate in the North-eastern states as an Index for measuring the changes in the level of living. The Table 6 certainly shows that infant Mortality Rate for these states in 2001 has fallen and except Assam 78 per 1000 infant baby and less than the all India. Yate 71 per 10000 which 49 for AP, 25 for Manipur, 52 for Meghalaya, 23 for Mizoram and 49 for Tripura.

The author index for these states is Poverty index for these states is Poverty Ratio for 1973-74 and 1999-2000. For whole India, the ratio has decreased from 54.88 per cent to

26.10 per cent which is also true for all North-Eastern Region States. Although except Mizoram, which is 19.47 per cent, all the states have higher poverty ratio in 1999-2000.

HUMAN DEVELOPMENT INDEX

The change in level of living in these states of North-Eastern Region can be known with the help of 'Human Development Index' which shows in the variables of human development index since the inception of planning for the human development, the government has devoted huge amount of money at though the effect on the human development has not been seen in comparison to the investment. In the north- eastern states, with the help of following table, we may explain in the changes of living due to changes in human index development.

The Table 7 reveals the fact that in 1991, the index value of Human Development, Arunachal Pradesh which index value in 1981 was 0.242 and ranking 31, where as in

TABLE 7

Human Development Index of North-Eastern States for 1981, 1991 and 2001 (with The Ranking States of 1991)

Sl.. No.	Name of States	1981		1991		2001	
		Index Value	Rank	Index Value	Rank	Index Value	Rank
1.	Arunachal P.	0.242	31	0.328	29	N.A	
2.	Assam	0.272	26	0.348	26	0.386	14
3.	Manipur	0.461	4	0.536	9	N.A	
4.	Meghalaya	0.317	21	0.365	24	N.A	
5.	Mizoram	0.411	8	0.548	7	N.A	
6.	Nagaland	0.328	20	0.486	11	N.A	
7.	Tripura	0.287	24	0.389	22	N.A	
8.	Sikkim	0.342	18	0.425	18	N.A	
	India	0.302	0.381	0.472			

Source : Human Development Report, 2001, Planning Commission, *Economic Survey*, 2002-03, p. 212.

1991 it is 0.328 and ranking 29, Mizoram –0.411 and 8 in 1981 whereas in 1991, it is 0.548 and ranking 7th, for Nagaland, it was 0.328 and ranking 20, in 1981, it is 0.486 and ranking 11th, ror Tripura, it was 0.287 and ranking 24 in 1981, whereas in 1991, it is 0.389 and ranking 22. But for Assam and Sikkim, the Index value has gone up from 0272 to 0.348, and 0.342 to 0.425 in 1981 and 1991 respectively but the ranking has not changed. (26th for Assam and 18th for Sikkim). But in case of Manipur, though index value has certainly gone up from 0.461 to 0.536 but ranking has gone down from 4th to 9th.

In India since 1991 comprehensive liberlisation measures have been undertaken for the development of the economy as well as for removing many obstacles so that the income and employment scenario would rapidly change. The 'Economic Reform' is being enforced with Industry especially the Public Sector, Balance of Trade, Information and Technology sector and Human Resources Development, etc. Since then, the government has undertaken both stabilisation programmes and structural reforms as two components of the economic reform package. But the desired objectives have been attained partly. Prof. Kirit Parikh observes, the reform have put the Indian Economy on a higher growth path, which it should continue to ride even without a lot of additional new reforms with more sensible policies. We have an opportunity to accelerate our growth further and take-off into a high growth trajectory. In 2005-06, it is observed that the growth rate of Indian Economy is almost more than 8 per cent overall. This rising growth rate has provided all round development of all sectors of economy which opens the flood gate of wide opportunity for the unemployed skilled and unskilled labor force which certainly affects the level of living in India. Today even in 'Rural India' it is explicitly visible with the level of clothing, housing, expenditure on non-food items, massive use of the two-wheelers, the Mobiles, the Radio, the T.V., etc. The thinking all round has gone a massive change and the awareness regarding health—Nutrition and Non-nutrition food is clearly visible in the activities of these people.

But it can not be denied that the impact of

'Liberlisation' and 'Economic Reform' are centered to certain pockets. As Prof. A. Ghosh has argued, the consequences of the NEP are likely to be extremely adverse for the future of the Indian Economy. The impact of the reformer, the performance of the economy has not been as huge or as sustained as predicted by its protagonists. But the growth of service sector since the reforms is highly important which contribution to the GDP has increased more than 51 per cent which was 15 per cent in 1950. Now this sector is providing employment to 25 per cent of the total work force, thus the fastest growing sector with the growth rate of more than 8 per cent during 2005-06. The growth in the service sector is attributed to increased specialisation, availability of a large population of highly-educated and fluent English-speaking workers on the supply side and on the demand side, increased demand from domestic consumers resulting from growth in personal incomes and from foreign consumers interested in India's exports or those looking to source their operation. This has a direct impact on the level of living. There is a migration of rural labour force to the urban areas, still there are some backward regions where the light of service sector does not reach, though there is awareness and the parents are always desirous to educate the child or to train them to be an efficient labour. But the level of living of Dalits, Backwards, Scheduled Castes, Scheduled Tribes, backward minorities and some poorer general castes in India suffer from the low level of living for which the government is marking special programmes for their upliftment. The level of living in 'Rural India' is found relatively worse than the 'Urban India' because the rural people more or less dependent on agriculture. The agricultural and allied sectors accounted for about 57 per cent of the total workforce in 1999-2000, down from 60 per cent in 1993-94. While this sector has been facing a stiff stagnation in growth, there is rapid rise in population which certainly affects the level of living of this sector. The NSSO survey estimated that in 1999-2000, 106 million, nearly 10 per cent of population were unemployed and the overall unemployment rate was 7.32 per cent with rural areas doing marginally better (7.21%) than urban areas (7.65%) unemployment in India is characterized by chronic under-employment or distinguished unemployment or even educated unemployment and the government is forgetting to eradicate both poverty and unemployment by providing financial assistance for setting up business, skill honing, setting up public enterprises, purchasing of milch cattle or bullock or tractors or other machines, etc. But in this financing, there is a lack of planning, enforcement method, inspection and more misuse of finance by the public themselves. All these have a direct effect upon the level of living and that's why the level of living, although enhanced, but still blocked either with certain rural families or pockets or villages, much is desired to be done for the upliftment of better level of living, it requires a second reform mostly associated for the rural-urban 'have-notes', Dalits, SC and ST and other poor families in minorities because they were poorer, more illiterate, have lower access to education, are relatively under-represented in public and private sector job and are finding it harder to access credit for self-employment. They must live in either a very poor house or under-trees in villages or having inadequate civic aid.

Thus we may conclude that the level of living in India is certainly affected with the regional development because the states of Punjab, Haryana, Maharashtra (Urban and some rural area), Delhi, shows marked changes over the year of independence but some backward states like M.P., U.P., Bihar, Jharkhand, Chhattisgarh level of living in rural areas and some urban people show a comparatively low level. But there is certainly a marked changes but still a lot have to be done for uplifting the backwards the poorer, the SC, the ST and the poorer of the minorities who do not have subsistence income for maintaining even the subsistence level of living. Moreover, these have been a great degree of depreciation of these poorer people of India. There is need for formulation of appropriate programmes to address the educational and economic backwardness of these people and for uplifting all of them, both educationally and economically, there must an effective programmes and measures which would be in accordance with the objective of our constitution to achieve growth with equity, to strengthen our pluralistic ethos and build an inclusive society. For this related data is the necessity for making an appropriate planning, formulating and implementing specific programmes to address issues relating to the upliftment of the socio-economic backward or any disadvantaged group of the economy and so the enhancement of a much accepted level of living.

References

Regional Development in India, M.L. Patel.

Role of Financial Institution in Regional Development of India, Dr. P.K. Kotia.

India's Development Experience, Edited by S. Subramanian.

The State of World Rural Poverty, "An Inquiry into its Causes and Consequences", Idriss Jazairy, M. Alamgir, T. Panuccio.

The Web of Poverty, B.D. Sharma.

Indian Economy, S.K. Mishra and V.K. Puri.

Demography, Dr. B. Kumar and Dr. S. Gupta.

Poverty and Famines, Amartya Sen.

Weaken in Welfare, Madhura Swaminathan.

Bihar Economic Journal, 2005, Conference Volume.

Wizard, Sept. 2006 Dl(n) 07/0/02/06-08.

Wizard, May 2006.

Yojana, Different Issues.

Kurukshetra, Different Issues.

Regional Disparities and Human Development

(A Case Study of Bihar)

T.N. Singh and Binodanand Bharti

INTRODUCTION

An overriding priority of the Government of Bihar since November 2001, when Jharkhand, an old part of south Bihar, bifurcated was to expand physical facilities to provide basic social services like education, health and nutrition to all sections of the people, particularly to BPL group. Entire part of mines, minerals and large scale industries, which were the major sources of revenue, had fully been shared by Jharkhand, so, over the years, the physical infrastructure in terms of schools, primary health centres, and other facilities have expanded enormously and variety of social and anti-poverty programmes have been introduced. Between 2001 and 2005, the pace of social sectors development had slowly and gradually moving up but after implementation the design of these programmes in the light of experience and to make social policies more responsive to the needs of the poor.

There is no doubt that the access of the poor to social service has improved enormously and now an average person in Bihar is, at present, significantly better-off than it was before June, 2006.

If any economy wants to achieve the objective of true development then it has to be viewed as people centre. It has to be designed at the accomplishment of human potentials and improvement of the social and economic well-being of the people and it has to be considered to secure what the people themselves perceive to be their social and economic interests.

The basic infrastructure sectors comprising primary, secondary and tertiary sectors are showing with a poor state of affairs. Primary sectors comprises Agriculture and Animal Husbandry, Forestry and Logging, Fishing and Mining and Quarrying, in secondary sectors, manufacturing, construction, electricity, water supply and gas have been covered while the tertiary sector also known as services sector consists of Transport, storage and communications, Trade, Hotels and Restaurants, Tourism, Finance and Real Estate, Public Administration and other services.

(a) GSDP at Current Prices

The 89.5 per cent of the total population of Bihar live in rural areas deriving their sustenance from agriculture and allied activities. The share of GSDP (Gross State Domestic Product) was the highest in primary sector and income accrued from this sector rose from Rs. 11129 crores in 1993-94 to Rs. 20977 crores in 2005-06 and this revealing a compound growth rate of 5.54 per cent during the period 1993-94 to 2005-06.

The income accrued from secondary sector increased from Rs. 2265 crores in 1993-94 to Rs. 7163 crores in 2005-06 recording a compound growth rate of 10.83 per cent during the entire period 1993-94 to 2005-06, and finally, income accrued from tertiary sector rose continuously from Rs. 9418 crores in 1993-94 to Rs. 32467 crores in 2005-06 thus revealing a compound growth rate of 11.07 per cent during the entire period 1993-94 to 2005-06. As a whole, total Gross state Domestic Product (GSDP) of Bihar increased from Rs. 22812 crores in 1993-94 to Rs. 60607 crores in 2005-06, thus indicating a compound growth rate of 8.7 per cent during the entire period 1993-94 to 2005-06. It is widely depicted in Table 1.

TABLE I

Gross State Domestic Product of Bihar at Current Prices

(Rs. in Crores)

Year	*Primary*	*Secondary*	*Tertiary*	*Total GSDP*
1993-94	11129	2265	9418	22812
1994-95	12756	2263	10926	25945
1995-96	10840	2452	11192	24484
1996-97	15628	2833	14080	32541
1997-98	14202	3838	15622	33662
1998-99	17452	3500	18081	39033
1999-00	16628	4824	20783	42235
2000-01	18637	4956	23376	46969
2001-02	18024	4685	24381	47090
2002-03	20883	5543	26735	53161
2003-04	18848	6129	27322	52299
2004-05	20571	6627	29947	57145
2005-06	20977	7163	32467	60607
CGR (%) 1993-94 to 2005-06	5.54	10.83	11.07	8.70

Source: Directorate of Economics and Statistics, Bihar.

(b) GSDP at Constant (1993-94) Prices

The income at Current Prices may vary from year to year due to changes in either the production or the prices of goods and services. In the context of an inflationary situation prevailing in the state, the estimates of GSDP at current prices are not free from the efforts of prices rise and, therefore, in order to indicate the real change in the availability of goods and services, the estimates are built up at constant prices also. The GSDP of primary sector in Bihar which was Rs. 11129 crores in 1993-94 with fluctuations though increased to as high as Rs. 15703 crores in 2002-03 and estimated to Rs. 13239 crores in 2005-06 as per advance estimate thus indicating compound growth rate of only 1.99 per cent during the period 1993-94 to 2005-06. The sub-sector of Agriculture and Animal Husbandry revealed a compound growth rate of 1.65 per cent.

On the other hand, the income from Secondary Sector increased from Rs. 2265 crores in 1993-94 to Rs. 4622 crores in 2005-06, thus recording a substantial compound growth rate of 7 per cent during the period 1993-94 to 2005-06. While the income from Tertiary sector rose from Rs. 9418 crores in 1993-94 to Rs. 18337 crores in 2005-06 and indicating a compound growth rate of 6.1 per cent.

In this Tertiary Sector, Finance and Real Estate alone recorded a compound growth rate of 8.26 per cent during the entire period 1993-94 to 2005-06. As a whole, the total GSDP of Bihar at constant prices rose from Rs. 22812 crores in 1993-94 though increased to a peak level of Rs. 36882 crores in 2004-05 but expected to be plummeted to Rs. 36198 crores in 2005-06 and thus recording a compound growth rate of 4.36 per cent during the entire period as can be seen from Table 2.

TABLE 2

Gross State Domestic Product of Bihar at Constant (1993-94) Prices

(Rs. in Cores)

Year	*Primary*	*Secondary*	*Tertiary*	*Total GSDP*
1993-94	11129	2265	9418	22812
1994-95	12961	2089	10252	25302
1995-96	10134	2071	9576	21781
1996-97	13506	2244	11210	26960
1997-98	10830	3117	11973	25920
1998-99	12836	2649	12403	27888
1999-00	11813	3495	13606	28914
2000-01	15146	3594	15771	34501
2001-02	12914	3079	15266	31259
2002-03	15703	3671	16785	36159
2003-04	12676	4028	16205	32859
2004-05	14825	4326	17731	36882
2005-06	13239	4622	18337	36198
CGR (%) 1993-94 to 2005-06	1.99	7.0	6.10	4.36

Source: Directorate of Economics and Statistics, Bihar.

CHART I

Growth of GSDP in Graphical Representation

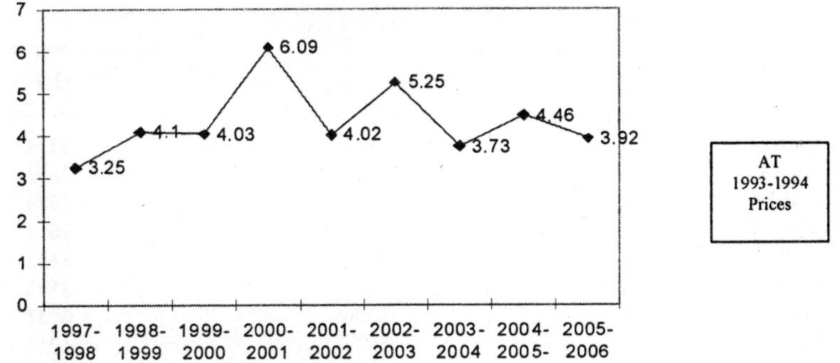

(c) Per Capita Income

The state income figures given in idea of total availability of goods and services. The per capita income figures give a better idea of the standards and levels of living of the people. The per capita income of Bihar at current prices, which was Rs. 3334 in 1993-94 with fluctuations increased to Rs. 6719 in 2005-06. But changes in real income can be understood where income estimates are available in terms of constant prices, the per capita income of Bihar increased from Rs. 3334 in 1993-94 to Rs. 4013 in 2005-06. The Table 3 will clear this.

METHODOLOGY

The present study used the data of Planning and Developing Department, Government of Bihar, 2004-05 to estimate human development and Gross State Domestic Product (GSDP) indices with simple modifications. The study used the GSDP at current prices as well as at constant (1993-94) prices and also per capita income on the basis of these prices. The concluding draft of recent Global Meet (January 2007) has also been considered to make a statistical analysis. State Budget 2007-08 has also finally made a part of study to give a final touch of this paper.

TABLE 3

Per Capita Income of Bihar at Current and Constant (1993-94) Prices

(In Rs.)

Year	*Current Prices*	*Constant Prices (1993-94)*
1993-94	3334	3334
1994-95	3703	3611
1995-96	3410	3034
1996-97	4421	3663
1997-98	4458	3433
1998-99	5036	3598
1999-00	5304	3631
2000-01	5737	4214
2001-02	5589	3710
2002-03	6212	4225
2003-04	6000	3775
2004-05	6444	4159
2005-06	6719	4013

Note: QE: Quick Estimates
AE: Advance Estimates

Source: Planning and Development Department, Bihar.

OBJECTVES

(1) To study the human development index for India to make a comparison study, before bifurcation and post-bifurcation.

(2) To know the levels of development in recent two years back to discuss the states plight having hope for a Bihari renaissance.

(3) To examine the standard of living at national level and regional level.

(4) To identify the main causes/reasons for the regional disparities in Bihar with respect to human development index (HDI).

HYPOTHESIS

(1) There is no relation between GSDP and human development in estimating regional disparities.
(2) There is no relation between A-13 parameter scale and regional disparities to yield a poverty line that corresponds to a bare minimum level of living.

Development Issues and Bihar's Economy

More than 600 non-resident Biharis for over sixty countries, representing all walks of life, gathered in Patna on January 19-21, 2007 for the Global Meet for a Resurgent Bihar. In this assembly comprising policy-makers, industrialists, academics, representatives of non-government organisations (NGOs), development specialists and trade, industrial and agricultural policy specialists discussed the plight of state, one of the most backward in the Indian Union. Director, Institute of Human Development provided a context to the newfound hope and stated "Institutions had more or less collapsed in the Bihar. The rule of law, the basic requirement for governance, had been completely eclipsed." Under the new government, there is hope. For the time in decades there is no open patronage of criminals, to the point that they have been kept out of the State Cabinet. Most critically, development now figures as a key issue in the political discourse.

The State Government of Bihar has constituted the Bihar Foundation of which the Chief Minister is the Chief patron. Although the main objective of the foundation is to facilitate the participation of the Bihari Diaspora in the State's Development, it is also to provide help to large Bihari migrant population settled and working across the countries, often in adverse conditions.

President APJ Abdul Kalam set out 10 point "Mission objective" for the transformation of state. In particular, he emphasised the importance of the agriculture sector along with infrastructure development and tourism, and of using Bihar's global human resource capital, "represented by its diasporas." He cited. "A developed Bihar is necessary for a developed India".

Bihar Burden

Bihar is perhaps India's least developed state the third biggest in terms of population; it fares poorly on almost every scale of human development when ranged against other states. Its plight has worsened since Jharkhand was carved out of it in 2001. It is the least urbanised state in India, with just 10 per cent of the population residing in urban areas. Literacy rates are abysmal. Just over half the population is literate more significantly, only one in three females in the state is literate. The situation among the marginalised communities such as Dalits and tribal people is far worse. Table 4 given the Bihar's share of BPL in Indian economy.

TABLE 4

Bihar's Share of Indians Below the Poverty Line

Year	*Rural*	*Urban*	*Total*
1983-84	16.58	6.25	14.31
1987-88	15.97	6.74	13.71
1993-94	18.48	5.67	15.40
1999-2000	19.48	7.33	16.36

Source: Planning Commission, 2002.

Bihar is a predominantly agrarian society. The creation of Jharkhand robbed the state of access of minerals while transferring the dominant portion of its industrial base to the newly created state. Although the state has the best alluvial soils in the country, the blight of feudal relations in agriculture have hampered prospects of any meaningful transformation in the countryside. Indeed, the social basis of agriculture, specifically agrarian relation, is believed to lie at the root of Bihar's malaise. The pressure on the agrarian economy has become acute, indicated by the fact that density of population in Rural Bihar (880 persons per square kilometer) is about three times that of rural India as a whole clearly agriculture holds the key to any kind of socio-economic transformation. The following table has made a comparison between Bihar and India.

Since the process of economic liberalisation hastened in 1991s Bihar's relative position has worsened considerably. In 1991s, when the Indian economy grew at the rate of about 6 per cent, Bihar's economy grew at only half this rate. While the rate of growth of the population between 1991 and 2001 slowed down in the rest of the country, in Bihar it increased. This meant a worsening of per capita incomes in the state. This has meant that income levels of an average Bihari has worsened when compared with the average Indian. In 1961, the national average Bihari income was about two-thirds of an average Indian, by 2006 this had fallen to less than one-third. This is shown in Table 5.

TABLE 5

Bihar and India: A Comparison

Sl. No.	Indicator	Bihar	India
(i)	Rural Population (in per cent)	89.6	72.02
(ii)	Birth Rate (birth per 1000 persons)	30	24
(iii)	Sex Ratio (tamales per 1000 males)	921.00	932
(iv)	Literacy Rate (combined) in per cent	46.96	64.59
(v)	Literacy Rate (female) in per cent	33.12	53.67
(vi)	Infant Mortality Rate (deaths per 1000 live births)	61	58
(vii)	Under Weight children (Below 3 years) in per cent	54.4	47.00
(viii)	Gross Enrolment (6-14 age group) in per cent	47.00	65.00
(ix)	Immunisation before (2 year of age) in per cent	12.8	56.6
(x)	Maternal Mortality Rate (Maternal deaths per 1,00,000 live births)	371	301

Source: Planning and Development Department, Government of Bihar.

Bihar has about 4.25 lakh people below the thoroughly discredited measure of poverty, the poverty line. This means that more than 40 per cent of the population earns less than what it takes to access the barest essentials of life. Denied any hope for decades, the poor have done only thing they possibly could in the face of such tremendous tribulations migrated. The ubiquitous Bihar migrant, visible as agricultural workers in Punjab or as construction workers all over India, has literally paid with his blood to escape the tyranny of feudal ties at home. The recent killing of Bihar migrant workers in Assam is only the latest example of the desperate Bihari's plight. The poor opportunities for higher education in the state have forced even sections of wealthier youth to migrate to study elsewhere. Moreover, the lack of industrialisation has forced the elite to move outside the state.

In Global meet, Government emphasised to the need for improving the social sectors and the human capital which would lead to improved living conditions and also enable Bihar's transformation. Improvements in education and health, it was pointed out, would not only improve the quality of life but also reflect in increased productivity and skill for motion and resulting to lay the basis for industrialisation.

Education

The abysmal levels of literacy are an obvious hindrance. In 2001 the gross enrolment ratio of children in the 6-14 age group, who have the fundamental right to free education, was only 56 per cent, compared with the national average of 85 per cent. In the 1990s, under the sway of several popular movements, there was a general expansion of educational facilities in the country. While the number of elementary schools increased by 40 per cent between 1990-91 and 2003-04, the intake of teachers increased by 37 per cent in India. However, in Bihar the number of schools fell by 10 per cent and number of teachers by almost 30 per cent during this period.

The gravity of this decline is best illustrated by the fact that there has hardly been any accretion to the number of government-run schools (5400) since such schools were "nationalism" in the late 1970s. According to the National Institute of Educational Planning and Administration (NIEPA), nearly one in five schools in Bihar are in "Urgent need of repair". Moreover, only one in five schools has a separate toilet for girl students, hardly an incentive in a situation of abysmal rates of female literacy.

Health

A similar situation prevails in the health sector. According to national norms, Bihar should have at least 533 primary health centres (PHCs), but there are only 398 PHCs in the state. Similarly, the state has fewer than 9000 functional health sub-centres, compared with at least 16,500 as per national norms. There are only 70 referral hospitals, though the norms stipulate at least 619 such hospitals in the state. This is reflected in the number of government medical officers, the state has only 3380 medical officers, whereas the norms stipulate 8500.

Neo-liberalism

Although the State Government repeatedly emphasised that the role of private-public partnerships is an urgent need in the fields of health care and road building. It is obvious that a sustained effort at poverty reduction requires a significant increase in public investment. This is required not only for the expansion of the social sectors such as health and education but also for programmes such as NREGS and the delivery of essentials to the poor through the PDS. Since agriculture represents Bihar's 'core competence' any effort at industrialisation would also require a significant scaling up of investment in agriculture. Such a strategy would recognize that Bihar's fundamental problem is conditioned by demand constraint. It would recognize public investment as a means of expending incomes, which can lay the basis for sustained industrialisation.

In global meet, it was highlighted the supply side issues and typically, it as considered as the problems of development as a matter of getting technique right. For instance, land reforms is only regarded as a problem of fragmented land holdings, not as a means of solving the acute problem of land hunger, which would increase demand. This attitude was best typified by the notion that Bihar's problem is just a matter of building better roads 'improving connectivity' improving the availability of electricity and cuirassing agricultural productivity.

The current strategy for agriculture productivity appears to rest on two factors, Firstly, since Bihar appears start from a low base, in a statistical sense, achieving a high role of growth of 7 per cent, at least in the short-term, ought not be difficult. M.S. Madhwan, Agriculture Director, describes this as a move to "harvest the low-hanging fruit first." The second aspect of the strategy appears to rest on the increasing commercialisation of agriculture, particularly through crop diversification, in a move away from food grain to cash crops. *Litchi* and *Makhana*, an aquatic plant rich in protein, have of such diversification. The government is also petting heavily on sugar, having approved the establishment of 20 new sugar mills in the state.

TABLE 6

Crop	*Bihar*	*All-India*	*National best*	*Bihar/National best %*
Rice	1,540	1,990	3,346 (Punjab)	46.03
Wheat	2,061	2,755	4,696 (Punjab)	43. 88
Coarse cereals	1,816	1,034	2,675 (Punjab)	67.89
Maize	2,004	1,785	3,182 (A.P.)	62.98
Pulses	804	630	965 (U.P.)	83.32
Oil seeds	808	856	1,417 (T.N.)	57.02
Sugarcane	41,665	70,825	1,05,757 (T.N.)	39.40
Potato	9,802	18,643	23,753 (W.B.)	41.27

Note: However, the compound annual growth rate of the agricultural sector as a whole (including livestock) between 1993-94 and 2004-05 has been only 2.91 per cent. Of course, the State government claims that the substantial gaps between productivity levels in Bihar and the rest of the country are indicative of the State's potential. Clearly, the success of the Eleventh Plan hinges crucially on whether Bihar closes the gap between it and the rest of India.

However, there are problems with such diversification, which are intimately linked to the nature of agrarian relations in Bihar. The first set of factors relate to the policy regime governing agriculture, which has a bearing on every conceivable aspect of farming, from input prices to the price at which the peasant sells his crop. The second set of issues relate to the process of commercialisation. Studies in Bihar show that there has been growing immiserisation of poor and marginal peasants, who are drawn to the risk-laden business

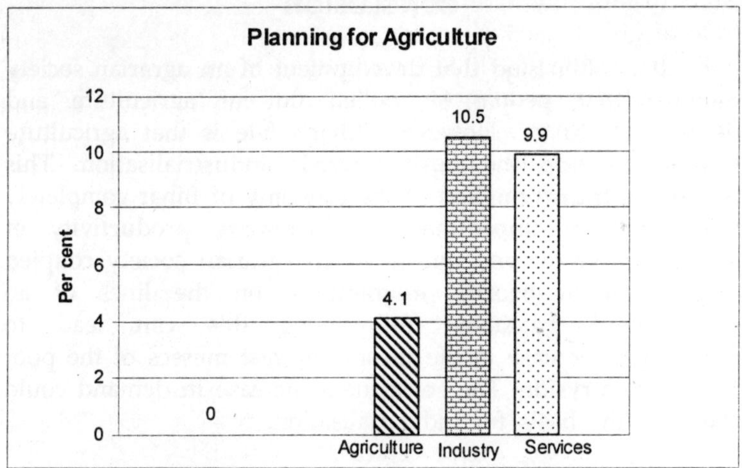

Note: The Planning Commission's Projection of 9 per cent growth rate during the Eleventh Five Year Plan period depends on the sectoral growth rates.

of commercial farming without being offered a safety net by the Government.

The Bihar Government's approach paper to the Eleventh Five Year Plan, prepared by the State Planning and Development Department, provides some dues about what it expect in the years ahead. The Eleventh Plan targets a growth rate of 8.5 per cent per annum, from less than 4 per cent in 2003-04. The targeted investment, corresponding to the targeted rate of growth of 8.5 per cent of gross state domestic product (GSDP), is about 24 per cent of the state's income, up from about 18.5 per cent in 2003-04.

The most striking feature of the plan is the sharp shift to emphasis on private investment as the prime mover of the economy. In 2003-04, private investment accounted for about 54 per cent of the overall investment, this is projected to increase to 65 per cent in eleventh plan period. In affect, the strategy adopted by the Bihar government appears to be to withdraw the state to facilitate private investment whether private investment will respond is, of course, another matter.

CONCLUSION

It is often said that development of an agrarian society requires that people be pulled out of agriculture and deployed industry. However, Bihar's fate is that agriculture has to provide the push towards industrialisation. This requires a transformation of the economy of Bihar completely which are in impediment to increasing productivity of agriculture sector and output in an agrarian society coupled with a public works programmes, on the lines of an employment guarantee programme this can lead to substantial increase in the income of vast masses of the poor in the countryside. The consequent increase in demand could then lay the basis for industrialisation.

REFERENCES

Rao, J. Narasimha and Bavdiah (2006), "Regional Disparities in Human Development in Selected State Analysis", *Southern Economist*, Vol. 45, No. 11, pp. 19-24.

Ram, Jaikumar (2005), "GSDP in Bihar", *Southern Economist*. Vol. 43, No. 13. pp. 17-19.

Sridhar, V. (2007), Wasting for Deliverance, *Frontline*, February 23 issue, pp. 113-17.

Sridhari, V. (2007), Betting on Farming, *Frontline*, February 23 issue, pp. 124-27.

Singh, P.N. (2004), Management Challenges of Bihar's Economy, Conference Volume of Economic Associaltion of Bihar, pp. 36-43.

21

Bihar's Road to Economic Development

Ugra Mohan Jha

P. Chidambram, Union Finance Minister in his Budget Speech has said that the main challenge of Indian economy is agriculture. Similarly, we can say that the challenge to Bihar's economy is agriculture. It is true that the formulation of the Union Finance Minister is swayed by temporary and transient consideration. He is a pragmatist and has to deal with agriculture because its development has nose-dived to an abysmal low of 2.7 per cent while manufacturing has registered 11.3 per cent growth rate and services 11.2 per cent growth rate. Agriculture is important in all times and in all countries and its importance never declines because it gives us four F, *i.e.—food for human beings, fodder for animals, fibre for clothes and fuel for cooking*. Still we can say that agriculture is not an end in itself. It is a means to higher ends which are faster employment generation, reduction of disparity across regions and thus achieving better standard of living and better social service for the masses of the country. If Bihar has to launch on a sustained growth trajectory we have to take a comprehensive holistic view of the economy of the country as a whole.

Bihar's economy is not an isolated and insular economy. It is vitally connected with Indian economy. There are some stumbling blocks to development which are common to the country as a whole and to Bihar also. These constraints deter the development wherever they exist and operate. The climate created in post-independent India is not healthy for development. Only a few days ago the two judges of the Supreme Court—Justice S.B. Sinha and Justice Markandey Katju—have made observations in a scam case of Bihar: "Everyone wants to loot the country. The only deterrent is to hang a few corrupt persons from the lamp post." The Judges regretted that the law does not permit them to do so. Left to themselves they would have preferred hanging the corrupt.

Development requires money and money is spent on projects. If, as our Late Prime Minister Rajiv Gandhi has said, 85 per cent of the development expenditure goes down the drain because it is pocketed by those who are the in-charge of the implementation of the project. Another estimate is that it is not 85 per cent but it is 90 per cent. In Bihar there are records in works like earthwork and digging that 100 per cent allotted amount is drained away and the purpose of the project is hijacked. Further, there are reports that the money allotted and earmarked is not spent. This is the case not with Bihar but also with Union Ministries. Many Union Ministries could not spend the money allotted to their departments. The department of Civil Aviation is the worst culprit. It spent only one per cent of its allotment. If such a state of affairs continues, development becomes a merage or a chimera. Hence three facts should be considered: (a) the government has no money for development because its revenue expenditure is always greater than its revenue receipts. If revenue receipt is greater than revenue expenditure the surplus is used for development; (b) even if the money is there the whole amount is not spent; (c) if it is spent a major portion of the allotted money fills the pocket of the monitors and guardians of the project. This is the great stumbling block in the development of Bihar. This feature is common to India as a whole and to Bihar in particular.

I now come to the Bihar's economy in the present time. According to the report of the World Bank "The poverty in Bihar—the highest among all states in India in terms of consumption measures is intensified by the deficiencies reflected in key human development indicators—the challenge of development in rural areas is even more acute since the aggregate figures subsume large rural-urban gap for most indicators". Bihar has a long history of fiscal and revenue deficit and they doubled since 1999. This means that Bihar is awfully dependent on borrowed funds. Relative to gross state domestic product expenditures soared to 28 per cent from 20 per cent and revenue rose by a half this share. They surged from 16 per cent to 20 per cent of GSDP. In the opinion of the World Bank this deficit is unsustainable—particularly speaking when the growth remains below 5 per cent per annum. The bifurcation of the state of Bihar took place in 2000. In pre-bifurcation stage debt rose from about 30 per cent to 42 per cent of GSDP and post-bifurcation it had jumped to 61 per cent. Thus, Bihar is groaning under the unbearable burden or debt service.

It should be born in mind that Bihar is the third biggest state in terms of population. It is also the least urbanised state in India. Only 10 per cent of the population of Bihar lives in urban areas. About 50 per cent of the population is illiterate. The condition of female literacy is worst. One-third of the female population is illiterate. The density of population in rural Bihar is nearly three times the density of population of rural India as a whole. That is why agriculture has special importance for the development of the state.

The economic development of Bihar has wider ramifications and deeper significance. If Bihar has to develop her agriculture has to develop and if Bihar develops the whole of India will develop because the development of Bihar will propel the development of the Indian economy. These are the minuses of the Bihar's economy. But let me come to some of her pluses. The first plus point is that it has the best alluvial soils in the country. The second point is that the people of Bihar are industrious, hardworking, persevering and enterprising. The people know how to survive under the most trying and adverse circumstances. They till the land of Punjab as migrant labourers. They are textile workers in Mumbai. The construction industry throughout the country is manned by Bihar's labourers. There are many foreign countries in North America and South-East Asia where migrant Bihari labourers are part and parcel of the economy of the countries.

Fortunately we have two documents which state authoritatively the present economic health of Bihar and point out the future road of development. The first is Economic Survey of Bihar issued for the first time by the present Government. This document mentions certain vital things. It points out that Bihar has lagged behind other states on all development indices. The state ranks at the bottom with respect to Human Development Indicators (HDI) with the HDI for Bihar being 20 per cent lower than the national HDI. Out of her estimated 90.2 million population Bihar has 536.91 lakh people living below poverty line whereas the national BPL percentage has dropped to 19.34 only. The state's total debt constitutes 71 per cent (Rs. 42,000) of her Gross State Domestic Product. The survey noted that the market size in Bihar is estimated to be worth Rs. 1,03,600 crore, i.e., 4.8 per cent of the country's market size. Bihar has a lower CD ratio than the national average, perhaps, the lowest one in the country.

The second is the Budget speech made by the Finance Minister of Bihar on February 27, 2007 in the Bihar Legislative Assembly. There are several good features and encouraging pointers about the future economic development of Bihar. The fact is that the state has contributed substantial amount of money for 11th Plan. In 2005–06 internal resources contributed only 8 per cent for the plan but in 2007–08 it rose to 29 per cent. Another good feature is the amount of debt provided in the budget in the preceding year was Rs. 5502.68 crores. Though the plan size increased yet the size of the debt went down and it came to Rs. 4776.38 crore. Formerly the debt was used for payment of salary, pension and establishment expenses but this year debt is being used for development works and creation of capital assets. These are the steps towards development of economy.

Another hopeful sign is that the closed state owned sugar mills, which are 15 in number, are being revived. Revival may assume two forms. The Government may hand them over to the private parties and the expectation is that they may become operational in the next season. The closed mills may be given on long-term lease to the private players or they may be even sold to them. It has been calculated if some money is invested, six mills can be rendered operational Mills. Government has appointed State Bank of India, Capital Market Ltd. to study the economic conditions of the mills and make recommendation to the Government. The recommendation will come in two parts and in 16 months.

Another silver lining is the attention which the Bihar Government has bestowed on milk production in the state. There is Bihar State Co-operative Milk Producers' Federation Ltd. This Federation has been scaling new heights of success under the present dispensation. It goes to the credit of COMFED that whatever it touches is turned into gold. The turnover figure exceeded beyond Rs. 400 crores during the last fiscal year. This time Rs. 50 crores is to be added to the turnover which is expected to total Rs. 450 crores. It is going to make huge leap. At present it supplies 5 lakh lts. of milk per day to the consumers. The level is likely to shoot up to 7 lakh lts. per day. Apart from milk the Federation is going to make forays in the sphere of vegetable production. It is contemplating to create Vegetable Co-operative Growers' Corporation. It is expanding its activities and proposing to make honey available to the consumers. The honey is known as *Sudha honey* and it will be superior in quality to other brands of honey available in the market. More important than availability of honey is its cheaper price. Further, the COMFED is going to launch Sudha brand of cow milk. It is going to produce *Ramdana lai* which has high content of pure *khoa* and which is processed and packed in presentable form.

The Government of Bihar is keen on making sufficient and timely credit available to the farmers. For this it is necessary that banks' services should be made available to all the villagers. It is reported that 48 blocks in Bihar do not have any branch of any bank. Further there are 50 blocks where there is only one branch of a bank. A rural bank in

Bihar has to cater to a large number of customers. There are 16 Regional Rural Banks (RRBs) in Bihar. There are Lead Banks also in every district. Bihar needs 1000 new branches according to the norm or criteria fixed by RBI. Reserve Bank of India wants that there should be one bank for 15 to 20 villages. There is another criterion also that the branch of a bank should serve 15,000 customers. The position in Bihar is that the branch of a bank in rural areas of Bihar serves 40 to 45 villages and more than 23 thousand customers. The Government is trying to remove this imbalance.

The linkage between growth and poverty reduction is very weak in Bihar. The question of growth is very complex one and depends on a plethora of institutional, cultural, historical and physical parameters. The relationship between non-farm growth and poverty reduction is also fragile. Recent research points out Bihar's low rates of literacy and overall weak human resource development are primary causes for the lack of adequate link between non-farm growth and poverty reduction.

According to World Bank the programme resources allocated to Bihar from the Centre were not fully utilised. This is surprising because the state is more dependent on Central allocation to finance public investment and development programmes. In view of Bihar's significant development needs there is necessity for the efficient use for the central funds. Unfortunately Bihar has the country's lowest utilisation rate for funds coming from the centre. According to one calculation Bihar forfeited 20 per cent of Central Plan assistance in the period from 1997 to 2000. The pitfalls plaguing Bihar are enormous due to persistent poverty, complex social stratification, unsatisfactory infrastructure and weak governance. These problems are well known but not well understood. The people of Bihar comprising civil society, businessmen, government officials, farmers and politicians also struggle against an image problem which is deeply damaging to Bihar's growth prospects. Hence an effort is needed to change this perception and to search for real solutions and strategies to meet Bihar's development challenges.

In Bihar the policy-makers must have living contacts with service recipients. They must know needs, requirements and aspirations of the persons who are at the receiving end of the services. The policy-makers must respond to the needs of the people effectively, quickly and comprehensively. If they fail the whole plan will go haywire. Again the policy-makers must be in touch with the service providers. Three things are required from the providers: (a) the policy-makers must see to it that the service is really provided, (b) the provision of service should be well targeted. It means that service is provided only to those for whom it is meant, and (c) the service provider is to further see that the service is in harmony with the needs of the community. There must be a living nexus between policy-makers, policy receiver and policy provider. Such a harmony will ensure hundred per cent implementation of any programme or project.

Further attempt must be made to avoid the poverty trap. High poverty rate leads to low level of literacy which in turn leads to poor health. The net result is ultimate poverty. This is the vicious circle. If the growth is low, there will not be any ability to generate resources to finance social and other services. At the same time it will cease to generate economic opportunities for households. What Bihar needs is pragmatic and affordable policy reform. A proper investment climate should be created to generate jobs and improve economic opportunities. There should be connectivity between people and market. Entrepreneurship should be encouraged. Technology in the rural sector should be adapted to the local needs. It should support human resource development.

In view of the discussions and formulations made in the preceding paragraphs the following policy prescriptions are recommended for the economic development of Bihar :

- Implementation machinery should be strengthened;
- There should be no political interference in the process of implementation;
- Those responsible for the implementation should not be allowed to line their pocket;

- Bureaucracy should not be allowed to subvert and pervert any proposal;
- Hydra-headed corruption should be killed;
- There should not be highly centralised authority which obstructs decision-making and implementation;
- In every stage there should be transparency in all actions and formulation of programmes;
- An attempt should be made to formulate programmes from the below and not from the top;
- Mass awareness should be created regarding the desirability and necessity of the programmes;
- State should do away with revenue deficit;
- Investment climate should be created;
- Where government cannot provide resources, public-partnership should be resorted to;
- Weak infrastructure should be removed;
- Law and order situation should be improved; and
- *Rangdars* should not be allowed to have a say and control in the implementation.

Index